DRILL TO WIN

12 Months to Better Brazilian Jiu-Jitsu

Andre Galvao

with Kevin Howell

Las Vegas

First Published in 2010 by Victory Belt Publishing

ISBN 10: 0-9815044-8-5
ISBN 13: 978-0-9815044-8-3

This book is for educational purposes. The publisher and authors of this instructional book are not responsible in any manner whatsoever for any adverse effects directly or indirectly as a result of the information provided in the book. If not practiced safely and with caution, martial arts can be dangerous to you and to others. It is important to consult with a professional martial arts instructor before beginning training. It is also very important to consult with a physician prior to training due to the intense and strenuous nature of the techniques in this book.

Victory Belt ® is a registered trademark of Victory Belt Publishing.

Printed in Hong Kong.

Cover design by: Haley Howell

Cover photo by: Gustavo Aragao

Photographs by: Brian Rule

Layout & Design by: Haley Howell

ACKNOWLEDGEMENTS

I dedicate this book to the honor and glory of Jesus Christ, who gave me the opportunity to be born again. Thank you, Lord, for supporting me and giving me life.

To my family and friends - thanks for helping and supporting me during both the good and bad times. You will never know how deeply I love and appreciate you all.

Finally, I need to thank my life long sponsors - Posto Acai and Vinac. Both of you took the chance with me when I was just starting with jiu-jitsu and I wish everybody could be as fortunate to have the support that you have provided me. Thank you.

-Andre Galvao

I dedicate this work to Haley and Oliver.

For Haley:

"I wonder what Piglet is doing," thought Pooh.
"I wish I were there to be doing it, too."
- Winnie the Pooh

For Oliver:

"You can know the name of a bird in all the languages of the world, but when you're finished, you'll know absolutely nothing whatsoever about the bird... So let's look at the bird and see what it's doing — that's what counts. I learned very early the difference between knowing the name of something and knowing something."
- Richard Feynman

-Kevin Howell

Contents

I was born in São Sebastian, Brazil, a quiet beach city off the coast of the state of São Paulo. When I was a preadolescent, around ten years old, my family moved to São Jose dos Campos, São Paulo, and this is where my brothers discovered judo and jiu-jitsu. Close to our new home was the Calasans academy, a judo school with links to jiu-jitsu as well. Both my oldest brother, Carlos, and my youngest brother, Gustavo, started training judo and jiu-jitsu because the academy was so close to our house and Master Calasans was always very generous to our impoverished family. My brothers would come home daily talking about the academy, but I had health problems with asthma, so instead of jiu-jitsu, my father enrolled me in swimming classes. This ended up being a blessing. I swam for three years to improve my asthma, and by the second year, I didn't need the rescue inhaler anymore. By swimming three kilometers a day, I had increased my cardiovascular strength and my lung capacity, making my next move into contact athletics far easier.

The more I swam, the more I wanted to become an Olympic swimmer, but my brothers would never stop goading me to try jiu-jitsu. They told me to train with them, and I chided them, saying that it was for girls and, "You guys have to hug men!" I really didn't like it, but they kept prodding me until I gave it a try. Finally, when I was around fourteen years old, I went with them to try a class. After the training session, I was exhausted and exhilarated. Both my brothers easily controlled and humbled me in class. I knew I was strong from swimming, but I had no idea about the type of strength I would need to learn this fascinating art. This was my first experience with the mountain of work I would take on to become proficient in jiu-jitsu. Not all my trials would be physical.

Although jiu-jitsu clicked with me and my brothers, it would not be easy for me to train. At the time that I finally gave it a try, my brothers were both training with Luiz Carlos "Careca" de Aguilar, a black belt instructor under Oswaldo Alves. Careca would be my first instructor as well, but only for three months. My family had financial problems, so I had to work in a pharmacy to help make ends meet. At the time, I was depressed because I felt like jiu-jitsu was slipping away from me. I worked at the pharmacy for over two years until I asked my dad if I could train jiu-jitsu again because I was young and I really loved it. He allowed me and my brothers to do it, but to ensure that we took it seriously, he said that if we did not win the championships, we would all have to go back to work. With the fire ignited, I began training in earnest at Careca's academy. I had just turned seventeen and knew that I had to train night and day to stand a chance at my first tournament. As an early white belt, my favorite move was the bull fighter, or torreando guard pass, and I used it exclusively to achieve my first tournament victory. With this, my father gave his blessing, and he worked hard to support our training as much as possible.

With my first instructor, Luiz Carlos "Careca" de Aguilar.
(Photo: Andre's personal archive)

At Careca's academy, my first real jiu-jitsu memory was that I was not one of the talented students. Careca confirmed this to me, and oddly enough, I beamed with pride. How strange to be happy about a lack of natural skill? For me, this elation stemmed from my strong performances, both in class and at my first few tournaments. When I had to work three times as hard as my classmates to learn something, I knew I was not the wunderkind. When I saw new students excel where I struggled, I understood that my time in jiu-jitsu would be all about determination. Nowhere was this more obvious than when examining my relationship with Chuck, one of my closest friends at Careca's. He was so flexible and fast (and flexibility is a talent), but he did not train like me. He didn't need to. What took me days of training to learn took him only minutes. However, as time went on, he drifted into drug use and focused less on training and more on his own talent. He knew that he could always "just pick things up." As a result of our two diverging attitudes, I started to win even more championships, while his performance plateaued. The reason is simple, I slept, trained, ate well, focused, resisted partying, and excelled. Talent can help so much in the beginning, but you cannot reach the top without hard work.

Careca supported me and my brothers very well. He took me from white to blue belt and did not ask for a dime. He knew of our family's plight, and all he requested was hard work and focus in return. I stayed with him until purple belt, but when I was a blue belt, I moved to Rio de Janeiro for six months and trained with Careca's master, Oswaldo Alves, a legendary Gracie family black belt who was known for introducing many moves from judo back into jiu-jitsu.

While in Rio, I trained daily with Alves and his top pupil, world champion Fredson Paixao. I trained hard while I was there, and I lived on the mats because I could not afford boarding. Though it sounds hectic, I look back at this time with fond memories. I would wake up, train hard, clean the mats, train yet again, clean once more, and sleep on the very same floors. I learned a lot from Alves about the importance of repetition and focus. Alves would often use closely related sequential moves that taught the transitions between jiu-jitsu techniques. For me, these sequences told the story of jiu-jitsu—movement. When it came time to compete, Alves had us on the razor's edge. Due to his emphasis on physical training and continuous drilling, we went on auto pilot to the championships. When I got to purple belt, I returned to São Jose and continued my training with Careca, my original master.

Shortly after I returned from Rio, Careca noticed that I was running low on training partners and that I needed something more than he alone

Me and my master, Fernando "Terere" Augusto. *(Photo: Kid Peligro)*

Visiting Terere's favela with Sussi Dahl and Kid Peligro.
(Photo: Leka Vieira)

could offer. At the time, I enjoyed training in my home academy, surrounded by old friends. However, Careca convinced me to reach farther, and he reminded me of my promise to my father. Feeling that I had the work ethic to go far in jiu-jitsu, Careca decided to send me to Fernando "Terere" Augusto, a famed jiu-jitsu world champion, who could train me hard to the next level. By the time I left for Terere's school, I was already a Mundial and World Cup champion at blue and purple belt in both my weight and the open category. On Careca's recommendation, Terere immediately took me in. Not only would I live with Terere, but I would receive private lessons and daily teachings from him at his Master Team–affiliated academy. Later, when I would go on to repeat my weight and open-class Mundial wins at brown belt, I would attribute this to Careca's willingness to see me reach my potential.

This time in my life is epitomized by Terere's graciousness and guidance. I don't think my jiu-jitsu today would be anywhere as good as it is if not for him. I was very fortunate because Terere taught me so many positions and he gave me private lessons for three years.

With Terere, I hit the jiu-jitsu lottery. He never charged me for any lessons, and he allowed me to live with him. He took me to his parents' home in São Paulo, where we all lived together for years. We trained hard, and I learned the intricate details and variations in positions. I also learned about the winning psychology. Terere gave me his best. I learned so much in this period, and it really opened my mind to jiu-jitsu.

While training with Terere, he splintered from the Master Team to form TT Academy (Terere and Telles Academy) and that's when people started learning my name. I was Terere's best student, and he would later give me the brown and black belts. TT was a competitive powerhouse, focused on a winning attitude. Terere would always let us know, "If you train hard, you will win." There were so many good fighters that came from here, and in many ways TT brought on a new era of jiu-jitsu champions. With other competitors like Rubens "Cobrinha" Charles, Lucas Lepri, the Langhi and Mendes bros, Ramon Lemos, and Gilbert "Durinho" Burns, we had a lot of hungry guys. Terere made us train hard, but train happy. His motto was simple, "If you watch TV, you have fun. If you run, you have fun. If you train, you need to have fun, too." He would always gauge us; if we were too focused and overtraining, he would mellow us out before we got angry or burned out. Terere understood the power of stress. So my training was more enjoyable than ever. Terere also put it in my mind that victory came from the submission. Everything was angled toward the finish and we became an academy full of submission specialists.

Me with teammates from Brasa. *(Photo: Galvao's personal archive)*

Although Terere's academy was a dream come true, it was also a dream that would not last forever. During a flight from the United States, Terere had some problems and was detained in the U.S. penal system for a few months. We were all worried about his deteriorating mental state, and when he returned, things were not the same. Unfortunately, my jiu-jitsu master succumbed to a cycle of drug use and personal torment. This was a hard time in my life because I felt like I was losing my best friend and mentor. Meanwhile, I had just competed at the 2006 Brazilian Nationals and lost twice to world champion Marcelo Garcia. Before the matches, there was a lot of talk about our matchup, and I went into the event confident because of Terere's own winning history against Garcia. My lack of training and overconfidence cost me; Marcelo beat me once on points and again via choke. Later that year, I lost again to Marcelo Garcia, this time by advantages, in the finals of the 2006 Mundials. Combined with the loss of my master Terere, my defeats at the hands of Garcia sent me on a personal jiu-jitsu soul search.

Winning my first black belt world championship at the 2005 Mundials.
(Photo: Marcelo Alonso)

With 2006 being such a tumultuous year, I knew I needed to make a change and get the training necessary to beat Garcia. I needed a coach, because I have always looked to great figures in my life for guidance. I chose Leo Vieira of Brasa Team because we had trained together before with Terere at Master Team and I knew I could trust him and his training methods as a coach. Training with Leo was incredible because every class was like a seminar to me. I learned so much from him, and my jiu-jitsu IQ started to explode. Every day, we would train together, and again I felt fortunate to see jiu-jitsu being created right in front of me. Competing for Brasa was like a reunion of old training partners. Instead of going it alone, now I had a team with the Vieira brothers, Demian Maia, Felipe Costa, Robert Drysdale, and Rodrigo "Comprido" Medeiros. My jiu-jitsu was alive again, and the championships started coming. In my time with Brasa, I took first in the 2007 and 2008 Pan Americans as well as the 2008 Mundials, making this my best year in competition and the antithesis of my troubles in 2006.

The following year, Leo Vieira decided to split from Brasa and

Hanging with teammates and Ramon Lemos (in white) at Posto do Acai, my sponsor. *(Photo: Jason Hunt)*

create his own team, Check-Mat. I was at another crossroads. Should I stay with my friends and teammates at Brasa or follow my coach? For the first time in my career, I decided to stick with my friendships and leave my training in limbo. At this time, I was a multiple-time world champion and did not know where to go with my jiu-jitsu. This is when my old friend and teammate from my days at TT Academy, Ramon Lemos, asked me to form a new team with him. I had always dreamed of my own jiu-jitsu team, and now the opportunity was finally in front of me. I knew that it would be a success and that I would also need coaching for my own jiu-jitsu needs. Ramon was the perfect fit. He understood my strengths and weaknesses and had already brought many of our teammates at TT to the world-class level. With the team set, we decided on a simple name, Atos, in reference to the biblical Book of Acts. With Atos, the dreams of my father have been fulfilled; I have achieved championships and become a professional in jiu-jitsu. Now, I get to pass on the knowledge given to me by so many great friends and coaches.

With Atos, I also have a responsibility as a dedicated Christian to live up to the true meaning of Acts. When I was younger, I just fought and trained hard and did not dwell on religion, even though I was born into a Catholic family. All of that changed when I met my wife, Angelica. Though she never forced me to go to church, I saw her as a shining example of God's will in action. Now I am a devout Christian, and I tell everybody that Jesus is the way to happiness. I know that others have different views, and that is okay, but I have to go with my experiences as well.

My mind-set changed a lot once I found God. Now I am happier because my life has changed for the better. I am married, I have a beautiful daughter named Sarah, a house, and a car. Before, I made money but had nothing, but with God, I now have everything. I think that God knows everything in your life. When I lost to Marcelo or Terere had his problem, I believe it was all in God's plan for me. All my experiences have led me to this point in my life. God brought me all my great coaches along the way, and pointed me in the right direction to achieve all my goals. He showed me that hard work will pay off and I just have to focus on what is important in my life. Of course, I will have a victorious career and life because I have God!

HOW TO USE THIS BOOK

Each chapter in this book represents a month in the year. Start at the first chapter and take each part day by day. There are four weeks per month, and five days of training per week. Some days have one drill, and others have more than one. Follow the directions to each drill and practice the suggested repetitions until you feel proficient with the movement. If at any time you're not confident in your skill level, repeat the day, week, or month until you feel you have mastered the drill. There are many drills in this book that focus on basic concepts that will come up over and over again in your training. Feel free to take drills from earlier months and use them as warm-ups for other drills later on. Once you have a good feel for all the drills in this book, piece them together in your own circuits to best suit your training goals.

While I believe whole-heartedly that doing drills is the most beneficial training method to get you ready for a competition, I do not mean for this book to trump your regular training regimen. Use these drills as warm-ups to class or with classmates during open mat. It is important to keep learning new techniques from your instructor and sparring with classmates to keep your jiu-jitsu experience active. My system of drilling will help you make leaps and bounds in your jiu-jitsu in addition to what you are already doing.

Against former rival, now Atos teammate, Gustavo Campos . *(Photo: Marcelo Alonso)*

BOOK'S GOAL

My immediate goal with this book is to take your jiu-jitsu to the next level by providing you with a one-year program of improvement. You will be training as I do and working what I know are the real "basics" of Brazilian Jiu-Jitsu: body movements. In my experience, there is only one way to program these neuromuscular transmissions, and that is through carefully designed drilling and sparring training. Although my personal aim is to use drills to get better at competition, it is just as important for noncompetitors to learn jiu-jitsu's invisible transitions. With drilling, your body learns the moves. Sparring is equally important. With sparring, you learn to fight. You need both to be complete. Many fighters master the guard but have holes elsewhere in their game. You need to practice everything from scratch and build yourself into a complete grappler. From standing, you will need both takedowns and guard pulling. From the ground, it is essential that you are well rounded in attack and defense, position and submission. If you have watched my fights you have seen that my jiu-jitsu has everything: takedowns, attack, defense, the guard, and top transitions. This book will provide you with a plan to fill your holes so that you become a more complete grappler, and it will only take two things: hard work and determination—the keys to success.

IMPORTANCE OF PARTNER DRILLS

I think most jiu-jitsu students drill just enough, but don't really get the most out of partner drills. They just follow the standard class structure of hip escapes, solo drills, technical instruction, and sparring instead of maximizing this useful tool. It is very important that you make good use of your partner because you will benefit from his body weight and immediate feedback. When drilling, you should try to use two- or three-movement sequences so that you learn both to see and feel what's around the corner. Once you start training in earnest, you will notice that this type of training takes the "edges" off your jiu-jitsu. Instead of sweeping and stopping and then passing and stopping, you will sweep, pass, and finish fluidly. This not only helps with the aesthetic quality of your jiu-jitsu, but it also results in a more overwhelming game.

HOW TO TRAIN

Obviously, you will not reach all your jiu-jitsu goals with drilling alone (though it will definitely help more than only sparring), so I have outlined three steps to training. Sometimes you will need to train seriously. In these situations, you should work hard, imposing your best positions or your "A game." This should not be everyday, just for tournament preparation, because most fighters have the tendency to avoid bad positions. Most of the time, you should be training for enjoyment. At these times, you will train all the positions, both offensive and defensive, transitioning a lot, and having fun. Other times you will test your skills by giving up advantageous positioning and trying to escape. You should practice like this with the best guys in the academy—not the white belts. This way, you will feel your jiu-jitsu improve. The final type of training, and possibly the most important, is positional sparring. This type of training is for perfecting a specific position or technique. You will train repeatedly from the same position to gain confidence and learn the ins-and-outs of a specific situation.

INTEGRATE CIRCUIT TRAINING FOR COMPETITION PREPARATION

Circuit training is for getting your heart rate to 170 beats a minute; this is essential for developing your competitive jiu-jitsu. If my next match is going to last ten minutes and I have ten moves that I would like to prepare with, I will use one minute per move or pick four moves and drill intensively for thirty seconds each for ten minutes total. Choose moves that get your heart pumping, moves that are constant and fast without letup. If you do the movements fast enough, you will pump your heart. As for creating the circuits, base them on the time of your matches. If you are a purple belt, your circuits will be seven minutes in duration. Then you recover for half or one full match before going again. If you can do this five times, you are in great shape.

Just be sure to always mix up your circuits. If you focus solely on one drill, your body quickly adapts to the workout, and though this is good for learning a move, it can be detrimental to your tournament preparation. You can create many styles of circuits. You can do the timed circuits that I mentioned, or you can work out intensively for thirty seconds, and then rest thirty seconds. Short intervals of intense work are great for building explosiveness, while long intervals at slightly lower intensity facilitate endurance. Depending on your training goal, circuit training can provide the necessary result.

COMPETING vs TRAINING IN THE ACADEMY

Many instructors emphasize competition, but they do not know when competition starts or stops. Oftentimes, an instructor will put so much pressure on his students to win that they feel they cannot lose in front of him, even if it is just in sparring during class. Whether you stall in class or win every day, either way, you inhibit your growth. Of course it is good for you to believe in yourself for championships and challenges, but eventually in a competition you may have your back taken. If you're not prepared because you have rarely experienced this in the academy, you'll get lost. I think you need to train everything—defense, attacks, everything. If your teacher does not set this up, you have to address this in your supplemental training.

Terere is responsible for how I see training in the academy. He told all of us that in order to make training fun, you must think of training like a game of soccer. When you make a goal, you celebrate. If your training partner submits, you laugh and make light of the moment. You train hard, but you enjoy yourself as you tap and win. This way, you can test yourself in the academy, but it is always a friendly competition. Terere's different training strategies also kept our egos in check. For example, we would often train with our eyes closed or exchange belts (Cobrinha gets blue, Terere gets purple, I get white) and then we would train. He instilled the idea that the white belt can submit you one day, and the blue belt too. You are not the best in the world just because you won the world championship; you just won a tournament, no more no less.

When it comes to training, people often ask me if I ever tap to lower belts. When I'm training my competition game, it is too hard for lower belts to get into rhythm, but when I open it up, it's possible. I see training as the time and place to attempt new things, so I don't really concern myself with who tapped whom. I've noticed this type of thinking while training in the United States, where people sometimes make a big deal about black belts getting tapped out to lower belts, but in Brazil it's normal. At my home school, the tapped black belt may have a few jokes thrown his way, but it's all in good fun. We all know the black belt is better, so we just laugh about it and move on. Sometimes, I get so exhausted in training that a fresh blue belt can definitely tap me, but at the end of the day, a black belt is still a black belt. I have my positions that are black belt positions, but when I tap to a lower belt, I really see no problem. That is why this is training, not competition. In competition, you need to change your mind-set and focus while implementing a smarter strategy.

SURPASS YOUR POTENTIAL

I believe that everybody has the potential to do well in jiu-jitsu. I also know that many people will not commit to the necessary hard work to reach their potential. Obviously talent helps; if you're very coordinated or flexible, you will get the position fast. However, if you are talented and do not train, you cannot get the gold medal. There are a lot of talented people in the academy, but they do not win the championships. Why? Talent never takes the place of hard work. These individuals are just talented. They win and lose and win and lose, but their stars do not shine. To do this, you have to train hard and be surrounded by the right mind-set. In addition, if you have the potential, but use drugs, you put your potential in the trash. To me, potential means you do everything 100 percent: training whether you want to or not, keeping a good diet, physical training, and sufficient rest. You always hear, "This guy is so talented . . ." but then some average guy beats him. I know this because I was that average guy, and I worked hard to beat talent.

MONTH ONE:
The Diet of a Champion

Once you make the commitment to competitive jiu-jitsu, one of the first things you have to focus on is your diet. I put this chapter before any physical training because it is one of the hardest parts of your journey to better jiu-jitsu. You must train your mind to have the willpower to eat what you need for success and to say no to the dessert after dinner!

I know junk food tastes good, but it is bad for your body. I like junk food! Sometimes, when I don't have a fight, I splurge on my diet and go to a fast food place. However, this is not everyday, or even every week, it's just sometimes! If you try to think about what you are eating before you eat it, and really think about junk food and how it could kill you one day, maybe you will think twice before chowing down on a burger and fries.

In secret, I love hamburgers and burritos. They taste amazing, but for the lifestyle I lead, they are unacceptable. I have to think of my future before I eat them. I want to be a champion. It is too hard to be a champion if you eat only junk food. When I'm in my training camp, I never allow myself to eat bad food. The tournament is everything! You must live and breathe the tournament. While you are training, eating, resting, or relaxing, keep a champion's mindset. Picture yourself as a winner. A good diet will only help your performance, and in the long run, it will be a part of your victory!

Let me preface this by saying that I am not a licensed dietician. I do not have formal training in nutrition, and by no means am I saying that my way is the only way to keep yourself healthy when training for a competition. Before beginning any diet or exercise plan, you should discuss it with your medical practitioner. Everybody is different and will have personal reactions to a different diet regimen. Look for a good and experienced doctor in your area who can help you find the perfect diet for you.

That being said, here is the diet and ideology I follow when it comes to training for competition.

First of all, I prepare my body before a hard workout. I like to drink a zero carbohydrate whey protein to give me energy before an intense training session. Right now, I use Endurox RX with Iso Whey Protein Zero Carbs. I also take an amino acid (BCAA) supplement before training. As many people know, amino acids are the building blocks of protein and are responsible for building your muscles. What some people don't realize is that amino acids, especially BCAA, can also become fuel to produce energy. This is why I find it important to take them before training.

After working out, I have a similar routine, but it varies slightly, depending on when I'm training. After a morning workout, I eat Iso Whey Protein with oatmeal. For other sessions during the day, I just take the whey protein. To both of these, I also add amino acids (BCAA) or glutamine, and I usually mix this with water instead of milk.

When I'm getting ready for a tournament, I follow a very strict diet plan. It's vital that you consistently regulate your meal pattern and never go more than four hours on an empty stomach. Also, if you eat fruit with your meal, either eat it first and wait fifteen minutes to allow it to digest before continuing with your meal or eat it last. Fruit does not mix well with other food types so it needs its own time to digest. It's also a good idea to vary your food everyday. Variation helps digestion and keeps you from becoming so bored with your diet that you quit. Finally, relax and eat your meals slowly. It doesn't help to inhale your food.

My diet is as follows:

Breakfast:
Fruit (Banana, apple, blueberries, strawberries, etc)
Whole wheat toast with olive oil or honey
Cereal (oatmeal or quinoa)
Whole yogurt or whey protein shake

Snack (3 hours after breakfast and 30 minutes to 1 hour before lunch):
One Fruit

Lunch:
One kind of complex carb (sweet potato, rice, pasta, etc.)
Animal protein (meat, fish, chicken, eggs, etc.)
Green salad and vegetables

Afternoon snack (3 hours after lunch and 30 minutes to 1 hour before dinner):
One fruit

Dinner:
Roots/carbs (Sweet potato or manioc, etc.) with a lot of olive oil and a little bit of salt
Fish, eggs, or mozzarella cheese
Green salad and vegetables

Before bed:
A handful of nuts, whey protein shake, or yogurt

I follow this diet to maintain weight while training, to gain energy through nutrition, and to stay strong with healthy protein.

When I am cutting weight for a tournament, however, I follow a different diet plan. It is extremely important that if you are going to cut weight, you do it safely and responsibly. You do not want to starve yourself, and it's not good for your body to cut weight drastically. Also, when you are cutting weight, avoid carbonated drinks like soda and mineral water. Drink water instead. Your body needs to e in constant state of hydration, and if you wait until you're thirsty, you are already too late. My method is to modify my diet slightly to cut out some of the carbohydrates and begin losing weight early. In this way, I cut weight little by little as I keep up my training regimen. My body adjusts to my new weight and my training does not suffer from dehydration or lack of calories.

I personally don't like to lose seven to eight kilos one week before a fight. I like to do everything as healthily and correctly as possible to avoid putting stress on my body. I started using this diet to cut weight before the 2007 ADCC trials and I have been a firm believer in it ever since. At the trials, I was the 77 kilos champion and I attribute a great deal of that win to my diet before the fight. Now, I only use this diet to cut weight.

I tried the high protein diet that is very popular, but my body didn't feel good from it and I didn't like it. I find this diet much better because I can maintain my energy and strength while cutting safely. This is especially important in gi matches where they weigh you right before your fight. If you cut too much weight the day or week before, your body cannot be its best. If you have already lost weight leading up to it, even after a hard fight, your body will recover nutrients and you'll be able to keep enough energy to fight the next round!

I start the following diet eight to nine weeks before a competition while I'm in training camp.

My weight cutting diet is as follows:

Breakfast:
One fruit
2 slices of whole wheat bread with olive oil
Cereal (quinoa or oatmeal)
Green tea
Whey protein no carbs shake

Snack (3 hours after breakfast and 30 to 60 minutes before lunch):
One fruit

Lunch:
Protein (meat, fish, eggs, or chicken) with salt
Green salad with vegetables
Green tea
Dessert: Diet gelatin

Snack (3 hours after lunch and 30 to 60 minutes before dinner):
One fruit

Dinner:
One kind of root (sweet potato, manioc, etc) with olive oil and no salt
Green salad and vegetables
Green tea

Before bed (2.5 to 3 hours after dinner):
Whey protein isolate shake, or yogurt mix and shake with a diet gelatin, or nuts (cashews, almonds, or peanuts)

I also find it important to take daily supplements because training hard can weaken the immune system. Here are the supplements I take on a daily basis:

Supplements:
Royal Jelly–in the morning
Vitamin C–2 grams per day
Multivitamin–2 times per day
B12 shots–2 times per week
Whey protein isolate (no carbs)–after workout
Glutamine–after workout and before sleep
BCAA (amino acids)–before and after workout
Endurox RX–after workout and before workout if I know I'm going to have an intense training session
Calcium Magnesium with Vitamin D–before sleep

Remember, too, that an important part of cutting weight is to rest. Spend time with your family, your brothers, your friends. Take naps and make sure you get plenty of rest at bedtime.

Because I take jiu-jitsu so seriously, I must also adapt to the real Brazilian Jiu-Jitsu lifestyle. Sure, you've all heard about the awesome life a professional fighter leads. Maybe you picture a training session here and there, healthy food before fights, and the rest of the time being spent lounging on the beach or partying at the best nightclubs.

This is not the real BJJ lifestyle. To me, health is life. I lead a healthy lifestyle, which means good food, plenty of sleep, no parties, no alcohol, and no drugs. I learned very early on that if you want to be a champion, you need a goal and a healthy lifestyle that enables success. My goal is trying to live in God's image and being the best person I can be. I want to enjoy my life just like everyone, but I don't need vices to do so.

Personally, I see my mental, physical, and spiritual well-being as equal contributors to my healthy life. I am a Christian this gives me confidence. I respect God's plans for me by eating healthy and living well, and in turn, I develop the confidence and willpower I need to succeed. Winning starts with willpower!

Of course natural talents and physical attributes will help a lot, but I believe more in dedication and discipline. Some guys have a natural talent for grappling, but if they don't have discipline, focus, and love for Brazilian Jiu-Jitsu, they will not succeed. It takes a combination of all three. In my experience, faith helps, too. Believe in yourself and in your talent. If you do not have an abundance of talent, don't worry; believe in yourself because Jesus believes in you!

In the beginning of this chapter, I mentioned that diet is one of the hardest parts of training. This may be true for some, but in fact, every part of training is hard. It's very complex. You need to do everything correctly and have discipline in every part of your routine. Is it hard? Yes, but I truly believe that this is why champions exist. To be a champion, you must have willpower, a desire, discipline, a focus, a clear mind, and, of course, humility.

While dieting may be hard for you to do at first, if you change your mind-set about food, it will become the easiest part. You will feel and see yourself getting in shape. In just a couple of weeks, you will already feel the difference. The food is often the hardest part for a lot of people because of the will of the flesh. This is natural, but if you make a good diet with a lot of variation in types of food, you will be okay! Don't think about the diet. Just picture yourself as the champion from here on out!

Give yourself one month committed to your diet and see it through. Stick to your regular jiu-jitsu training if you are already a practitioner, or any other physical activities that you usually do. With your diet on track, you're ready to turn the page and radically transform your jiu-jitsu in one year's time.

MONTH TWO:
Strength Matters...
Balance Does Too!

I don't want you to get the wrong idea about what it means to drill. Sure, it is highly important to drill specific techniques and movements to get your body used to them. In fact, the following chapters in this book are solely focused on specific technical drills to improve different aspects of your game. However, don't overlook the importance of getting your body in shape, your muscles strong, your ligaments flexible, and your equilibrium stable. I purposely put strength and balance drills ahead of technical ones so that your body will be ready to perform common jiu-jitsu movements in the following months. This month, you will focus on developing a strong core, a good base, and flexibility, and in the mean time, repetitions will grant you great conditioning.

In week one, the drills center on general strength and conditioning. The goal is to start working on your basic conditioning for jiu-jitsu with special attention paid to the core section of the body. Your core is important because it is crucial for standing, squatting, and sitting up to your opponent. Together with your hips, your core is responsible for controlling the fight. Because this is the first week of actual physical exercise, take these movements slowly until you feel comfortable with them. As you practice, your body will get stronger and you can use these positions as a warm up to training.

Week two's goal is balance. As any jiu-jitsu practitioner knows, balance plays a key role in your top game. This week's exercises work to develop your positional balance, especially while standing and squatting, but also while you are in any other top position. It is important to understand the idea of a "base" or, in other words, stability while your opponent is trying to unbalance you. In a real match, you may not always have all your limbs to help stabilize you. This section will help you focus on staying balanced even in difficult situations.

Week three is an advanced guide to strength and conditioning incorporating what you learned in weeks one and two,. You have been drilling for two weeks now, and your body is getting stronger. Now, the goal is to add explosive power

Training strength and conditioning in a weighted vest with Alejarra. *(Photo: Galvao's personal archive)*

and isometric strength to your game. In competition, you will need to use short bursts of energy to catch your opponent off guard, and this week's drills will help you train your body to do so. Along with explosive power, you must also maintain some constant strength so you can control your opponent. To be successful in Brazilian Jiu-Jitsu, you must have a nice balance of these two energy systems.

In week four, you will learn the importance of gymnastics for jiu-jitsu. If you observe my competition style, you'll notice that I do not like to stay in one place for too long. Agility is a trait that is often overlooked in the academy, but it is highly responsible for contributing to your base, guard passing, and improvisation skills. Gymnastics is about understanding your own body and how to use it to its full potential. This radically equates to better success in training and in competition. Once you know your body, you can then exceed what you thought were your limitations. Remember, Brazilian Jiu-Jitsu is about movement – not just holding your opponent! Learn to do these drills well and your game will become more flexible and acrobatic.

At the end of this month, you will feel an overall improvement in your strength and conditioning. It is very important that you do not stop here, though. Just because the following months do not outline it, doesn't mean you should stop the strength and balance drills. Add them to your warm ups to keep your body agile and your base solid. Each chapter in this book should act as a building block to the next. Do not abandon drills from month to month. Simply add them to your workout and you will see tremendous gains.

I had to pull from my conditioning as I tried to attack Roger Gracie's back at the 2008 Mundials. *(Photo: John Lamonica)*

DAY ONE:

BACK LOOSENING

FREQUENCY: 5 360-degree turns to each side or 2 minutes total

Start the first week of strength training by stretching. This is one of the best drills for lengthening the upper and lower back as well as loosening your shoulders and neck for training. I originally started doing this after watching one of my old instructors, the turtle master Eduardo Telles, flow around in circles with this stretch before training. It took a little time for me to figure out the mechanics, but at its heart, the move is fairly simple, especially if you are familiar with front shoulder rolls and back breakfalls (month 3). As you get more familiar with this roll, you should feel your lower back stretching out, making it easier for your feet to stay in contact with the mats as you roll. The same is true for your upper back muscles, which should also gain some flexibility, allowing your neck to feel more relaxed as your knees and head collapse toward each other. As for training, this should help you in both your inverted guard recovery as well as defending any type of stacking pass.

FREQUENCY: 10-20 rotations at a medium pace

Along with the previous technique, this is a warm-up that I love to use before training. This move is straight from the Leo Vieira classroom warm-up and was one that I immediately implemented after spending some time training with him while at Brasa in São Paulo. Basically, you will be spinning on your rear and hips as you pendulum your body from side to side. It is very important that you warm up your hips and core before training, and this is one of my favorite ways to do so while incorporating jiu-jitsu-related movements. This drill should also help your ability to scramble, regain guard, and move with more fluidity while sparring. Practice this daily as a warm-up!

Developing Side Control Movement

As I roll onto my left shoulder, it is vital that I push off the mat with both feet while opening up my shoulder by tilting my head away from my left collar. This allows me to safely get on my shoulder while saving my neck from abuse. To get my right shoulder to the mat, I tuck my chin to my chest and rotate my legs square to my head and then past it toward my other shoulder. In this situation, my body follows my legs and I end up on my right shoulder, still in a stacked position. From here, I can come back to my knees and execute another roll as I continue my 360-degree spin.

LEG SWINGS

Starting facedown on the mat with my feet behind me, it is important that I arch my chest and feet off the mat, creating a fulcrum point at my hips for balance. Next, I must lean onto one hip; this is the hip that I will spin 180 degrees on. Keeping my legs straight and locked together, I swing my legs to where my head was, ending in a seated position. To return, I lean onto my other hip and swing my legs back to the starting position. It is vital that you feel yourself rowing from hip to hip to open up the proper angle for the swing. Once finished, repeat to the other side and mix it up (full 360 revolution, 180 spin and return, etc).

DAY TWO:
BALL PUSH-UPS

FREQUENCY: 2-3 sets of 12-20

Regardless of your previous fitness level, Swiss ball push-ups can be challenging and rewarding as you work on your core grappling muscles and upper-body strength. As with many of my drills, I prefer to do standard push-ups with the assistance of a Swiss ball because I have to use more muscle groups to stabilize my balance as I do my repetitions. On a jiu-jitsu level, I like to imagine knee on belly or guard pass training as I do this, picturing the ball as my opponent, trying to upset my balance. To get the most out of these, explode upward with your push-up and descend back to the ball with a slow count of four to six.

FREQUENCY: 2-4x the length of the mat

This is a drill that I have been doing since I started jiu-jitsu training, but I think it got more popular when people saw Jacare using a modified version of it after he won his championships. This drill combines coordination, core strength, and an incredible upper-body workout. The key is to get as low as you can without resting your body on the mat to ensure that you keep constant muscle tension throughout the drill. When you apply this to jiu-jitsu, this drill is wonderful for guard passing pressure and hiding the back leg from being sucked into the half guard while passing.

Arms & Core

I begin my upper body Swiss ball workout in base, with my legs spread beyond shoulder width apart and my hands in front of me on either side of the ball. Slowly, I inhale as I lower myself to a slow six count. With my breath ready, I exhale sharply and explode upward, extending my arms without locking my elbows completely. This counts for one repetition. It is very important that you lower yourself steadily and as low as possible without resting on the ball – overall muscle tension is key!

ALLIGATOR CRAWL

Although these often look somewhat tricky, alligator crawls are actually very easy once you try them out. I always begin by walking forward with all fours as if I were bear crawling. As I step one hand forward, the opposite leg steps forward as well. Once here, I turn onto the hip of my rear leg and I lower my hip to the mat like a push-up. To continue, I simply finish the push-up and walk my other hand and leg forward, turn my hip, and complete the next alligator crawl. Just remember the most important element – breathe!

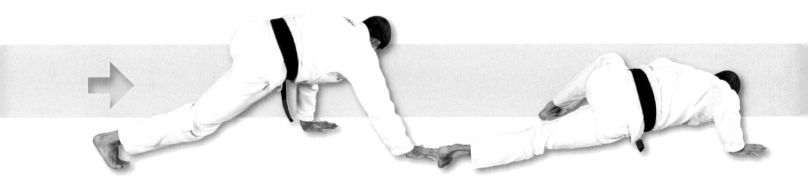

DAY THREE:
BALL SIT-THROUGH

FREQUENCY: 2-3 sets of 20 or timed sets

As we get to the midpoint of this first week of strength training, it is important that we continue to do exercises that focus on our most important jiu-jitsu muscles, the core – the upper quadriceps, hamstrings, and hips to the upper abdominals and lower back muscles. In this set of exercises, you will get a great core drill and hip mobility exercise along with an isometric workout on your upper body. In terms of jiu-jitsu, these moves are directly applicable to passing the guard, escaping the sprawl position, maintaining top position, and transitioning to other positions. In other words, this is a jiu-jitsu master move that everybody should be adding to their warm-up and workout routines, whether it is week 1 or week 501.

FREQUENCY: 2 sets of 12-20 at a medium pace

With your hips loose from the previous drill, it is now time to do some inverse crunches on the ball. This is an excellent workout for your upper and lower abdominals, and you can even flex your hips downward a little to get some lower-back benefits. Regarding the pace of this drill, I like to change the pace regularly. Sometimes, I try to explode into the curled position and slowly stretch into the plank, and other times I will do the inverse. I would advise mixing it up to ensure that you are working your explosive muscles as well as your muscle endurance. Incorporate extra repetitions of this if you are working on guard passing or mount retention.

Abdominals & Core

Although this drill more or less illustrates itself, there are two movement variations that can be incorporated into the same drill. The first one is shown above. Start on the ball with your legs spread to hip width apart, your hands on the mat, and your knees pinching slightly for balance. Roll slightly to one hip and then use that leg (the bottom leg) to switch your hips so that your hip lands on the mat. Next, return to the square position and repeat to the other side. For the variation, let the ball carry you off axis as your hip pushes the ball to the side. Next, switch your hips and bring the ball to the other side. I like to do this drill to music to help with my rhythm with this move.

PLANK CURL

Starting from the plank position with my legs straight and about hip width apart and my hands directly in front of my shoulders, I breathe inwards to prepare for my crunch. At the apex of my breath, I explode my rear upward while exhaling sharply, using my knees and shins to pull the ball toward my face. Once here, I hold the crunch for a few seconds. Then, I slowly breathe in and stretch my body to the original position.

DAY FOUR:
CLOSED GUARD WALKING

FREQUENCY: 2-3 mat lengths

As we start day four, your diet and earlier stretches and abdominal work should have you feeling energized and ready for a challenge. This drill is that challenge. I originally practiced this with my first jiu-jitsu instructor, Careca, and I have used it ever since white belt. The objective of this drill is to lift your partner while in his closed guard and walk the distance of the mat. Your partner should maintain the guard for the entire length of the mat. If either person fails by losing balance or opening the guard, the drill should start over. This is an incredible workout for both me and my partner holding the guard.   Just be safe and pick a partner that you can lift and carry a manageable distance. Walk at a slow and controlled pace.

Legs & Core

Before practicing, I choose Marcel because he is a similar size and weight. Marcel pulls me into his closed guard and I stand for closed guard walking. As I stand, I pull Marcel up with me using my front hand. Steadily, I begin walking, making sure that my hips and knees are always in balance under Marcel. Do not get sloppy with this move or try to lift too much or push it too hard — this move can result in serious knee injury if done improperly. If you are uncomfortable with this drill, practice lunge walking instead.

TURTLE HURDLE

FREQUENCY: 2-3 sets of 15-20 or timed

You should be tired from the closed guard walking, and now you are going to tax both your cardio and lower-body systems with the turtle hurdle. When I started training with Fernando "Terere" Augusto at purple belt, I knew he was already an amazing competitor, and it was drills like these that showed me why. We would use this drill as both a warm-up in class and as part of the between-rounds conditioning during competition sparring. There is no better picture of torture than doing turtle hurdles for half of your rest (the other half is for your partner) after and before a hard sparring round.

With Marcel on all fours in the turtle position, I start on one side with both feet pointing forward. I breathe in as I crouch, and then I quickly exhale while jumping as high as I can over Marcel. I need to try to bring my knees to my chest at the apex of my jump and, more importantly, clear Marcel to the other side. Once I land, I collect my breath and repeat.

DAY FIVE:
STANDING CLOSED GUARD SIT-UPS

FREQUENCY: 3 sets of 12-20

First of all, day five's title is a little bit of a misnomer. All of the workouts so far have been full body, although most of our focus has been on specific areas. The standing closed guard sit-up is great exercise for both partners as I work my legs and abdominals and my ability to keep the closed guard, and my partner gets to work his balance and standing base as my swing disrupts his equilibrium.

Full Body

I start the position with Marcel standing in my closed guard. My legs are securely locked over his hips. I breathe in and then exhale as I sit up toward Marcel's chest. Once I hit his chest, I contract my abs and I slowly lower myself while inhaling. If the partner standing starts losing control, he can step forward to regain his posture, but being careful of his knees. The person using the closed guard should try to sit up with control so that he does not throw his partner too much out of balance.

KANGAROO HOPS

FREQUENCY: 2-4x the length of the mat

Now that you are comfortable with alligator crawls, kangaroo hops should be a walk in the park. They are also the close of your first week of jiu-jitsu conditioning. These drills are great for developing balance, coordination, explosiveness, and total body strength. Often, I use these as a classroom warm-up to get everybody's juices flowing for class. As for jiu-jitsu applications, this is great for passing the guard and having confidence in your passing base and balance.

I begin the kangaroo hop by dropping into a seated squat position. Then, I walk my hands forward until I am in a coiled plank position. From here, I keep my rear high and my feet underneath me. Once ready, I drive off my feet, using my hips to swing my body forward while pushing forward and off the mats with my hands. I land with both feet flat on the mats with my hands up in front of me. Now you are ready to repeat the position. If you do not land with your hands off the mat, you are not exploding enough to get to the upright position.

FREQUENCY: 2-3 sets of 10 or timed sets

With some basic strength and conditioning out of the way, it's time to get into some basic balance drills. This is a move that you should be familiar with from your closed guard sit-ups and walking. For this movement, I really want you to work on your mechanics of standing up. Make sure that you do this slowly and use your bent knees to keep pressure off your lower back. This drill will contribute greatly to both your balance and your ability to open the closed guard, especially against taller opponents, as well as the strength and conditioning of your partner's closed guard. For day one of balance training, this drill is key and should be repeated at least a couple of times a month.

FREQUENCY: 3-5 minute timed sets

This is an incredible drill for developing standing posture balance and better body movement. The key to this position is to use a twisting body motion to stand straight up and return in an alternate-leg sitting position. You should do this at a slow to medium pace until you are comfortable with the motion. Once you are comfortable, you can increase the pace a little, but only go as fast as you can without sacrificing great posture. Make sure you have warmed up and stretched your legs, knees, and lower back before doing this drill.

Squatting Balance

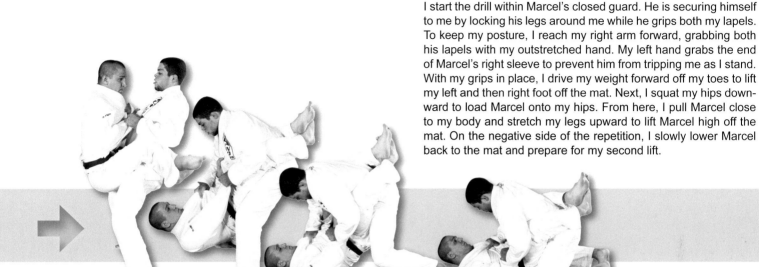

I start the drill within Marcel's closed guard. He is securing himself to me by locking his legs around me while he grips both my lapels. To keep my posture, I reach my right arm forward, grabbing both his lapels with my outstretched hand. My left hand grabs the end of Marcel's right sleeve to prevent him from tripping me as I stand. With my grips in place, I drive my weight forward off my toes to lift my left and then right foot off the mat. Next, I squat my hips downward to load Marcel onto my hips. From here, I pull Marcel close to my body and stretch my legs upward to lift Marcel high off the mat. On the negative side of the repetition, I slowly lower Marcel back to the mat and prepare for my second lift.

TWIST & SPINS

I begin the drill in a cross-legged seated position. To initiate the drill, I begin leaning forward to transfer my weight to my legs. Once my balance is far enough forward, I can start standing to my feet. To assist, I squeeze my knees together to propel my body upright. As I squeeze my legs, I uncoil them until I am standing with my face away from my starting position. Do not stop here; continue with your momentum as you wind your legs in the opposite direction. Slowly lower your hips as your legs cross and return to a seated position with your legs crossed.

DAY TWO:
Single-Leg Balance

ONE-LEGGED HOP

FREQUENCY: 3-5 minutes timed sets

Day two is all about focusing on single-legged balance drills. Why do I dedicate an entire day to developing single-legged drills? Because you will often find yourself against an opponent who wishes to take you down or reverse you with the single-leg takedown and many judo style takedowns require balance on one leg. If you want to buy yourself some time to defend against such attacks or learn throws like ouchi gari, uchimata, kouchi gari, or harai goshi, you will need to learn how to balance yourself on one leg before you throw yourself to the wolves.

For this simple yet invaluable drill, I begin with Marcel and me holding each other's extended right legs. For the basic version of this drill, start by hopping in a circle to the left and then to the right, making sure that the standing leg is bent at all times for balance. Switch legs after a couple of rotations to ensure that you balance train both legs equally. For the more advanced version, hop in erratic patterns in an attempt to unbalance your partner. The partner left standing is the winner.

SCORPION KICKS

FREQUENCY: 2-4x the length of the mat

The scorpion balance is one of my favorite pre-class warm-ups for single-leg balance and is one that I practiced repeatedly while I trained with Terere at TT and Leo Vieira at Brasa São Paulo. When you practice this drill, you need to focus on speed and the "scorpion" leg that helps you keep your momentum going forward while serving as a counterbalance. On a practical level, this drill is good for your balance during a scramble, failed throw, an uchimata throw, and for freeing the legs during a guard pass. One last piece of advice – don't go so fast that you fall or you are liable to go face first into the mat!

Just as with last week's kangaroo hops, I start by going down to all fours with my rear elevated. I lift my right leg and hop forward with my left. This leaves me out of balance as my base collapses toward my hands. I must hop my hands forward to regain base. Once comfortable, I increase speed for the remainder of the mat. When I have finished one length, I must switch legs. As with all balance drills, it is important that I become as dexterous as possible in my ability to balance on either leg or side.

DAY THREE:
Abdominal & Hip Balance

SIT-UP MOVEMENT

FREQUENCY: 1-2x the distance of the mat

As you hit the midpoint of week three, it is time to put those abdominals and hips that you've been working out to some good balance training. This is a great drill that I learned with Leo Vieira that I love to use to develop the holy trifecta: balance, coordination, and movement. With the sit-up movement drill, you will learn the necessary coordination, balance, and movement to sit up from the guard and generate forward drive from previously awkward positions. This translates to better guard transitions and more driving takedowns.

I begin this drill in a mock sit-up guard position; I am seated with my right foot on the mat with my left leg crossing underneath it. Instead of trying to stand up from here, I allow my right knee to collapse to the mat. From here, I utilize my hip and abdominal balance as I open up my left leg and swing it forward to a standing position. Once in position, I can continue the drill for the remainder of the mat. Keep one rule in mind while you practice this drill: you can never touch the mat with your hands while making your way forward. This would weaken your balance and abdominal training and is just cause for restarting the drill from the beginning.

TOE TOUCH

FREQUENCY: 3 sets of 12-20 or 1-2 minutes timed

For your second balance drill of week two, you will do an incredible abdominal workout masked as balance training. Whether you train jiu-jitsu or not, this is an incredible drill for core power, but when applied to jiu-jitsu, this drill is very useful for developing balance in the sitting/butterfly guard. If you feel that it is too easy for you to be pushed backward while sitting, this drill will develop the necessary strength and balance you need to overcome this problem.

I begin in the sitting position with both feet in front of me on the mat. Once ready, I lift both feet off the mat. For my first repetition, I bring my left hand to my right foot and then I continue by bringing my right hand to my left foot, all without touching my feet or hands to the mat. If you are having trouble with this drill, I suggest working on just holding the balance position without touching your feet for a couple of minutes at a time. Once you are confident with your balance, move on to the actual drill.

WEEK TWO: Balance

DAY FOUR: Basic Props

BALL BOARD BALANCE

FREQUENCY: Keep track of your time and beat it!

For the first prop of week two, you should try out the ball board when working on balance. If you cannot find one, you can substitute this balance training by using an Indo Board or make your own using a thick piece of PVC pipe and an old skateboard deck or thick plywood. What I like about the ball and board is that the fulcrum is fixed in the middle, making it much easier to find your balance point as you dive into supplementary props. Pertaining to jiu-jitsu, this drill is wonderful at all things standing, whether it is guard passing or posture. In addition, this helps your overall game as you strengthen your large stabilizing muscles: the quadriceps and hamstrings.

With the ball firmly within the walls of the balance deck, I am ready to stand up and work my balance. I start with my right foot on the board and then place my left foot on the elevated left side. Once here, I put some pressure on my left foot to bring myself to the ball board's equilibrium point. From here, I simply relax and focus on keeping my balance for as long as possible. As with all props, be sure to practice on a soft surface that you are confident to do a breakfall on. You might fall, so you should be prepared to fall safely.

NOSE RIDER

FREQUENCY: Keep track of your time and beat it!

This is a much more advanced drill than the previous one and it is the first to introduce the Indo Board as a prop. In Brazil, we love to use the ball board, Indo Board, and Swiss ball to supplement our training, and it is common to see mini-competitions in the academy to see who can create the best trick. Although this would not qualify as the best trick in my academy, it is a difficult move at first and an essential one to master. Mimicking a surfer on a long board, you work with a staggered stance as you constantly check and recheck your balance while moving atop a large pin. As with most board prop techniques, this is great for developing standing posture, but this move is unique in that it greatly assists your balance development when fighting with a staggered stance or in a combat base.

Once you are comfortable with this stance, try to play with this staggered stance and create your own drills and movements to further your balance training. You can only get better!

Before I hop on the board, it is essential that I move the pin all the way to the front of the board. Do not put the pin at the board's midpoint when getting on at first; you will likely lose your balance and fall! Once the board is in place, I place my back foot on the tail of the board and step forward with my right foot. In position, I slowly lean forward until I feel my back foot lift off the mat. Now that the board is in balance, I can slide forward and backward while maintaining this stance. If you want to nose ride in style, try to get your toes over the nose and get the pin under your front foot!

DAY FIVE:
Advanced Props

BALANCE BOARD SQUAT

FREQUENCY: 2 sets of 12-20

This is one of the more advanced drills and it is key to developing your quadriceps and hamstrings. For those who are struggling at day five of balance training, don't fret because the following drill for the day should be a little more relaxed and is not dependant on such perfect balance and muscle stability. Here's the good news: if you've made it to this point, you have already made great leaps in your passing game without even rolling.

As with the nose ride drill, I begin with the board in the ready position, the pin under the "nose" section of the board. I step my right and then left leg onto the board as I roll the pin toward the middle and then right side of the board. To begin my squat, I first roll the pin back to the middle. Once in the sweet spot, I squat down slowly, making sure to keep my form as solid as possible. From here, I can even lightly touch the board with my hand and then stand up to finish the repetition. Following this, I can either roll back and forward before my next pressure or continue from the sweet spot position.

BALANCING KNEE SWITCH

FREQUENCY: 2-5 minutes timed

As discussed last week, the Swiss ball is one of my favorite tools for strength and balance development. In this drill, you will mimic a faux knee-on-belly movement that really puts your balance to the test. Unlike the previous drill, you are offered a little more leeway in your practice. If you stumble or fall, try to land your hip on the ball and improvise until you can re-stabilize. Half the fun with Swiss ball drills is the improvisations that you will make to save yourself from an error. This is a drill that you should train regularly, but especially during knee-on-belly, side control, and mount training.

I begin on top of the Swiss ball in an all-fours position. Using my hands to pedal the ball forward, I slide my knees forward and balance in a kneeling position. Next, I put both hands on the ball and kick my left leg to the side. Then, I return my foot and repeat the same action to the right side. Try to hold these knee-on-belly positions and get comfortable with your knee balance.

DAY ONE:
Upper Body Warm-up

SIDE-TO-SIDE PICK UP

FREQUENCY: 2 sets of 10-12

To start off day one of week three, you should already be feeling great increases in strength, balance, and agility. For your first day of drilling this week, I want you to work on this classic wrestler's drill. The goal of this drill is to work on your gi-less grip with hands clasped together, your upper-body strength, and your hip explosion. When you combine explosive hips with a strong core and upper body, you are on your way to becoming a nightmare grappler for anybody.

As with all lifting drills, I choose a partner with a similar weight and build. Do not injure yourself by lifting someone you cannot comfortably handle. I start with Marcel hunched over in front of me. I grab both of my hands over his back and clasp my hands together. I keep my elbows tight to him as I hug his body. In one explosive action, I penetrate my hips into Marcel in a bridging motion while lifting Marcel's tailbone toward my head. From here, I use my upper body strength to swing Marcel's hips from my right to the left, until I can safely return him to the opposite side. Repeat to the other side. Always be extra careful that you keep your knees bent and use good posture to prevent injury.

BEAR CRAWL TO PUSH-UP

FREQUENCY: 2-4 x the length of the mat

Your second upper-body warm-up this week is the bear crawl to push up. This is an excellent warm-up exercise, especially when you have a long mat to work with. As you may have noticed by now, I really like working a lot of drills that run the length of the mat. The reason is simple; you get to incorporate realistic movement into your drills, along with an infusion of cardio, strength, and balance training. This is also a great drill for learning to escape the single-leg takedown where you try to run away and for working on your side control to knee-on-belly transitions.

I begin on one side of the mat with my feet square. Squatting down, I put both hands on the mat and I bear crawl my hands forward until I am in a push-up position. From here, I execute a push-up, breathing in as I lower myself, exhaling sharply as I explode upward. Following the push-up, I walk my feet back to my hands, stand, and repeat for the length of the mat. Again, I cannot reiterate this enough – focus on your breathing, and never hold your breath!

DAY TWO:
Squatting Power

BALL SQUAT

FREQUENCY: 2-3 sets of 8-12

This is easily one of the most difficult Swiss ball exercises in this routine and it should be handled with extreme caution. The stand and squat is a dynamic exercise that will put your balance and squatting power to the ultimate test. I originally started doing this while training at Terere's TT Academy, and this exercise has followed me with all my travels. As for jiu-jitsu, you should expect to see great results with your passing balance because this exercise really focuses on those stabilizing leg muscles in conjunction with the workout from the standard squat. Practice this in a safe environment on a very soft surface – you may fall!

As with all balance-ball exercises, I begin by placing the ball on a soft surface, free from obstructions. I place both hands on the ball and in one motion, I jump my feet to a squatted "owl" position. I make sure that my feet are stable and will not slip downward before I stand upright. Once I am sure of my position, I slowly stand up while slightly pinching my feet into the ball for stability. Once I reach the zenith, I pause to collect my balance and drop myself downward to finish off the repetition. Until you are comfortable with this drill, you may wish to use a spotter to help with your balance and confidence.

SUMO SQUAT

FREQUENCY: 5-10 minutes timed

For your second squatting power drill, you will be incorporating wrestling movements with forward pressure and a level change. The wrestling pressure comes from the forward shoulder drive that you and your partner will exert toward each other via the ball. The level change is in reference to the squat, which will enable you to get underneath your opponent's defense as you shoot in for a takedown. This drill is resistance training at its finest and is a must have in anybody's drill routine.

Marcel and I begin facing each other, both on dropped knees with the ball pressed against our right shoulders. While pressuring the ball into each other, we stand up from our kneeling posture. In a coordinated effort, both Marcel and I switch the ball to our left shoulders and immediately drop to a kneeling posture, effectively changing our level. To continue, we would stand again and rotate the ball to the original shoulder. As you get more advanced, try to really drive into each other and beat the other opponent to the level change.

DAY THREE:

TURTLE TUMBLE

FREQUENCY: 2-3 sets of 12-20

For the beginning of day three, it is important that you continue to progress into more difficult strength and balance exercises. This a great drill that I learned from the legendary Oswaldo Alves during his brutal conditioning and drilling classes. The goal here is to work on your flexibility and total body strength while your partner must keep his balance as your swinging weight disrupts his base and equilibrium. On a purely jiu-jitsu level, this drill teaches one very important lesson: when you dedicate your entire body to one thing in jiu-jitsu, it is incredibly difficult to resist. Imagine if you were to use a similar roll against someone who was not prepared with as strong a base? In that case, your opponent is likely to get rolled as he feels all your weight pull him off balance. As you will discover while practicing as the turtled partner, even in a based-out position, with your knees wide and your hips weighted downward, it is still very difficult to balance yourself without falling to your side.

DAY FOUR:

FREQUENCY: 2-3 sets of 12-20

Day four includes a body weight exercise that is essential for becoming a back attack master. This is the drill that you should focus all of the day's supplemental training on because you will need this motion to move on to tomorrow's variation. This is also a master drill that works everything. You should expect to gain coordination, balance, strength, and conditioning through this drill. You will also get a great feel for your own weight and your partner's hips, letting you know exactly where you should be to successfully take and maintain the back. As a general rule, stay above his hips and keep the middle of your chest glued to his upper back – this should keep you above his hips.

Abdominal Power

Before I jump into this move, it is vital that I showcase the proper grip that I have against Marcel. As shown in the close-up, I have both my arms under Marcel's near-side arm with both hands gripping his far-side lapel with a thumb on the inside grip. With this grip in place, Marcel goes to the turtle position with his knees pointed slightly outward for base. In one motion, I roll my head over his left flank and then kick my feet to vertical. To finish the first phase of the flip over, I hide my head under Marcel's left side as my feet come down to the mat. To return, I pull on his lapels while horse kicking my feet upward. Once my head is out from under him, I continue to throw my feet to Marcel's right side until I land in the original starting position. From here, I continue to finish out my set.

CLOSE UP: GRIPS

Beginning Gravity Workout
ADVANCED MONKEY CLIMB

As with all standing drills, I pick a partner that is equal in size and weight. It is important that he can stay in posture while I climb around his stationary body. I start the drill with Marcel standing in my closed guard with my weight sitting up toward him and my right hand clasping his left shoulder. In one motion, I duck under his right arm while pushing it away with my left hand. My left hand then clasps his shoulder as I lock his arm in a faux head-and-arm triangle. The next part is the key to getting around Marcel; I unlock my feet and hook my right foot over Marcel's right knee. Using this hook, I climb my body higher while I pull myself toward his back with my arms. Safely on his back, I switch my grips so that my left arm is now under his armpit and my right arm is over his arm. I duck under his left arm while hooking my left leg inside his as a clamp. I keep pressure on his back with my right leg to keep my hips high, and then I swing my left leg to Marcel's front to pendulum my body back into the guard.

DAY FIVE:

ALL-FOURS MONKEY CLIMB

FREQUENCY: 10x each side

After you have mastered day four's advanced monkey climb, you are ready to try your hand at the all-fours monkey climb. This drill is both more difficult and easier than the prior move. For the opponent on all fours, it is easier because you have developed the necessary strength to hold yourself in this position for quite sometime and you do not need to balance with a standing base. For the bottom player, it is easier because you have a rest stop when you get to the back. However, the difficulty is amped up in the beginning because more of your weight is hanging downward and you really have to fight gravity to get to the back. In addition to this, you have more repetitions, so you should really pace yourself. Beyond this, the technique offers great benefits to your all-fours base and exponential leaps in your ability to take the back and close off gaps in your attacks.

DAY ONE:

WEEK 4: In Focus

You may be thinking, "Why do I need to learn gymnastics or any acrobatic moves for jiu-jitsu?" especially when so many of our moves are based on simple and easy-to-perform techniques. Well, the answer is in agility and total body strength. For a long time, gymnasts have been master-level athletes known for their incredible body control, strength, flexibility, and agility. It is these attributes that we wish to tap into while retaining the same mindset of using movements that are related to our core jiu-jitsu concepts and techniques. This way, when you are faced with a wall in training you will have more options — you can slowly smash through it, step around it, or in the case of gymnastics, jump over it!

FREQUENCY: 3 sets of 20 or timed sets

Although this movement jumps ahead a little bit to month two, it is still an essential movement that should be showcased this week. It is the back roll with handstand. When doing this, first focus on executing a proper back shoulder roll with your chin glued to your chest to prevent injury, your head to the side to open up your shoulder, a proper breakfall slap with your hands at forty-five degrees away from your hips, and a roll over your exposed shoulder. Once here, the handstand will come easily – just focus on horse-kicking your feet upward as you come up to your hands. This movement can also save you from a slipup, where you have fallen but do not want to start on the bottom. Do this movement explosively and get out of trouble!

Advanced Gravity Workout

I begin with an open all-fours base similar to the one used for bear crawling; Marcel has me in his closed guard and he is locking his body to me by underhooking both his arms under my own and clasping his hands behind my back. In his first step, Marcel changes to an over-and-under grip around my right ear. Just as in the previous move, Marcel ducks under my left arm and clamps his head and body to it as he shimmies his hip to my left side. From here, Marcel releases his grip and grabs my right lat with his right hand. With this grip in place, Marcel puts weight on his right leg, lightening his left, making it easy for him to pull his body to my back with his lat grip. Once here, he takes the back position, switches grips, ducks under my right arm, and slides to the closed guard in the much easier return trip.

Introduction to Handstands

BACK ROLL W/ HANDSTAND

I begin on one side of the mat, facing the starting point. I sit my rear to my heels with my hands in front and my chin pointed into my chest. As I sit my rear to the floor, I slap the mat at a forty-five degree angle to break my fall. Continuing with my momentum, I turn my head to the right to open up my left shoulder. As I do this, I roll onto my shoulder and horse-kick my feet upward. My momentum carries me upward to my hands and I pause for a moment in an erect handstand. From here, I throw my feet back, landing in the original position and ready to continue for the remainder of the mat length.

DAY TWO:
Hand Walker

WALKING HANDSTAND

FREQUENCY: 1x the length of the mat

Once you are comfortable with yesterday's backroll and handstand, it is time to move on to the hand walker. Remember, you have built a lot of strength, balance, and coordination over the past few weeks, so you should be feeling ready for different challenges. When it comes to walking on your hands, it is natural to experience a little trepidation, and it is even more natural to fall a lot as your learn to balance on your outstretched arms. Don't let this stop you. If you feel that you are going to fall, simply tuck your chin to your chest and round your back as you fall forward; this will force you to ball up and flow into the fall (making this a great precursor to our week on breakfalls). Although this is a very advanced movement to get used to, it will definitely pay off in your ability to prevent the sweep and improvise while passing the guard. If you are feeling especially confident with the walking handstand, add a push-up every now and then for an extra challenge.

I begin on one side of the mat with my feet square. Kneeling over, I drop my hands to the mat directly in front of my face. Now is the time for commitment; I jump my feet off the mat and point my feet skyward, keeping my toes pointed. I am vertical and ready to walk. As I start stepping my hands forward one at a time, I allow my feet to "scorpion" slightly over my head, this allows me to walk forward and to keep my momentum heading in the same direction. So, the "scorpion" serves as my tail or my counterbalance. I continue walking until I reach the other side of the mat. When learning this move, I find it helpful to have a spotter hold your legs vertically as you learn to balance. You can use a wall as a substitute, but I often find that you depend far too much on the wall and do not develop the necessary balance and confidence to walk. Remember, if you fall, tuck your chin to your chest, round out your back, and easily roll out of it. Soon you will realize that half the fun of getting down the mat is rolling out of your forward falls.

DAY THREE:
Cartwheels

CARTWHEEL

FREQUENCY: 2-4x the distance of the mat

If yesterday seemed a little too tough with the walking handstands, don't worry! Day three is much easier. The reason you started with the walking handstand instead of the cartwheel is because this is a movement that really benefits from a strong upright posture. If you decide to use the cartwheel for a guard pass, as in the famed star pass created by my former coach Leo Vieira, you need to make sure that your feet can clear your opponent's outstretched legs and hooks. If your legs are too low and your opponent can follow you, you are at risk of reversal as he kicks or pulls you off balance. Once you are confident with the motion, it's time to move on to the jiu-jitsu application: the round-off.

I begin in a sideways stance with my left side facing the end of the mat. Bending at the knees, I drop my left hand to the mat on the same line as my feet. This coils me up for the cartwheel. I release this energy by jumping off the mat with my left foot as my right hand touches the mat. Once completely vertical, I continue with the momentum until my right and then left foot touches the mat. I return to a standing position and continue for the remainder of the mat.

ROUND-OFF

FREQUENCY: 2-4x the distance of the mat

Now that you are confident with the cartwheel, it is time to do the real jiu-jitsu application of this gymnastics movement: the round-off. Think of the round-off as the end of the guard pass where you need to face your opponent instead of being on your side. Mastering the round-off allows you to pass and face your opponent very quickly, setting you up for the north-south position if he fails to recover or another guard pass if he does recover. You can also practice this and the cartwheel in a smaller environment by completing one round-off or cartwheel and then doing another to return to your original starting position.

Just as with the cartwheel, I begin in a sideways stance with my left side facing the end of the mat. Bending at the knees, I drop my left hand to the mat on the same line as my feet. This coils me up for the cartwheel phase of the round-off. I release this energy by jumping off the mat with my left foot as my right hand touches the mat. Once completely vertical, I change the move from the cartwheel by twisting my hips so that my belly button faces the end of the mat. This aligns me to land square instead of sideways. I try to bring both feet down as close to the same moment as possible and I finish by looking at my starting point. Now I am ready for my next repetition.

DAY FOUR:
SPIN WHEEL

FREQUENCY: 2x the distance of the mat

As you get toward the end of week four, I really want to put your agility and balance to the test. The spin wheel is a great move to start with and it is far less intimidating than the back handspring. Although there are not too many situations where you will use this identical movement in jiu-jitsu, it will help you develop the necessary agility and total body movement to get out of many tricky situations. Practice this movement until you are very confident before moving on to the back handspring.

FREQUENCY: 2-3x the distance of the mat

The capoeira handspring is always scary during the first half of the movement and easy on the second. What it calls for is a leap of faith where you cannot see where you are going. The good news is that once you can see the mat, you can also see your landing. Just as was the case with the spin wheel, the back handspring will pay off huge dividends in both your balance and agility and that is why I challenge you to learn it. If this is proving too difficult or scary, use a spotter for the back roll until you gain some confidence. Once you learn this, throw a back flip at the end and you have a victory dance worth showcasing!

Agility Master

I begin in a square stance with my back facing the end of the mat. To initiate the drill, I crouch down and put my left hand behind me with my fingers facing the end of the mat. From here, I look down to my left side, coiling up my body for the action phase. Now, I jump both feet off the mat and spin to a square stance with my back facing the end of the mat. Once I stand, I have completed one repetition and I am ready to continue.

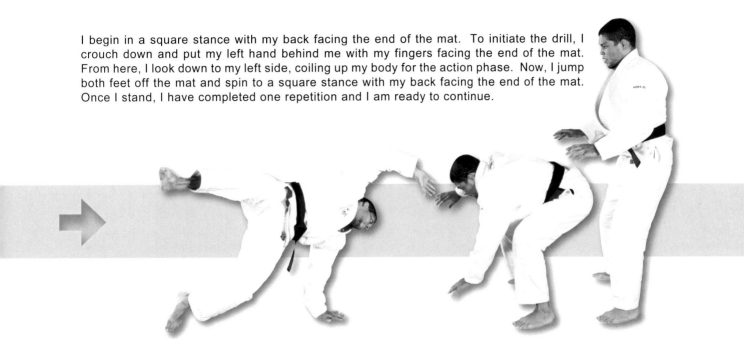

CAPOEIRA HANDSPRING

As was the case with the spin wheel, I begin in a square stance with my back facing the end of the mat. To initiate the drill, I crouch down and put my left hand behind me with my fingers facing the end of the mat. Instead of looking down as I did in the spin wheel, I now have to look over my right shoulder so I can spot my right arm landing and where I will drop my feet. This is the leap-of-faith phase. I go with confidence and let my head lead the way. Then, I land both hands to the mat and jump my feet to a square stance with my back facing the end of the mat. Now I am ready to continue. Needless to say, you should practice this on a very forgiving surface with safety as your focus.

WEEK FOUR: Gymnastics for Jiu-Jitsu
DAY FIVE: HEAD POST TRAINING

FREQUENCY: 2 sets of 12-20 or timed

The end of Month One is in sight! Now that you are comfortable with back handsprings, cartwheels, and spin wheels, this movement should come easy. Basically, it is a headstand with a twist and not quite dissimilar to moves that you would see in break dancing. As with the cartwheel, you want to imagine yourself jumping over your opponent's legs. If his legs can follow you because your legs are too low, you will have to go to plan B or perhaps get reversed. This is an easy drill to start out our last day of gymnastic training and it serves as the necessary introduction to more advanced head post training.

FREQUENCY: 2 sets of 10-20 or timed

This is an excellent drill that I learned from wrestling and tweaked a little for jiu-jitsu training. It is a continuation of the head post training, but it involves throwing yourself into a bridge position (you will focus on this next month) and then turning your hips over to get back to all fours. The great thing about this drill is that it accurately follows one of the tangibles of acrobatic guard passing. Sometimes when you do a head post to pass the guard, your opponent manages to sweep you to your back. Instead of giving up the points and falling to your rear, you train yourself to land on your feet and scramble over to side control. This is an essential drill to have in your arsenal.

Head-to-Head

I begin with the top of my head and both palms on the mat with my thumbs next to my ears. Both feet are on the mat with my legs close to my left elbow. To start the drill, I jump my feet to vertical, using my hands and head to keep my balance. I keep my feet as vertical as possible to mimic guard passing. I return my right leg to the mat and then my left leg. From here, I will jump again to the other side to continue my training.

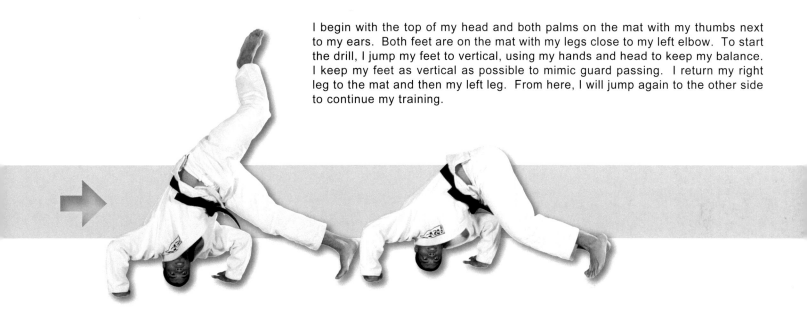

ADVANCED HEAD POST TRAINING

From a square stance, I put both hands on the mat with my thumbs next to my ears. As I lean my head to the mat, I jump my feet directly over my body, overshooting vertical and landing on my toes in a bridging position. To setup my turn, I open up my right arm to expose my right shoulder. Then, I step over with my left leg while pivoting on my shoulder to get back to all fours. Usually, I like to do the head post jump at a slow to medium speed and the turnout very fast. It is important that you develop that speed so that you can get out of a potentially bad position before your opponent has time to pressure you.

MONTH TWO: In Review

This month, you took a very athletic approach to Jiu-Jitsu. You worked on gaining muscle memory and getting your body conditioned to do certain exercises that will appear time and again while sparring and drilling. When it comes to competition, strength, cardiovascular endurance, flexibility, and balance will pay off in spades.

Remember, Jiu-Jitsu is a full-body workout. Do not make the mistake of overworking any one muscle system at the detriment of another. Even if you prefer a certain guard or pass, it is important to have your entire body strong and ready to move however you will need it in Jiu-Jitsu. Sure, your core and legs are major components to most positions, but your arms and neck are just as important. You will see in the coming months that muscles you didn't even know you had will get a workout with Jiu-Jitsu!

An important lesson to take from this month is to be honest with yourself. If you are struggling with your strength and conditioning in week four, you may wish to return to week one and go through this month one more time. This is entirely okay! Don't rush it! You have your entire life to perfect Jiu-Jitsu - it is more important that you get your body and mind ready before jumping in too deep!

Whenever you workout, be ready to replenish your body within 15-30 minutes of your routine. I like to drink protein shakes to help build new muscle fibers. The most important thing to do is rehydrate! Always have water nearby to help you recover!

WEEKEND WORK:

Supplement your training with weekend runs. My personal favorites are anything short interval with high intensity runs. Try bleacher climbs, hill runs, or 100 meter sprints, with lower intensity return laps. This will help create fast twitch muscle fibers while mimicking the intensity of a grappling match. I believe running is the perfect complement to Jiu-Jitsu because it keeps up your cardio and gets you in shape to finish the match!

MONTH THREE:
Mastering the Basics

Now that your body is strong and flexible and you are improving your base, it is time to start mastering the basics. This month is about training your body to move in ways in which it is not accustomed. Although children pick up jiu-jitsu very quickly and many of the movements come natural to them, as adults we lose that ability to adapt our bodies so easily. We must train our bodies to move the way we want them to, and a big part of that is attributed to muscle memory. For the most part, when you learn a move in class, your body doesn't automatically do it right the first time. You have to drill it several times to make sure you are putting your hands in the correct place and you are doing every part of the technique in the right order. When it comes to the basics, the most important aspect of muscle memory comes with basic movements. Instead of being particular about where to place your hands and remembering every small detail, it is more important that you learn to break your falls so you don't get hurt, and move your hips so you can have a more agile guard and more effective escapes. The bridge is an important movement that you must get used to doing, and the technical lift will assure you always stand up in base and do not get hurt in the process.

This month, view the basics as the fundamentals of jiu-jitsu. Movement, not cross-chokes, armbars, and simple guard passes, is the key to learning the fundamentals. There is a difference between simple and advanced techniques, but any movement relevant to Brazilian Jiu-Jitsu should be considered a basic or fundamental for the art. What is more fundamental – a bridge escape from the mount (upa) or the bridge movement itself? Obviously the bridge movement is the fundamental because it can be applied to many different techniques.

In week one, you will be focusing on breakfalls and sprawls. We focus first on breakfalls because they are the most important form of self protection in our daily lives. Once you learn to break your fall correctly, you can practice all types of standup without the fear of hurting yourself if you get taken down. Sprawls are important because they are your first line of defense when your opponent shoots in at you to take you down or reverse the game. When you sprawl correctly, you can spend more time deciding where the match will progress to and less time lying on your back with your opponent dominating you. In addition, I like to focus on breakfalls and sprawls first because they help to build a fighting spirit as you continually pick yourself up off the mat. Mental training like this is as important as physical training and could be the difference between you and your opponent in a competition.

Week two introduces one of the most important movements in jiu-jitsu: the hip escape. Learning to hip escape is key to all lateral movement in jiu-jitsu, and it is essential in building a great guard as well as defense. As you will discover, the more hip movement present, the greater the appearance of fluidity in your game. Usually, blocky or awkward-looking styles are due to stiff hips. As you learn to hip escape, practice all variations and not just the simple "shrimp across the mat." If you are only doing this, you are missing out on many of the hip escape's useful applications. You must master the hip escape to different angles for different purposes. For example, you will hip escape laterally or away for the elbow escape from the mount, downward for a tighter half guard, and upward for certain attacks like the triangle choke. As I mentioned before, it is the principle of the hip escape, not each individual technique that is the most important lesson this week.

In week three, you will learn the upa and combine it with other movements from earlier in the month. The upa is another name for the bridge, and it is the key to many finishing techniques and escapes. Once you train your body to use it, the upa can be a powerful tool for the armbar and triangle choke, as both are stronger when you bridge into them. As you will notice in doing the drills this week, the upa should be combined with the hip escape early in training so that you always see the two as interrelated and contiguous instead of as solitary movements.

In addition, the upa can level the playing field when it comes to strength and size. The hips and legs of smaller students are often more powerful than the arms and chests of much heavier guys. Once you learn to use the upa to your advantage, it will also act as a weight multiplier. The pressure from bridging can make the person on top feel much heavier than he actually is while he is pinning his opponent on the ground. As you can tell, the upa is a powerful movement that allows your hips to control and disrupt your opponent, leaving your hands free to go to work.

Week four introduces an essential movement for changing positions from the guard to standing. It focuses on the technical lift, a very important movement for both self-defense and competitive jiu-jitsu. While often seen as defensive, it has just as many offensive options and variations. With the technical lift, a competitor can choose between offense and defense based on standing back (the master lift) or forward (thrusting techniques). I introduce the technical lift in week four because it can be combined with bridges and hip escapes in many different forms to create drill combinations. The technical lift can also be used as a baiting technique. You can stand with the master lift, and then counter as your opponent predictably lunges toward you! As you will find out, there are more variations to the technical lift than most would imagine – sit-throughs, thrusts, hip crumbles, hip heists, and lifts. You will see all of these styles in the weeks to come, and hopefully you will begin to train your body to use them interchangeably.

In this chapter, try to focus on your body mechanics. Repetition will play a major role in training your body to do what your brain tells it. Eventually, you will not even have to think before attempting these movements. Your body will automatically hip escape when it is supposed to and bridge without hesitation or even combine the two and create a seamless combination effortlessly.

DAY ONE:
Back & Shoulder Rolls

═ BACK BREAKFALLS ═

FREQUENCY: 4 sets of 20

The back breakfall is an essential maneuver that all students must not only learn, but master. My first exposure to the technique was through my first instructor, Careca, who in turn learned it from his master, jiu-jitsu and judo great, Oswaldo Alves. This move will not be new to most; it is practiced in most jiu-jitsu and judo dojos, but regardless, train every single repetition as if it were your first exposure to the drill. The smallest movement, like tucking your chin, breaking your fall to forty-five degrees, and rolling your back are essential to your longevity in the sport and your overall preparation to deal with most other slips or falls.

I begin the back breakfall in a crouched position with my hands crossed in front of me and my heels touching the mat. Falling backward, I first make contact with my rear, then lower back, and finally my upper back. As I hit the middle of my back, I forcefully slap the mat with my arms at a forty-five degree angle from my body. I allow my legs to continue the backward momentum and then I rock myself forward and back to my feet. Be sure that you do not hit the mat at a higher than forty-five degree angle; it could result in injury.

═ BACK ROLLS ═

FREQUENCY: 2-4x the distance of the mat

Now that you know the proper mechanics of the back breakfall, it is time to expand our horizons this week with the back roll. The back roll is an essential movement in jiu-jitsu, and it is often used to prevent your guard from being passed, to recover guard, and to sweep to the mounted position. Actually a shoulder roll, the back roll will also help you develop the proper mechanics to expose your shoulder for a backward roll. In addition, you should expect to gain some neck, upper- and lower-back, and hip flexibility as you get comfortable loosening up during the rolling phase.

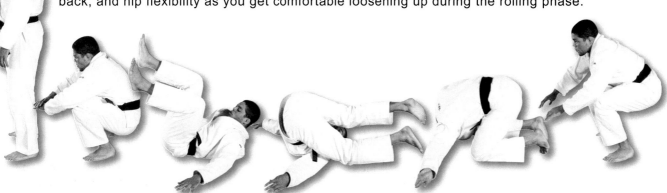

I begin with my back to the end of the mat in a square stance. I initiate my back roll by first crouching with my hands crossed in front of me and my heels touching the mat. Falling backward, I first make contact with my rear, then lower back, and finally my upper back. As I hit the middle of my back, I forcefully slap the mat with my arms at a forty-five degree angle from my body. I allow my legs to continue the backward momentum as I turn my head to the side, opening my left shoulder for the back roll. I roll over my left shoulder until my knees touch the floor. Once my head comes free, I stand and repeat the drill. Emphasize the opening of your shoulder and never roll over your neck while doing this drill!

FREQUENCY: 2 sets of 12-20

This is a very simple drill that could be added to almost any warm up. It is also a great precursor to the extended shoulder roll, back breakfall, and back roll. Of special importance is the concept of opening up your shoulder for any type of back roll movement. While you practice, be sure of your movements, expose your shoulder and work on your flexibility until you can safely touch both toes to the mat. Once you have reached this point, try to relax in this stacked position for a few seconds. Soon, you will be so flexible here that your knees are likely to touch your face. Again, this is an essential drill for back falls, rolls, and guard movements.

From a stomach-up position, I have both feet and palms on the mat with my knees bent. Using my hips and lower abdominals, I swing my legs upward and slightly to my right. I shift my head to my left, exposing my right shoulder. As I roll onto that shoulder I touch my feet to the mat on the right. From here, I swing my feet back to the starting position and repeat to the other side. Remember, throw your legs in the direction of your exposed shoulder. Do not make the mistake of exposing your shoulder and then throwing your legs the wrong way – you will end up stacking yourself and adding undue pressure to your neck.

EXTENDED SHOULDER ROLL

FREQUENCY: 2 sets of 10-20

Before you dive into standing break falls and back rolls, you will definitely want to try your hand at the extended shoulder roll. At the heart of this drill, you have the same shoulder roll as before, but you get the added benefit of rolling completely to a prone position. This offers the benefit of teaching your body what to do with your arms during a roll while emphasizing the importance of flowing between defense and attack. The sparring application to this move is a guard pass defense to a single- or double-leg takedown.

Once again, I begin in a stomach-up position. I have both feet on the mat with my knees bent. Using my hips and lower abdominals, I swing my legs upward and slightly to my right. I shift my head to my left, exposing my right shoulder, as I roll onto that shoulder, touching my feet to the mat on the right. From here, I turn both arms and shoulders out so that I can free my arms as I finish my roll. I continue to roll and land in a prone position with both arms open, ready to grab an imaginary leg. It is very important that you get used to opening your arms here. Besides setting up the single- and double-leg takedowns, your open arms serve as a barrier, preventing your opponent from possibly taking your back.

DAY TWO:
Front Rolls & Side Falls
FORWARD SOMMERSAULT

FREQUENCY: 2x the distance of the mat

You covered a lot of back breakfalls, back flexibility, and rolling on day one and now it is time to continue to front and side breakfalls for day two. As a starting point, you should focus on the front somersault. This is a square roll, meaning that you will execute from and return to a square stance instead of a staggered one with one foot in front of the other. The benefits of this roll come in the form of confidence and agility. Just be careful that you never actually roll onto your neck. Jump to your shoulders instead of initiating a death dive onto your own neck. Expect to get a little dizzy after a few of these!

I begin in a square stance with my back facing the end of the mat. To initiate the drill, I reach down and place both palms on the mat. Remembering my handstand training, I put my weight onto my hands, lean farther forward and tuck my chin to my chest. This forces me to fall to my upper back. I keep my back curled and use a back breakfall to absorb any shock. Maintaining my momentum, I flick my legs downward, using the force to carry my body back to a crouching position. Just to reiterate, do not dive onto your head or neck, but your shoulders. In all likelihood, you already have some experience with this rollout while practicing hand-walking.

FREQUENCY: 2 sets of 12-20 or timed

Now that you have learned the forward somersault, you are more than prepared to learn the standard front roll, otherwise known as the front breakfall. This is a common technique in most academies, but I prefer to teach my students to land with the breakfall instead of trying to come up to their feet every time. This way, you will learn to break your fall and you will not develop bad habits as you tumble with your legs awkwardly beneath you. Develop the ability to break your fall first; this is far more important. Later you can make adaptations for the roll-out version.

I stagger my legs with my left leg a little forward as I bend down to attempt the roll. I place my right hand on the mat and begin shooting my left hand toward my right hip. This opens up my left shoulder for the roll. I roll onto that shoulder and slightly tense my rear leg. As I finish the roll, I land on my right side, slapping the mat at a forty-five degree angle with my right hand. My rear (right) leg lands flat and elongated while my left leg ends in a bent position. I stand and repeat the drill for the remainder of the mat. Remember, the fall is broken by your arm and leg in this case. Do not land flat on your back or you will absorb too much shock.

ONE-SIDED BREAKFALL

FREQUENCY: 2 sets of 20 or 2x the distance of the mat

It is not good enough that you know how to breakfall forward and backward, you must learn to breakfall to the side as well. This move should be trained in combination with the front roll, because the two techniques share so many similarities, especially in the ending position. Once you begin sparring from the feet, this is the fall most people use when thrown with deashi-barai foot sweeps. Furthermore, this movement gives you a sneak peek into the technical lift, which will be drilled in detail later this month.

From a left-foot-forward staggered stance, I bring my left hand to my abdomen as I swing my right arm and leg outward and slightly forward. Keeping my weight on my left leg, I swing both my right leg and arm in front of me, forcing me to fall toward my right hip. As my body makes contact with the mat, I emphatically hit the mat with my right hand to absorb the shock of the fall. My arm is close to my body to prevent injury. Next, I sit up to my right hand and post my left foot on the mat. To do the technical lift, I stand up on my left foot and right hand, lightening my hips and right leg. Then, I swing my right leg under me and stand up in base. Now, I am ready to continue with the one-sided breakfall.

DAY THREE:
Sprawling Basics

SPRAWLS

FREQUENCY: 3 sets of 20

Now that you are familiar with breakfalls, it is time to get to some more preventative maneuvers. This is where the basic sprawl comes in. In contrast to the following sprawl, this is the sprawl that you will want to use most often, because you focus your hip pressure on the exact point where your opponent is attacking. This makes you feel much heavier while retaining a high level of mobility. Many mixed martial artists have made careers of sprawling against their opponent's wrestling takedown and then pounding on them as their failed shot leaves them exposed, so you should learn to do the jiu-jitsu version of the same thing. Develop a sprawl in drilling and then add chokes and top transitions to make your opponent pay!

I begin in a staggered stance. Quickly, I kneel down as if I am doing a lunge or a wrestler's level change. I place both hands on the mat and then sprawl my left leg backward, touching my left hip to the mat. Then, I swing my left leg back to the front and prepare for my next sprawl. With this drill, always sprawl your front foot backward, because this is the exposed leg that your opponent is likely to attack.

SQUARE SPRAWLS

FREQUENCY: 2-3 sets of 12-20

The square sprawl shares a lot in common with a regular sprawl, but this time, you focus on driving both your hips to the mat. I have also added a two-legged hop to recover the standing position to increase the cardio burn. As you can feel by now after training the previous sprawl, these drills are excellent for adding a high-intensity burn to your workout while teaching your body combat-effective motor skills. Whenever you fight in a square stance, you can use this sprawl as you drive both hips to the mat to defend against a wrestler's takedown.

I begin in a square stance. Quickly, I kneel down in a squat and then touch my hands to the floor. Then, I sprawl both legs backward, dropping my hips to the mat. I try to put a strong back arch into the position to increase the weight of my hips. Immediately afterward, I lift my rear to the sky and jump my feet up toward my hands. Now, I can safely stand up and continue to another sprawl. For a more cardio intense workout, run in place and have a friend or instructor call out intermittent sprawls for a select time.

FREQUENCY: 2 sets of 12-20 or timed

This movement is a continuation of the square sprawl and it calls for more explosiveness in getting back to your feet. Not only is this great for your jiu-jitsu, but it also works wonders for your hip mobility and leg/core strength. While training this movement, try to do the whole movement at a rapid-fire pace. Do not sit and recover when you get back to your feet. If you choose to do this as a timed exercise, choose a short time like one minute or less and really try to keep up the intensity throughout. This is a real leg burner!

From a square stance, I crouch into a deep squat with my hands to my front. I should kneel deep enough so that both my elbows are between my knees. Immediately, I drop my hands to the mat in front of me at shoulder's width. I sprawl both my legs back and away from my body to land in a wide push-up position. Once I have lowered my body to the floor, I push off the mat, exploding my torso upward. I continue this momentum, jumping all the way back to the starting position. Now, I can continue with my second repetition.

SQUAT & ELBOW SPRAWLS

FREQUENCY: 2 sets of 8-20

The elbow sprawl is the final sprawl drill for today, and you should be very tired before you get to this one. I originally learned this move from my first instructor, Careca, and it is so great because the sprawl mixes in a judo style breakfall, where you fall onto your forearms, with a regular square sprawl. This is a total body exercise that really works the upper body and core muscles along with the standard leg burn.

From a square stance, I crouch down toward the mat. In one movement, I dive my forearms to the mat, touching my hands together to form a triangle. As my hands get to position, my hips and legs are already sprawling backward. From the plank position, I keep my rear high and I explode off my forearms while jumping my feet forward. My hands should be off the mat before my feet arrive. This makes the move far more explosive and effective for jiu-jitsu conditioning. I stand upright and prepare for the next repetition.

DAY FOUR:

LEAPFROGS

FREQUENCY: 3-4x the distance of the mat

This drill is easy and fun, and, more important, it's effective at bridging solo sprawl training with a live opponent. Think of this movement as a forward sprawl where you try to incorporate all of the same mechanics as your previous square sprawl training. As you practice, try to focus on smashing the Swiss ball with your body weight and hips while getting a far forward leap out of your legs. Oftentimes, the jiu-jitsu application to this technique comes after you have defended the shot and your opponent tries to back out of his uncomfortable position. Once you have mastered the leapfrog, you don't have to let him out! Follow him with the sprawl and keep the game where you want it to be!

I start the drill in a square position facing the end of the mat. I am leaning over and hugging a Swiss ball with both hands with my legs coiled up under my rear. Explosively, I spring my body forward. I must focus on jumping forward instead of upward, because upward movement gives my opponent too much space. Landing on the ball, I smash my hips and bodyweight downward while sprawling my legs back. With the sprawl completed, I recoil my legs and prepare for the next repetition. As with everything in my top game, I am always on my toes.

DAY FIVE:

FREQUENCY: 1-2 sets of 20

To begin the day on partner sprawls, I usually like to choose a solo sprawl warm-up as I mentally and physically prepare for the drills I have ahead. This is a great drill to that end. In the square sprawl and turn around, you will be incorporating a square sprawl with a hip-pivoting technique. It is a very dynamic drill and you should feel more in control of your body than had you just committed yourself to sprawl repetitions. Work this movement at a medium pace and save your explosive energy for the partner sprawls. This is an excellent drill for developing further hip control and improvisation during stand-up fighting.

Ball Sprawl Repititions

FREQUENCY: 3-4x the distance of the mat

This is the second drill for day four's ball sprawl repetitions and is the inverse of the leapfrog. Where the leapfrog is a following-sprawl maneuver, the backward ball sprawl is a classic sprawl that can be developed for the use of takedown defense. My favorite way to practice this technique is side by side with the leapfrog. I do frog leaps the length of the mat and then return using backward sprawls. As with the previous drill, make sure that you squish the ball with your hips to really simulate an opponent underneath you. Also, as you suck the ball underneath you to mimic a deep shot, fling your legs back as fast as possible to build your timing and reaction speed in preparation for the real thing.

As with the previous drill, I start in a square position facing the end of the mat. I am leaning over and hugging a Swiss ball with both hands and my legs coiled up under my rear. I lift my hips off the ball, spread my legs to create space, and pull the ball all the way under me to simulate a deep wrestler's shot. Forcefully, I throw my legs backward, sprawling my hips down as my chest drives into the ball. With the sprawl finished, I return to my coiled position and ready myself for my next action.

Partner Sprawls

WEEK ONE:
Breakfalls & Sprawls

As with the square sprawl, I begin in a square stance. Quickly, I kneel down in a squat and touch my hands to the floor. Then, I sprawl both legs backward, dropping my hips to the mat. From here, I turn my hips so that my right hip lifts from the mat while my left penetrates toward the floor. I make my left hip my balance point and spin my legs to my right and around to the front of me. Using my arms, I help myself to my feet, crouch into the starting position and continue the drill.

FREQUENCY: 5-10 minutes timed

For the first actual partner sprawl, you should work with your partner to develop rhythm and speed in getting to the mat. The purpose of slapping hands is to coordinate with each other, serving as an encouragement for both to keep up the pace, and to approximate proper takedown distance. If you can hit each other's hands, you are in range for the takedown, which also means you are in range for a sprawl. Treat every slap like the initiation of a takedown, and sprawl quickly to develop your wrestler's intuition, that special timing where every shot is met with an early and heavy sprawl! I like to work this exercise to time, so that you can challenge both yourself and your partner to more and more repetitions as you get better conditioned.

Marcel and I begin facing each other in staggered stances. At the same time, we both reach forward with both hands and slap palms. Immediately, we retract our arms and sprawl to our hips. Both Marcel and I sprawl our forward legs back in defense of a mock attack on that leg. Remember, the other leg is further back, making it relatively safer than the forward one. Get used to the angle that your opponent wants to shoot from and prepare your defenses around your exposed points.

WEEK ONE: WRAP UP

After completing breakfall and sprawl training this week, you may not be ready to defend every throw or stuff every shot, but you are ready to practice your stand-up game with some confidence. The number one thing I want you to remember is that you need to have confidence in these areas. Do not fear the takedown to such a level that your throwing game becomes fearful, stiff and stagnant. Though the side of you that leans toward self-preservation may think that avoiding the standing game by hunching over and frantically pushing the opponent away is a good way to prevent big throws, it is also a deadly trap when faced with someone who is comfortable on their feet.

So my advice is this: get out there, stand up, and fall. You are going to get taken down, but hopefully after you break a few falls and sprawl on a couple of shots, you will gain a little confidence. Next time, go with someone a little more challenging that you know will throw you with ease. With preparation in breakfall and sprawl training, there is nothing left to fear about stand-up training.

For the end of this week, find a partner with some throws and try your luck with some stand-up sparring. Make sure you are supervised by an instructor who knows throws and then start hitting that mat!

Partner Sprawls Continued

PARTNER BALL SPRAWL

FREQUENCY: 2 sets of 20 or timed

Now that you have finished slapping sprawls, it is time for the partner ball sprawl. This is an incredible drill, where the Swiss ball represents your opponent as he shoots in for the takedown, and without having to wear him down, you crush him repeatedly with your 100 percent intensity sprawls. For beginners, stand far apart to give yourself more time to see the ball come at you. For more advanced practitioners, get close and try to get the ball to each other with some speed. You should see a great leap in your ability to stuff telegraphed shots, even if the takedown is only apparent for a fraction of a second. Once you get moving with this drill, change things up with fake kicks and see if your partner falls for the bait and does a "ghost sprawl." The pace of this should range from medium speed to high, and the sprawl itself should always be done with maximum effort to stop the shot.

To start the drill, I have the Swiss ball and I am facing Marcel. Because we are used to this type of training, we close the distance to speed up each other's reaction time. With two hands, I push the ball to Marcel. Marcel prepares for the arrival, and sprawls as soon as he makes contact. As with all sprawling techniques, Marcel drives his hips and all his weight downward while crushing the ball with his mid torso. Immediately after, Marcel will recover and push the ball back to me to continue the training.

DAY ONE:
STATIONARY HIP ESCAPE

FREQUENCY: 4 sets of 10-20

The stationary hip escape is one of the most important and fundamental movements in Brazilian Jiu-Jitsu. From the time you begin training until the time you are a black belt and beyond, you will need to practice this movement. I originally learned this the first day I started training with Careca, and the last time I practiced this was the last time I trained. While doing this technique, be sure to escape your hips to the side and not the rear. Learning to escape more to the side will allow you to gain better penetration for side control and mount escapes as you use your hips to create openings in your opponent's top position.

Beginning from a stomach-up position, I keep both legs bent with my soles on the mat. To initiate the drill, I turn my body onto my left hip while I keep my right foot on the mat with my right knee chambered. In one motion, I extend my right leg, pushing my hips away while I push forward with my hands. Once I have finished, I pull my hips back to the center position and roll to my back so that I can practice the other side. It is essential that I learn to hip escape by pushing with my outside leg instead of the bottom one. This allows me to use the bottom leg to slide under and reestablish the guard.

FREQUENCY: 2x the distance of the mat

The guard recovery push and shrimp is an excellent drill that really puts your hands into practice while hip escaping. You may have been wondering about the pushing movement that you were doing earlier and as you can tell from the movement below, there is a real application to that movement. However, it is equally important to understand that you will not be pushing with much force. Instead, your hands are in place to block your opponent and impede his forward progress. With the arms in place as a block, you can freely use the rest of your body to escape your hips backward and recover. Once you make space with your hips, your arms keep that space open until you have realigned the guard.

Basic Hip Escapes

FREQUENCY: 2 sets of 12-20 or timed

The moving hip escape applies the body movement that you learned with the stationary hip escape to the length of the mat. This time, however, your goal is not to escape your hip to the side and then pull yourself back to the center position, but to penetrate your hips to the rear and then realign your body with your hips. This makes the moving hip escape a great technique for defending the guard. When your opponent almost passes your guard, you move your hips away and when you realign your head to your hips, you will notice that you have gained considerable distance while reestablishing your guard on the same line as your opponent.

Once again, I begin from a stomach-up position with both legs bent and my soles on the mat, but this time, my head is pointing to the end of the mat. To initiate the drill, I turn my body onto my left hip while keeping my right foot on the mat with my right knee chambered. In one motion, I extend my right leg, pushing my hips away and up the mat while I push forward with my hands. Once I have finished, I scoot my shoulders back, elongating my body to realign the guard. I continue by bringing my knees back toward my body and rolling to a flat back position. Following this, I will roll to the other side and continue my hip escapes for the remainder of the mat.

GUARD RECOVERY PUSH & SHRIMP

I begin in a stomach-up position with both legs bent and my soles on the mat. Marcel is standing over me, blocking both my hips with his feet. To initiate the drill, I turn my body onto my left hip and keep my right foot on the mat with my right knee chambered and both my hands on Marcel's lower leg. In one motion, I extend my right leg, pushing my hips out from under Marcel while I lock Marcel in place with my hands. Once I have escaped my hips, I scoot my shoulders back, elongating my body to realign the guard. As I pull my knees off the mat, Marcel steps forward toward my hips and I repeat the drill to the other side.

DAY TWO:
Sit-Up Hip Escapes

SIT-UP HIP ESCAPE

FREQUENCY: 2-3x the distance of the mat

The sit-up hip escape and its variations are just as important as the back flat variations that you covered yesterday. Day two's lesson is that you cannot ever have enough hip escape drills in your repertoire. The goal of this movement is to transition from a flat posture to a seated posture. You still escape your hip like a moving hip escape, but you also post on your elbow to essentially hip escape into a guard position. This movement can serve as a precursor to the technical lift to help guard players get to their feet against stalling opponents. In addition, it is also a great technique for recovering guard when your opponent passes your leg toward your backside. Practice this drill often and your guard recovery and transitional acumen should skyrocket.

Beginning from a stomach-up position, I have both legs bent and my soles on the mat with my head pointing to the end of the mat. To initiate the drill, I sit up to my left elbow and keep my hand in front. In one motion, I extend both legs, pushing my hips away and up the mat while I push to the front with my hands. With my hip escaped, I shift to a square, seated position with my rear flat to the mat. I return to the starting position and continue the movement to my right side. Every time I do this escape, I must move once I get to my elbow to emphasize the urgency to transition to a better position.

SIT-UP HIP ESCAPE VARIATION

FREQUENCY: 2-3 x the distance of the mat

This is a variation of the previous technique and I like to practice the two in combination. Sometimes I do the sit-up hip escape with the elbow and other times I focus on getting all the way to my hand. While sparring, you may wish to do this to hide your arm from your opponent, who may try to grab it to destabilize your position as you try to escape. The key to any good grappler is adaptation and variation so practice this one with your other hip escapes often.

From the stomach-up position, I have both legs bent and my soles on the mat with my head pointing to the end of the mat. To initiate the drill, I sit up to my left hand while keeping my right hand in front of me. In one motion, I extend both legs, pushing my hips away and up the mat while I push to the front with my hands. With my hip escaped, I shift to a square, seated position with my rear flat to the mat. This time, I bring my knees to my chest to bring my defenses back to my body. I fall to my back and continue the drill to the other side.

DAY THREE:
Mobile Hip-Switching

SIDE-TO-SIDE HIP ESCAPE

FREQUENCY: 3 sets of 12-20 or 2 min timed

For day three, you will work on the side-to-side hip escape, a movement that is vital to developing a strong sitting guard position. To perfect the drill, focus on using your posting hand to lift your hips off the floor, this way you will have the mobility to jump your hips to the alternate side. The side-to-side hip escape drill is great for developing any type of defense technique, like arm drags or simply moving out of the way of your opponent. Remember, the arm drag is useless if you cannot get your hips out from underneath your opponent and attack his back, so make sure your hips are mobile!

My starting point for the side-to-side hip escape is the seated position. Both of my legs are bent with my soles on the mat. My right hand is posted on the mat and my left hand is protectively hovering in front of me. To initiate the drill, I push off the mat with my right hand to elevate my hips. With my left hand, I mimic an arm dragging motion as I pull my hand to the right while I jump my hips to the left. This is important: I always pull my opponent to where I was while I escape to where he isn't. Once I finish the hip switch, I shift my hips to the other side, drop my left hand to the mat and set up my next hip escape to my right.

HIP ESCAPES: In Focus

Although the name implies differently, hip escapes are total body movements. If you have never done one before, simply hearing, "Just move your hips!" is not good enough. First lets look at the legs; they are the first of two grounding points. They are also what propel you into hip escapes. Next we arrive at the hips and core. It is core strength that you will need as you crunch your body to get your rear away from your opponent. This brings us to the arms. Arms are your brace, and you will need to use some strength. This strength is reserved to holding your opponent in place as the rest of your body coordinates its escape plan. Finally, we have the shoulders. The shoulders are your secondary grounding point and will serve as your axis. So, next time you think of the hip escape, do the hip escape, or deal with an opponent who is hip escaping, take a second and understand the movement. You need your entire body to commit a successful and seemingly effortless escape. In this case, it is not all in the hips.

DAY FOUR:
Full Body Movement
HIP ESCAPE TO STOMACH

FREQUENCY: 3 sets of 10-20

Getting to the prone position from the hip escape is another must-master move in Brazilian Jiu-Jitsu. This is a drill that teaches your body how to move to your belly when escaping the side control or preventing the guard pass. The key to this movement is a secondary hip escape that gets your body far enough away so that you can slide your inside leg under your body, allowing your body to end parallel to its starting position. If you want to try this movement in sparring after you have mastered it in drilling, wait for your opponent to block your hips while you are hip escaping. This is the signal to escape your hips again, free your bottom leg, and go for the reversal.

I start with the standard hip escape. Once I have finished my first escape, I post my left leg further from my body and escape my hip a second time. If I do not do this, I will come up to my knees very awkwardly, and in sparring, I will be put back onto my back. With my hips escaped far, I slide my right leg under my left until both my knees are on the mat. From here, I can swing my right arm free as if I am attacking an imaginary double- or single-leg takedown. One final point – I must hide my inside or right arm by keeping it close to my body while I go to all fours. Otherwise, it will impede my transition, giving my opponent precious time and control to thwart my escape.

FREQUENCY: 4 sets of 20

To continue the final day of week two, it is essential that you work on your inverse or reverse hip escapes as guard recovery. If you do not work on this technique, you will severely limit your mobility, making it easier for your opponent to take your back after passing the guard. Basically, the reverse hip escape is tailor-made for two specific situations: recovering guard when your opponent passes toward your exposed back, and scooping your hips inside of your opponent to create more leverage for stronger sweeps and reversals. After practicing mobile hip switching, this movement should come easy.

DAY FIVE:
Advanced Hip Movements

SHOULDER ESCAPES

FREQUENCY: 2 sets of 20 or timed

The shoulder escape should serve as an introduction to guard inversions and inverted recoveries, but most importantly it is a highly effective guard maintenance technique. The key to this position is your ability to push off the mat with your inside foot to propel yourself onto both shoulders. With the shoulder escape, you take on a rocking action as you sway to the side and then roll back in the opposite direction. While rolling with your partner, an opportunity for this move often appears as your opponent runs to your back. From here, just rock away from your opponent and then roll your hips to him. Though your back will be momentarily exposed, by the time your partner tries to attack it, he will already be facing your legs as they transition to the front. Once you are comfortable, practice with your partner trying to pass your guard.

 From a stomach-up position, I imagine that my partner has passed my guard to my right side. I roll away from my imaginary opponent, pushing off the mat with my left leg to roll onto my right shoulder. I continue to push off the mat while tucking my chin to my chest to allow both my shoulders to touch the mat. From here, I swing my hips over my head to square up my body position. To finish, I swing my feet down, finishing 180 degrees from my starting point. It is important that I imagine my opponent passing all the way around my guard as my feet come around to meet him.

REVERSE HIP ESCAPE

I start in a near fetal position with my back on the mat. My knees and elbows are close to my body for protection. To begin, I turn to my left side with left toes on the mat while imagining that my opponent has jumped my guard toward my exposed back. Next, I push off the mat with my toes, propelling my hips down and to my right. I kick my right foot upward to help steer my hips to a square position. I bring my right leg to the mat on my right side and restart the drill with my right foot on the floor. Again, it is important that I imagine an opponent attacking my back so I never expose too much of my backside while using the proper amount of explosiveness to make my transition.

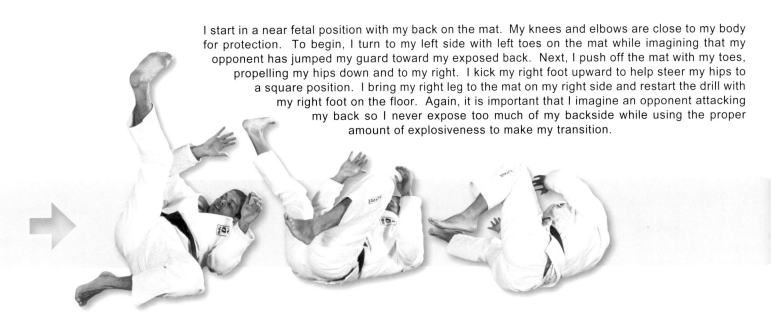

WEEK THREE: The Upa

DAYS I&II:
THE BRIDGE

FREQUENCY: 4 sets of 20

For week three, you should absolutely dedicate yourself to the bridge, or upa, escape. Although it may seem dull to do two days straight of classic bridge maneuvers, your core strength, explosiveness, and technique should all see drastic improvement by week's end. Once you are done with this week, continue warming up with this move – it is an essential. As you practice, make sure to explode your hips upward and then have a slow two-three-second negative phase as you return to the mat. When it comes to jiu-jitsu training, this movement is a technical wonder: using the power of your hips and legs in conjunction with your back and shoulders, you can lift a person far heavier than your arm strength alone could handle.

DAYS III&IV:

FREQUENCY: 4 sets of 20

The latter half of this week on the upa includes the extended bridge. Once you have mastered the previous movement, it is time to make some small tweaks and perfect it for both repetition training and sparring. This movement accurately mimics the bridging action necessary to bridge your opponent off of the mounted position. Unlike the previous movement, you will not need to lift your feet to gain momentum. Instead, keep your feet close to your body, explode into the bridge, and then turn over your shoulder to get to your knees. This should be in every grappler's repertoire. To this day, I still get bumped off an opponent's mount from this movement, so I know it is necessary and effective.

The Master Bridge

My starting position is with my back flat on the mat and both feet on the floor. To coil my body for the bridge, I bring both my feet off the floor and crunch my knees to my chest. Immediately, I slam both feet to the mat as close to my rear as possible. As I drive my feet into the mat, I explode my hips upward. I keep my head out of the way of my left shoulder as I bridge onto it, arching my back to the point where I can actually look down at the mat. I return to the flat position and repeat the exercise to the other side. Notice that as I drive my feet down, I don't lift with my hips. I lift with my legs as if I am pushing the world away from me.

WEEK THREE:
The Upa

The Long Bridge
EXTENDED BRIDGE

My starting position is with my back flat on the mat and both feet on the floor near my rear. Unlike the previous move, I do not lift my legs off the mat – doing so could give an opponent control of my hips and legs. So, I drive my feet into the mat and explode my hips upward. I keep my head out of the way of my left shoulder as I bridge onto it, arching my back to the point where I can actually look down at the mat. This time, I continue turning onto my left shoulder and I swing my right leg to the mat. I finish with both legs posted on the mat in a firm base. Once finished, I return to the starting position and practice to the other side.

DAY FIVE:
BRIDGE TO HIP ESCAPE

FREQUENCY: 2-3 sets of 20 or timed

To finish the week on the upa, you have to start thinking of the bridge and the hip escape as interconnected systems. One movement will not always work on its own. Instead, you will have to teach your body the ability to seamlessly transition between both. If the bridge fails, you have opened plenty of space for an effective hip escape. Whenever you need to make room for something, the bridge should always be one of your go-to options for loosening things up a little. Practice this movement often and when ready, practice with a partner in the mounted position to get used to his body weight.

DAY ONE:

FREQUENCY: 3 sets of 20 or timed sets

To finish our month on the basics of Brazilian Jiu-Jitsu, it is absolutely imperative to learn one of the best skills for changing position in grappling, the technical lift. For your first day of training this week, you will be tasked with the master's lift. This movement is ideal for self-defense, sport jiu-jitsu, and MMA, where you are faced with the need to stand out of the guard. As you try this out for yourself, be sure to keep your base strong over one leg and the opposite arm. This allows you to elevate your hip and free leg while blocking any possible kicks with your front hand. It also lets you use the kick to get your opponent away from you, making space for you to stand up and change position. As with all basics, this movement must be mastered before moving on.

Bridge & Hip Master

My starting position is with my back flat on the mat and both feet on the floor. Using the movements mastered over the previous four days, I bridge onto my left shoulder to separate my hips from the mat. Immediately, I push my hips in the opposite motion, getting drive with my legs. This effectively escapes my hips into the space created by my bridging technique. With my hips escaped to the maximum distance from my starting position, I bring my hips back and transition to my original starting position. From here, I can continue my repetitions to either side.

The Master's Lift

MASTER'S LIFT

To start the master's lift, I am lying with my back flat on the mat with both feet close to my rear. Using our sit-up movements from this month, I sit to my elbow and then to my hand. I put my weight on my right hand and left foot. Next, I lift my hips and right foot off the mat. With my leg light, I can swing it underneath my body until I can stand it behind me in base. I take my hand off the mat and end in a strong stance. With this repetition finished, I will return to the mat and continue to the other side. Detail: It is important that I stand up with my feet staggered and not in the same line when I stand. Otherwise, my base will be compromised and I will fall.

DAY TWO:
SIT-THROUGHS

FREQUENCY: 3-4 sets of 12-20

The sit through is a master's lift in reverse. Instead of pulling your forward leg out from under you as in the master's lift, you will be doing the opposite as you slide your rear foot forward. The practical implementation of the sit through can be seen in half guard pulling, escaping or changing position from the bottom of the sprawled position, and when breaking down an opponent and taking his back. As a rule of thumb, when you see a master move that has so many different applications, I sincerely advise you to master such a maneuver and think about all of its different uses.

FREQUENCY: 3 sets of 20 OR timed sets

Once you are comfortable with the sit-through, you should move on to the four points movement. This is a great drill for small spaces that integrates both a sit-through and a master's lift. You will be swinging your leg both forward and backward and your goal should be to develop speed, timing, and strength. Before you know it, your arms will start burning and your core muscles should feel like a brick wall. Beyond the workout and attribute training, this movement works in a similar fashion to other complementary moves. When sparring, if a sit-through isn't working, slide your leg back for the master's lift. Turn your drills into combinations and then bring these skills to your training.

Sitting Through & Leg Mobility

To start the drill, I go to all fours in a bear crawl position. Both my feet and hands are on the mat with my hips pointed upward. Once ready, I balance myself on my right hand and my left foot, allowing my left leg to lighten and my hips to move freely. I swing my right leg forward, while I lift my left hand off the mat. As I land my right foot, my hips are pointed upward. Following this, I place my left hand on the mat, return my left leg to the floor, and now I am in position to continue the drill to either side. Once you are comfortable with this drill, try to pick up some speed and feel how your hips are carried through by the inertia caused by your swinging legs.

FOUR-POINTS MOVEMENT

I start from a belly-up position with my hands and feet on the mat and my hips elevated. While keeping my weight on my right hand and left foot, I swing my right leg under me while my left hand switches positions to finish a master's lift type of movement. Immediately, I swing my left leg under my body while my right hand switches positions with my hand in a sit-through movement. From here, I can continue by doing another master's lift to either side. I will try to keep a strong pace for the duration of the drill.

DAY THREE:
SITTING THRUSTS

FREQUENCY: 2-3 sets of 20

For your third day of technical lift training, you will practice this sitting thrust. The sitting thrust is a great technique for standing from the bottom position and creating forward momentum. This is a great movement for offense-minded players. Instead of standing away from a mock opponent as is the case with the master's lift, now you will be standing into your opponent with the goal of creating drive. This is a great move for learning takedowns and leg-pick sweeps from the guard. Once comfortable with this, you can integrate master's lifts into your sitting thrust training. Again, I am always looking to train complementary drills together.

FREQUENCY: 2-3 sets of 20

The master's thrust is a great continuation of the sitting thrust drill that you just completed. The goal with this movement is to use your hips and legs to thrust yourself all the way to your feet. This is a great movement for dealing with athletic opponents who just will not quit when you try to finish with the sitting thrust. From your feet, you can use even more drive and keep on the offensive. As you train, focus on developing the speed, balance, and power to offensively stand from the seated position. As with the sitting thrust, this can also be practiced with a master's lift to bridge offense to defense.

The Technical Thrust

I begin in the seated position with both feet forward. I curl my right foot toward my body as if I were doing a butterfly stretch while I reach my hands forward for balance. I continue to curl my right leg under my body until my toes touch the ground. From here, I start to push off my toes and drive my body weight toward my left knee. I continue until I am completely upright with both knees bent at ninety-degree angles. To return, I re-chamber my right leg and sit back to the guard position. Now I am ready to drill the sitting thrust to the other side. Detail: When I sit all the way up, I cannot lead with my head. If I do, and my head crosses my knee, I will be severely off balanced forward and an opponent can pull me down toward my face.

THE MASTER'S THRUST

Once more, I begin in the seated position with both feet forward. I curl my right foot toward my body as if I were doing a butterfly stretch while I reach my hands forward for balance. I continue to curl my right leg under my body until my toes touch the ground. From here, I start to push off my toes and drive my body weight toward my left knee. I continue thrusting until I am completely upright with both knees bent at ninety-degree angles. I do not stop here but continue to push off the mat with my right foot until I am standing completely upright. To return to the mat, I bend my right knee to the floor, sit my body back over my right knee, and finish in the original starting position. From here, I can continue the drill to my other side.

DAY FOUR:
ROCKING SINGLE-LEGS

FREQUENCY: 2-4 sets of 20

For day four of technical lift training, you will use a sitting thrust and rocking chair type of movement to sit up as if you were attacking a single-leg takedown. While sparring, you are likely to use this drill when defending the guard pass, sweeping from the half guard, and escaping the side control. This is an incredibly versatile drill and it combines elements of defense and attack. It is important that your body learns to combine these two, because often enough, your window of opportunity is small while grappling. You have to be able to seize every opening so make sure you are drilling this movement enough to be able to do so when the time comes.

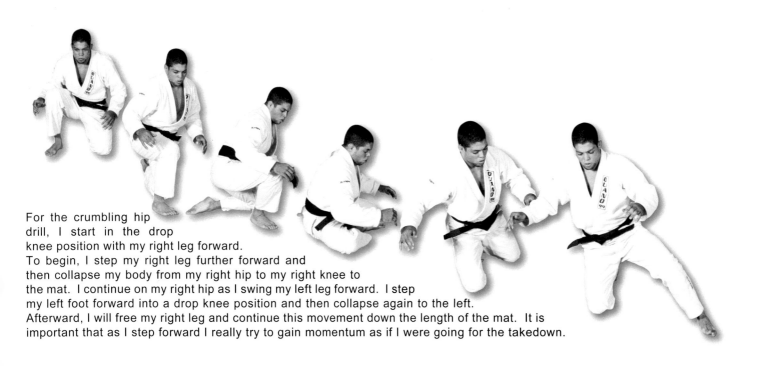

For the crumbling hip drill, I start in the drop knee position with my right leg forward. To begin, I step my right leg further forward and then collapse my body from my right hip to my right knee to the mat. I continue on my right hip as I swing my left leg forward. I step my left foot forward into a drop knee position and then collapse again to the left. Afterward, I will free my right leg and continue this movement down the length of the mat. It is important that as I step forward I really try to gain momentum as if I were going for the takedown.

Penetrating Hip Skills

I start on my back in a fetal position. I fall to my right side and lift my left foot up toward my head. Forcefully, I swing my leg down, letting the momentum carry me up to a kneeling position. Immediately, I swing my left leg around what would be my opponent's exposed near side leg and then clasp my hands together. I lean slightly forward in a mock takedown. Once finished, I release my grip and fall backward toward my right thigh. I end on my back and am ready to do the same drill to the other side.

CRUMBLING HIPS

FREQUENCY: 2-4x the length of the mat

This is a really fun drill that I learned while training with Leo Vieira at his school in São Paolo. He had us do this stationary and moving, but in this situation you should first learn how to do it while moving down the length of the mat. The purpose of the crumbling hip is threefold: You should develop your sitting thrust to offensively get up to your knees, your hip mobility and agility to land in base and open up your leg, and your driving momentum to finish takedowns. Aside from these, you may wish to picture yourself attacking one of your opponent's legs and then the other as he manages to escape each leg away from you. Practice this with a slow to medium intensity and make sure your hips and legs are warmed up prior to the drill.

DAY FIVE:
HIP ESCAPE TO MASTER'S LIFT

FREQUENCY: 4x the distance of the mat

For your final day of this month on the basics, it is important for you to do some integrated training. Although the combinations are nearly limitless, one good starting place is to integrate one hip escape with one technical lift. Whether you use a basic hip escape to a master's lift or a sit-through to a reverse hip escape, the point is the same – integrate your basic hip and lifting techniques to better control the space between you and your opponent. For this drill, you will do a standard sit-up escape combined with a master's lift. Focus on fluid, continual movements. If you are too boxy or clunky, go back to the move and work it until it is absolutely seamless.

Beginning from a stomach-up position, I have both legs bent and my soles on the mat with my head pointing to the end of the mat. To initiate the drill, I sit up to my left elbow while keeping my hand in front. In one motion, I extend both legs, pushing my hips away and up the mat while I push to the front with my right hand. As I fully extend, my left elbow should still be on the mat. With my hip escaped, I shift to a square seated position with my rear flat to the mat as I base my hand out to my rear left to keep my base. At this point, my left hand becomes incredibly important. I must keep it posted on the floor so that I can keep my base. Otherwise, an opponent would gain the ability to disrupt my base by pushing on my head and I would have to use far too much abdominal strength to keep my upright position. Now I am in a great position for a master's lift.

Integrating Hips w/ Lifts

Before I continue to the master's lift, I commit myself to a second sit-up escape without falling back to the mat. Then I flow directly into the master's lift by putting my weight on my left hand and foot. Next, I lift my hips and left foot off the mat. With my leg light, I can swing it underneath my body until I can stand it behind me in base. I stand my hand off the mat and end in a strong stance. With this repetition finished, I will return to the mat and continue to the other side. Detail: Whenever combining drills, work your hardest to blend the seams, making your transitions unapparent. Now you are ready to add these transitions to your other techniques and sparring.

ROLL & SPRAWL

FREQUENCY: 2x 5 minutes

To end your first quarter of training, it's time to prove to yourself how much you have learned and just how far your jiu-jitsu movements have come along. This is the first of two master moves. For the rolls and sprawl, you will incorporate all of the essentials from this month of training: the forward roll, master's lift, basic sprawl, back breakfall, and back roll to the feet. You are ready for this movement and I want you to look at this as your first major test. Use this as your benchmark to see where your basic movements are before moving on. If you are failing at this and the following master move, I recommend repeating this month until you're comfortable with your motion.

For the first master move, I begin with my right leg slightly forward. I roll over my right shoulder and land in a sitting position. From the seated position, I put my weight on my right leg and left arm and immediately execute a master's lift. Without delay, I sprawl my right leg back so that my hip falls to the mat. Explosively, I stand to a square stance, keep my hands in front of me, tuck my chin down and fall backward. To break my fall, I slap the mat at a forty-five-degree angle and then roll over my left shoulder to get back to my feet. To finish this repetition, I immediately sprawl down and then jump back to my feet to start my second repetition with the forward roll. It is important that I keep a very strong pace throughout this routine. The sprawls should add some more intensity and explosive energy so I really throw myself wholeheartedly into every single one.

BREAKFALL, LIFT & SPRAWL

FREQUENCY: 5 minutes timed laps

Though the last master move was longer and included more rolling, this one is far more intense. The movements are shorter and more direct, and you will be doing two core exercises back to back: The master's lift and the sprawl. While the minutes tick on during the drill, do not sacrifice your good form or safety. Keep your body in a strong base, tuck your chin while falling, and breathe! You are almost done with this month and after all this breakfall training, it is time to put it to some use by building your takedown skills as well.

MONTH THREE:
In Review

The drills from Month Three should never leave your periphery. You will see these moves come up again and again throughout your jiu-jitsu career. In fact, every routine in every day of the rest of this book can benefit from drilling one or more basic movement exercises prior to training. Be sure you conquer these techniques so you can always keep them in your back pocket for a rainy day!

Do you ever see students that can "plug-in" the most complex movements and use them only minutes after learning them? For the most part, these are people that have mastered the basic body movements necessary for ALL jiu-jitsu techniques. All you need to do in order to be one of these students is to drill these basic movements a lot. Drill them more than you feel like you need. Even when they start to feel second nature, keep drilling them. There will come a time when you no longer see them as drills, but instead as natural body movements you do without thinking.

On the other side of this, any simple technique can become endlessly frustrating if you cannot plug the proper movement into the maneuver. It is important to master the movements first, and the techniques second. As you drill the basic movements, you can start piecing them together to create your own technical chains, and before you know it, you'll be mastering the basics!

Here's a helpful tip to get the most out of this month: While drilling, seek out a better economy of motion. For example, if your hips are slowing you down, you may have to bridge your hips higher off the mat before you move them or lean more onto your shoulder. You will spend less energy bridging your hips than you will trying to drag them on the mat! Always keep in mind the best way to get from point A to point B. It is not always the easiest route, but that's where drilling comes in! You will find that eventually, a simple basic movement done correctly and at the right time will pay off more than an explosive power move that gets you in the same place. Always aim for the most technical, smart positioning and it will save you from years of fixing bad techniques you've picked up along the way!

Remember, this is the most vital month to your overall progression. Do not pass this month until you feel mobile and loose on the mat. It's okay to repeat this month or certain weeks in this month as many times as you need until you feel very confident with these motions. And don't worry! If later on in the book, something is not working for you, you can always return to Month Three to refresh your basics and keep drilling them!

I begin the second master move in a crouched position with my back to the end of the mat. Falling backward, I tuck my chin and break my fall. I rock myself to a sitting position with my weight on my right foot and left hand. I use this base to stand with the master's lift, staggering my left leg to my rear left. Without standing all the way up, I immediately lean forward, throw my right leg behind me, and sprawl to my right hip. To finish this repetition, I stand to my feet and continue down the length of the mat. To make your master move a little more realistic, try to throw your hips farther back as you really try to imagine the would-be wrestler's shot. This will move you down the mat faster, but don't worry about that, this is a timed move and your finishing line is based on the clock, not your distance.

WEEKEND WORK:

As a review exercise, take some alone time on the weekends to do an endless flow drill with your basics. Move from one movement to another continuously to develop fluidity. This will take the jerky edges off your movement and create a cohesive, beautiful jiu-jitsu style that works!

MONTH FOUR:
Get Down!
Throwing & Pulling Guard

Month four is a comprehensive plan to get better at takedowns and pulling guard. This month's emphasis is to get comfortable on your feet. No matches magically start on the ground so you will have to master this part of the game in order to be successful in competition. The standing portion of a match can make or break a competitor. Whether it leads to a takedown or guard pull, stand-up plays a large role in whether or not you can get a leg up on your opponent or vice versa. If you are unable to get a takedown or you fail at pulling the guard, you will always be working your way out of a negative hole in the match points-wise. Even great players sometimes lose because they are unable to impose their games during the standing portion of a match. Use this chapter as a starting point to improve your takedowns.

Week one introduces a very important part of the standing game: grip fighting. I placed this early in the month because it will play a role in every other aspect of this chapter. Getting a dominant grip should always be your first goal, and this week you will learn how to fight for the best possible grip in any given situation. A dominant grip allows you to set up throws much easier. With a dominant grip, these throws will require a lower level of athleticism and the window of opportunity for success is much wider.

Gripping also allows you to read your opponent, making it easier to pull guard or block his guard-pull attempt. For example, if you grab both his arms, you can jump guard because he cannot block you with his hands, or if you grab with one hand, you will leave the other free to knock off his leg if he attempts to pull guard on you. In addition, if you feel your opponent trying to pull guard, you know he is probably a "guard guy," meaning he feels most comfortable there and will probably aim most of his attacks to end up there throughout your match. As you can see, grip fighting is not only important for the advantages it gives you if you do it correctly; it also sets up a mental strategy for the rest of the fight by giving you an idea of your opponent's game plan.

As you will learn this week, you always want to have an inside grip. This is the same in both judo and wrestling. When you have the inside grip, you are in control of the game and you can feel confident in setting up your takedown. It is also important not to limit yourself to just judo or just wrestling grips. You must learn them all because there will always be moments when one is more appropriate than the other.

Remember, many matches are won and lost by a small margin. Two points from a takedown are all you need to win a tough match! Grip fighting is just the beginning to build a great takedown strategy.

Week two focuses on wrestling throws. These types of takedowns are dependent on inside control, drive, and changing levels. The drills this week will get your body used to doing all three of these things interchangeably so that you can build a very strong wrestling game. While you work through the drills this week, get used to changing levels with your legs and hips, not your back. Bending down in wrestling is a no-no! Always crouch down or lunge down instead. This way you keep your base strong and you can always keep an eye on your opponent's next move. If you can develop a wrestler's shot and a wrestler's tenacity to push through the defense, you will be a nightmare on the mat. Every jiu-jitsu student should know how to pummel the inside grip, double-leg, and single-leg takedown. Drill all these moves this week so that by the end of this month, you can swap them with judo and guard pulling to create a dynamic stand-up game.

In week three, I introduce judo takedowns. I trained judo with the Brazilian national team, and one of the best things I learned from them was that drilling footwork is the single most important aspect of judo. This week, you will focus heavily on footwork. Take a lot of time with it. As you begin to learn the dance, you can speed it up and get in a lot of repetitions. Train it repeatedly until you are comfortable with judo's insertion techniques. As you apply this footwork to your stand up game, use tripping techniques or foot sweeps (called Ashiwaza) to set up your bigger hip and shoulder throws.

Once you are comfortable with judo and wrestling, it is time to integrate the two in controlled sparring. Because the two have much more in common than they have differences, you will find it is easy to incorporate both into a strong takedown routine. Throwing in both judo and wrestling is usually more explosive than ground grappling so be sure to build your hamstrings, quadriceps, glutes, lower back, and abdominals to stay strong and be able to keep training tomorrow! Feel free to play around with the drills this week and create your own chains to develop a takedown strategy that fits your game. And remember, just like grip fighting had a mental side to it, so does the rest of judo. A big throw often has a negative psychological effect on your opponent. If you can pull off a takedown right from the get-go, your opponent will be thinking, "Oh no! What did I just get myself into?" There's nothing better than mentally dominating your opponent from the very first minute.

Finally, week four discusses pulling guard. I focus on developing guard-pulling skills last because it shouldn't be seen as a crutch – it is a weapon! Learn to throw well and then you have the power to decide where the match will go. You can take your opponent down or pull to your guard depending on how the match is going and whether or not you feel your opponent attempting to drive the game in his favor. You should also practice flying attacks to develop your explosive jump. This not only helps for incredible submissions, but it gives you the confidence to jump to the guard more easily. Try to think of guard pulling as a throw. Once you pull guard, sweep immediately, or better yet, knock your opponent down with the force of your momentum.

By the end of this week, you will have an arsenal of drills to improve your stand-up game. Like every chapter, be sure to keep drilling the techniques, even when this month is through. The more you practice, the more your body learns the mechanics of the move and it becomes a natural part of your muscle memory.

DAY ONE:
Developing Grip Strength - Curls

COLLAR ROWS

FREQUENCY: 2 sets of 8-12

Just as you conditioned your body prior to learning your basic Brazilian Jiu-Jitsu drills, you will also condition your grip-specific muscles before you dive into the grip fighting drills. All of the technique and movement of grip fighting will be lost on you without some level of hand, forearm, and upper-arm strength. This is even more so the case in competition. For your first drill, you will do a couple of sets of standing collar rows. As with all of these partner lifts, keep your knees bent to prevent lower-back injury and always choose a partner you can safely lift. This exercise has a great benefit for your ability to latch onto an opponent's collars during sparring.

I begin bent over Marcel with my feet to either side of his waist and my hands gripping each of his lapels. I drop my rear and bend my legs for back support. Next, I lift Marcel by bringing my elbows to my side. To finish the repetition, I slowly bring Marcel back to the mat over a deliberate two- to three-second count. While I am doing my curls, Marcel should keep his whole body flat in order to prevent any cheating on my part. If Marcel's upper body bends, the lift will be too easy and will not yield the same results.

BICEPS ROWS

FREQUENCY: 2 sets of 6-10

Now that your heart rate is undoubtedly up, you should move on to an even more difficult row. The biceps row is a nightmare for most, even me. This is because the kimono makes grabbing on the biceps incredibly difficult. As you commit to your lift, you will notice that you really have to pinch your fingers together to prevent your partner from slipping free of your grip. This is a much harder drill than the previous one and you should probably tell your partner to keep his chin tucked downward in case your grip fails. Get strong with this position and you are on your way to becoming a grip-fighting beast. As for practice, continue with an explosive lift and a slow negative return.

The biceps row begins with Marcel underneath me and my feet on either side of his waist. My hands grip the outside of each of his biceps. I drop my rear and bend my legs for back support. Next, I lift Marcel by bringing my elbows to my side. To finish the repetition, I slowly bring Marcel back to the mat over a deliberate two- to three-second count. Detail: To ensure a noose-tight grip, focus on pinching with your pinky to middle fingers – these fingers are capable of pinching much tighter than your thumb and index fingers.

DAY ONE:
Developing Grip Strength Cont.
BICEPS ROWS VARIATION

FREQUENCY: 2 sets of 6-10

Your second routine of biceps row incorporates one major difference – you do not return your partner all the way to the mat. This increases the time that you will have to hold your iron grip and it will make the transition from the negative phase (letting your partner down) of the curl to the positive (lifting him to you) all the more difficult. Again, as you get tired, be sure that your posture or form does not get sloppy. Keep your elbows close to your body and make one full breath cycle per repetition. Practice with a medium to medium-high intensity – explosive on the pick-up (positive) and slow on the return (negative).

I begin bent over Marcel with my feet on either side of his waist and my hands gripping his outer biceps. I drop my rear and bend my legs for back support. Next, I lift Marcel by bringing my elbows to my side. To finish the repetition, I slowly bring Marcel back down (two- to three-second negative phase) until he is just hovering over the mat. I will finish my set before I return Marcel to the mat.

CROSS-CHOKE CURLS

FREQUENCY: 2 sets of 10-12

The cross-choke curl should be your cool-down exercise, as it is much easier than the biceps rows that you have been doing over the last four sets (though still difficult in its own right). Besides being great for your overall gripping strength. These will help your situation specific grip strength for cross-collar chokes. As with all cross chokes, you need to finish close to your opponent and if you can lift your opponent using a similar form to the choke, the choke will be exponentially easier when you are faced with a live opponent (once you can get your grips of course). Practice this with the same intensity as all previous curls.

For the final curl of day one, I begin bent over Marcel with my feet on either side of his waist and my hands cross-gripping each of his lapels as if I were executing a cross choke. I drop my rear and bend my legs for back support. Next, I lift Marcel by bringing my elbows to my side, simulating the choking action. To finish the repetition, I slowly bring Marcel back to hover over the mat as in the previous biceps curls. I will finish my set before I return Marcel to the mat.

DAY TWO:
Developing Grip Strength - Pull Ups

SPIDER GRIP PULL UPS

FREQUENCY: 2 sets of 8-12

Day two of grip fighting continues grip strength development by combining different forms of the pull up. The first form is the spider grip pull-up and this is a great exercise for grip fighting and later, the guard. The key to all of these pull-ups is your ability to keep your body perfectly flat as you lift yourself up and down. Practice with the same intensity as yesterday – medium to medium-high with explosive pulls and slow returns on the negative side.

To start the spider grip pull-up, I roll each of Marcel's sleeves to create a grip for my four fingers. While standing over my hips, Marcel keeps his body in upright posture; he should stay upright throughout the exercise. For my first repetition, I lift my chest to Marcel and hold for a second. Slowly, I return to the starting position with my back on the mat. I continue until I have finished all of the repetitions in the set.

WRIST GRIP PULL UPS

FREQUENCY: 2 sets of 8-12

To continue your pull-up training, you should switch your grips to the wrist grip variation. This grip should be more difficult because your wrist breaks upward. As you practice this, get a strong grip with your pinky to middle fingers and focus on keeping your own wrists strong. As with all grip exercises, this movement immediately translates to how your opponent feels you while training. If you have strong grips on your opponent, he will fear the takedown. I have never had an instructor or known a world champion in jiu-jitsu that had weak grips, so make sure you are supplementing your standard technique time and sparring with some type of grip training to make sure that you are the one that comes out on top!

To start the wrist grip pull-up, I grab along Marcel's sleeve with my four fingers, thumbs pointing up. My pinky should be closest to my body and my wrists should be tight. While standing over my hips, Marcel keeps his body in upright posture, he should stay upright throughout the exercise. For my first repetition, I lift my chest to Marcel and hold for a second. Slowly, I return to the starting position with my back on the mat. Again, I continue until I have finished all of the repetitions in the set.

DAY TWO:
Developing Grip Strength Cont.
JOYSTICK GRIP PULL UPS

FREQUENCY: 2 sets of 10-12

This is the final drill of your second day on grip training. This is also my preferred grip when fighting on the ground. The reason I like it is because it takes the slack out of my opponent's gi and it makes it much easier to control his arms. If my opponent has this slack, he can follow my arm, constantly circling his hands until he can break my grip. With this in mind, I have to get this grip strong as well. Does this mean that I should ignore the training of the grips in the past two drills? Of course not! You never know when you will end up in a particular situation so it is best to be prepared for anything or any grip!

For the joystick grip pull-up, I take the slack out of both of Marcel's sleeves and I hold the excess as if I were holding an arcade joystick. Once more, while standing over my hips, Marcel keeps his body in upright posture and he should stay upright throughout the exercise. For my first repetition, I lift my chest to Marcel and hold for a second. Slowly, I return to the starting position with my back on the mat. I will continue these repetitions until I have finished the set.

DAY THREE:
Introduction to Grip Fighting

GRIP FIGHTING

FREQUENCY: 2x 10 minutes timed

You're onto day three and it is time to dive into some actual grip fighting. This is not only good for your stand-up fighting, but it also translates to far more control on the ground phase. For beginners, start slowly and try to feel the technique as you "pop" each of your opponent's grips off. This type of training should be done at a slow to medium pace. For the more advanced students, have your opponent grip at 100 percent strength and as you remove his grip, have him immediately jab into you with another grip. This type of training should be at a medium-high to intense pace. For both groups, start one handed and then move on to two.

I start with my left hand grabbing my belt and Marcel grabbing my left lapel with his right hand. With my right hand, I cup Marcel's right sleeve and pop it down and away from me. This goes against his thumb grip and makes holding very difficult. Immediately, Marcel grabs my right elbow with his left hand. To combat the grip, I bend my elbow to remove the slack from my gi and then punch it away from him. As Marcel counters by grabbing my right lapel with his left hand, I grab under his sleeve and punch it upward, again diffusing the power of his thumb grip. Once finished, I can repeat the drill until I am ready for both hands. When I am capable with both hands, we increase the intensity.

DAY FOUR:
ARM DRAG GRIP FIGHTING

FREQUENCY: 2x 10 minutes

Although I like to do kimono-specific grip fighting, it does not complete you as a grip fighter in the world of grappling. This is where the following two days of drilling come in handy. For your fourth day of gripping, you should work on the arm drag drill. This is an excellent maneuver for learning to control the arm and it has many applications. While stand up fighting, you can use this movement to open up the back or set up upper- or lower-body takedowns. While on the mat, you could use the arm drag to expose the back, reverse positions, or set up the sweep. It is dynamic and effective in all levels and types of grappling. Therefore, it is an essential drill, and you should constantly make sure that your arm drag is honed to a razor's edge. For the beginners, just practice this movement at a slow pace. For advanced students, try to arm drag grip fight at a more intense pace with the opponent resisting at around 70 percent or more.

DAY FIVE:

FREQUENCY: 2x10 minutes

Your second non-kimono-specific grip fighting drill will help with two of your skills: pummeling and ducking under the arm. The purpose of pummeling is to escape your opponent's inside or body control and to get to the inside or body control yourself. From here, you can attack his legs for the takedown, trip him or go for an upper-body throw, or slip under the arm and go to his back. With his elbows separated from his body, you are in a great position to do so. Ducking under the arm is your second skill. It depends on acute timing to feel when your opponent's elbow is open for you to slide under and go to his back. Both pummeling (esgrima) and ducking under are difficult skills to come by, and that is why you need to drill this. Once familiar with the esgrima to the back drill, work this at a medium to medium-high intensity, with both partners really trying to gain inside control and slide under to the back.

Arm Drag Grip Fighting

Marcel and I begin the arm drag grip fighting drill facing each other in square stances with Marcel's right hand on my left shoulder. Circling my left hand from the inside to the outside, I deflect Marcel's hand off my shoulder and grab his right wrist with my left hand, cupping his right triceps with an inside grip. Immediately, I have to pull his grip across my body. Marcel counters the pull by grabbing at my shoulder with his left hand. Already, I have countered his counter and am ready to arm drag his left arm. I continue the drill for the set duration of the round at a predetermined pace. Detail: As with all arm drags, I cannot just drag the triceps without holding the wrist. By holding the wrist, I create a leveraging action as I pull his triceps. This gives Marcel the sensation of being shoulder locked as his elbow is forced forward. If I do not grab the wrist, Marcel can simply lift his hand to escape the attack, making my arm drag a wasted effort.

Pummeling Drills

WEEK ONE: Grip Fighting

PUMMEL TO BACK

Marcel and I are facing one another with both our left arms under each other's right armpits. Both our heads are on the right. To start the drill, we move our heads to the center to open up space under each other's left arm. Immediately, we both pummel our right hands into the space under the left pit. However, before Marcel can finish his pummel, I lift his right elbow away from his body. Immediately, I duck my head under his elbow and lunge forward with my left leg. I arch my head upward, burying it into Marcel's right shoulder. Then, I continue to step around to Marcel's back and control his waist with my grips. Afterward, we will restart our esgrima training with periodical duck-under maneuvers to keep things fresh.

WEEK TWO: Wrestling Throws

DAY ONE:
Wrestling Drive

BALL WRESTLING

FREQUENCY: 2x 5-10 minutes

For your first day of wrestling throws, this is a great drill, and it can be repeated throughout the week as a warm-up. The purpose of the drill is to use your leg power and, if necessary, sprawl to stop your opponent's advance with the Swiss ball as you attempt to drive the ball into him. Ball wrestling is a great way to develop that forward drive and to stimulate your wrestling power muscles—the legs and core. For the more advanced students, you can make this exercise more dynamic if you make a ring that you can push each other out of. Feel free to use forward, backward, and lateral movements to get your opponent out of bounds! For beginners, you may choose to have one person resist while the other drives the ball in one direction. Next time you shoot in for a takedown, make sure your legs have the power to finish the job!

To do ball wrestling, both Marcel and I hug the Swiss ball from a low or kneeling level. When the instructor says, "Go," we both push the ball into each other as we seek to move both the ball and one another around the mat. A second way to practice (pictured above) is to have Marcel push forward into the ball while I try to slow down his progress with resistance. This is a great way for both of us to gain some experience with drive and resistance.

SUMO SPARRING

FREQUENCY: 2x 5-10 mintues

Sumo sparring is the standing equivalent of partner ball wrestling. This time, the goal is to use your balance, forward lean, drive, and footwork to keep the ball pressed into your opponent while you both work for the standing position. Just like partner ball wrestling, you should also change up your goals. Sometimes you will want to have a ring to make the training more sportive and other times you will want your partner to charge forward while you impede his progress through resistance. However way you play it, there are only a couple of rules: you cannot drop the ball, you cannot drop to your knees, and you must hold on to each other, not the ball. This means you will have to use your body weight to keep the ball up as you fight to control your opponent. One last item—if the ball falls, both partners should do 10 push-ups.

Sumo sparring begins with Marcel and I holding each other's forearms while trapping the Swiss ball between our torsos. Immediately, we start jockeying for position as we both drive forward. As I gain a slight advantage with my drive, Marcel stops my progress with his base. We will continue this drill for the set duration, resetting every time one of us is pushed out of the training area's boundaries.

DAY TWO:
Changing Levels

WRESTLER'S SHOT TO LEAPFROG

FREQUENCY: 2 sets of 20 or 3-5 minutes timed

For day two of wrestling throws, you will work on a drill that should tax your cardiovascular system, work on your explosiveness, and most important, emphasize an extreme level change. Changing levels is the key to any good leg takedown and your ability to quickly transition from the standing or head level to the kneeling or waist/leg level will be a large determinant of your success. While practicing, make sure your opponent ducks his head after you shoot through the legs. Otherwise, you could hit him in the back of the head as you jump over! If you choose to do timed rounds, let the time dictate your intensity. Less time always equals higher intensity.

I begin facing Marcel at head level. To get through Marcel's legs, I lunge forward to change my levels. Still, I am not low enough, so I go to all fours as I shoot through his leg. As I pass through Marcel's legs, I stand up and quickly face his back. At this point, Marcel ducks, and I place both hands on his shoulders and jump over his head. I turn to face Marcel. From here, I can continue by changing levels and shooting again or Marcel can immediately shoot under my legs for a more relaxed warm-up.

DAY THREE:
DOUBLE-LEG TAKEDOWN

FREQUENCY: 4x the distance of the mat

For day three of our wrestling training, you should focus entirely on the double-leg takedown. This drill builds on your balance and agility from the sitting thrust and crumbling hip training and adds the proper movements to finish the takedown. As with your level-changing training, you will need to focus on your ability to move from the head to the hip/leg level as quickly and smoothly as possible. Also, you should notice that I return to my starting level at the end of the technique. I return to the upright position so that I can get my whole body and the power of my legs driving into the takedown. Once finished with this drill, add it to your solo warm-ups in class. Focus on changing your levels and not extreme speed at first. As you get more comfortable, try to explode into the shot and the finishing phase.

I begin on one side of the mat, facing the end. I step forward with my left leg and immediately drop all the way to my left knee. As my body drives forward, I catch myself by standing up with my right leg. This is my level change and penetration step. From here, I make a mock grab with my hands as if I were grabbing both of my opponent's legs. I stand my left leg up and then commit to the throw by pulling my arms to my right while I drive my head to the left. If I were practicing with an opponent, his legs would be pulled one way while my head would push him over.

The Double Leg

FREQUENCY: 2 sets of 12-20 or 3-5 minutes

So far, you have been focusing primarily on the level change, which is still your first essential movement to master. However, what happens when you get to the double-leg? Obviously, you need enough power in your reservoir to finish the takedown. Otherwise, you may be faced with an immediate sprawl. The double-leg lift spin is the right drill to help with your explosive finish while continuing the progress you have made with your level-change training. As with all lifting drills, choose a partner that you can safely lift throughout the duration of the exercise. To add some more intensity, adjust your shooting range so that you have to cover a greater area. Just keep in mind that you are always trying to get as close as possible when you attempt takedowns in sparring.

To set up the double-leg lift spin drill, Marcel stands in front of me with both arms outstretched. I change levels and lunge forward with my left leg, taking me underneath Marcel's arms. I clasp my hands together under Marcel's hips to form a bodylock. As I do so, I step my right foot forward so that it is even with my left; my knees are bent. Explosively, I lift Marcel completely off the mat, turn him 180 degrees and then place him down. I quickly reset my position, Marcel repositions his arms and I am ready for my second repetition.

DOUBLE-LEG TAKEDOWNS: In Focus

Without a doubt, changing levels is the most important wrestling element that you should initially master. Dwell on your posture with every repetition. If you bend your body forward without lowering your stature at the hips and legs, you will outstretch your torso too far and will inevitably be sprawled on. If you lower your hips and then shoot in for the takedown, you will have the power of your hips to drive through to the finish. As with everything, changing levels is about mastering your hips!

DAY THREE:
DOUBLE THREAT:

With my back facing the beginning of the mat, I start with my left foot forward in a staggered stance. As I crouch downward, I step forward slightly with my left foot and then follow with my right foot. Unbalanced, I fall to my right side in a side breakfall. Once I have broken my fall, I post my right hand and left leg on the mat, take all the weight off my left foot and stand in the master's lift. Instead of standing to the upright position, I immediately shoot forward with my left leg, fall to my left knee, and penetrate with my right foot. While grasping my would-be opponent's mock foot, I step up with my left foot, pull my arms to my right and drive to the left with my body and head. When practicing this move, I put it into my head that my timing is critical. If I stand straight up from my master's lift, I will lose the moment to attack the double-leg. This is why I am always thinking offensively, even while recovering my composure with a defensive action. Your time to attack is often limited, so always be prepared to change the tide of battle.

The Double Leg Continued
MASTER'S LIFT TO DOUBLE-LEG

FREQUENCY: 2x the distance of the mat

Whenever you take a fall, you must not only be thinking of escaping back to your feet or surviving the fall, but changing the tide of the match. This is why I love to do this drill. As with many of my solo techniques, I know just how important it is to bond defensive and offensive actions together. In this case, you will be covering a wide range of jiu-jitsu techniques as you break your fall, do a master's lift, and finish with a double-leg takedown. While practicing, focus on the transition between standing and shooting for the takedown. Your success in immediately going for the throw will often determine how deep you penetrate against a live opponent. So don't wait until you are all the way upright. Once you have your feet underneath you, go for it. Not only will you develop your legs, core, and technique, but you will also develop your fighting spirit as you make yourself focus on the offense. Practice at a low intensity and only explode as you shoot in for the takedown and drive to the side.

DAY FOUR:
SINGLE-LEG BALANCE

FREQUENCY: 2-3 sets of 20

Two months ago, you practiced the single-leg hop as you worked on your overall balancing skills. Now, it's time to put this to the test in a movement that mimics a defensive action while sparring. Basically, you will be turning away from your opponent while keeping your balancing leg at a distance to prevent the possible double-leg takedown. Use this movement to learn how to turn your hips to slip the knee out of his grasp. Your goal is not to run from the single, but to use swiveling to break up the hold. Obviously, this is also great for your balance and coordination.

To set up the single-leg slip drill, Marcel stands in front of me with both arms outstretched. Before I change levels, I deflect Marcel's hands upward to expose his legs. I change levels as I lunge forward with my left leg, taking me underneath Marcel's arms. I clasp my hands around Marcel's left leg and pinch my head to his left hip. As I do so, I step my right foot forward so that I can drive even more pressure into his hip. Explosively, I stand up with my left leg as my head continues to duck through to his back. I end up on Marcel's back with a bodylock. Once here, I release the lock and repeat the drill by shooting toward Marcel's back. I change levels by dropping to my right knee and step in with my left foot. This time, my left hand hugs his left leg, while my right arm controls his hip. Marcel drops his arms so that I can force myself underneath with a returning duck-under maneuver. I finish with a front bodylock on Marcel. Now, I am ready to release my grips and set up my second repetition.

The Single Leg

We start the single-leg balance drill with Marcel grabbing my right leg above the knee in a single-leg position. His head is pushing into me, and he is tight on my leg. I am keeping my balance with my left leg. As I begin to turn away from Marcel, I push his shoulder down slightly to shimmy him lower on my knee. This frees my hips and allows me to turn so that I can bring both hands to the floor. I keep my left leg far from Marcel so that he cannot transition to a double-leg takedown. My hips are high to prevent him from jumping onto my back. With my knee escaped, I can turn back to Marcel and restart the drill. If it is too easy to escape my knee, I will ask Marcel to add a little more resistance so that I can work on finding space with my hips.

SINGLE-LEG SLIP

FREQUENCY: 3 sets of 20 or 5 minutes

Just like the through the legs to leapfrog drill, this movement emphasizes changing levels to execute the single-leg while slipping your body to the outside to finish the takedown. As with most leg throws, it is vital that you teach your body to move after you have grabbed the leg. In this case, I am training my body to move to the outside so that I can drive into Marcel's leg to finish or take his back if he defends. What I like about this drill is that it makes going to the back a priority. Often enough, it is hard to finish the takedown, and you may waste a lot of energy if you continue to fight for it. Instead of burning yourself out, you should train your body to move around your opponent and at least threaten the back position. If your opponent does not react, you have a clear path to his back. If he does react, usually the single-leg takedown is ripe for the picking. Train this drill with a medium to medium-high intensity. It is important that you learn to use your head and outside foot to step around your opponent while sliding under his arm.

DAY FIVE:

TAKEDOWN TO BACK

FREQUENCY: 5-10 minutes timed

After yesterday's single-leg training, you should be aware of the interrelation between single- and double-leg take-downs and the back. Your first drill for our last day of wrestling training is a pickup to the back. You will develop the necessary explosiveness to bring your opponent to all fours as well as the technique to put your opponent at an angle where you can take the back and the timing to immediately take his back. For the bottom player, you will learn to keep your hips high and head low to sneak out of a back attack. With you and your partner training both positions, you should both expect to get a dynamic and mutually beneficial workout. Do this move with explosiveness on the pickup and speed with the back attack.

FREQUENCY: 3 sets of 20 or 5 minutes

This is a great drill that combines your esgrima to the back grip fighting with an explosive high crotch pickup. This routine will get your heart rate going, so be ready for a workout. The goal is to develop the speed and timing of your duck-under while immediately exploding into the high crotch pickup. Try to make the whole movement one motion. It shouldn't be too difficult because you only have one grip change and a big step. Your pickup power should be there by now, but I want to see more than power. I want you to be able to launch your opponent upward. If you have to struggle to lift your opponent, choose a partner that you can lift with some zeal. If you are still having problems, make sure that your hips are penetrating enough. The explosive lift will come from your hips and legs, not your upper body. Try to do your repetitions at a rapid-fire pace for a very tough workout.

Pick Ups & Exposing the Back

I start the pickup to back with my hands clasping each other around Marcel's back. While squeezing my grips into his navel and keeping my elbows tight, I bring my hips forward and explosively lift Marcel off the mat. Instead of dropping Marcel down anywhere, I turn his hips in the air so that his legs land at a perpendicular angle to my own. Immediately, I put my left hook in front of his left quadriceps. Without delay, I jump onto Marcel's back and place my right hook inside. From here, Marcel drops his head lower and I slide off him to my front. Marcel slides out the backdoor and grabs around my waist to start his repetition. We will trade pickups and back attacks for the duration of the drill.

FIREMAN'S CARRY LIFTS

I begin facing Marcel with my right hand on Marcel's collar and my left hand gripping his right elbow. Marcel has a mirrored grip. In one motion, I lunge forward with my left leg while I lift Marcel's right elbow skyward. Afterward, I turn the corner, square my legs and hips, and grab Marcel's upper thigh with my left hand. With my base underneath me, I can immediately explode upward, lifting Marcel with the power of my hips and legs. Once finished, I return Marcel to the starting position and move back to his front. Each repetition should be done seamlessly and explosively. I work one side first, keeping my hand on his collar at the same place throughout the drill.

DAY ONE:

FOOT SWEEPS

FREQUENCY: 2x 5-10 minutes timed

Foot sweeps, or ashiwaza, as it is called in judo, are usually the signs of amazing throwing technique. Both simple and hard to master, foot sweeps require a basic movement and incredible timing. If you sweep at the wrong time, you are usually faced with what feels like a brick wall. When done perfectly, they feel effortless. I remember doing this drill for hours with my old master, Terere, as he often used this as a Kouchi Gari throw to set up even more throws, such as his ippon seoi nage. The key to this first day of judo takedowns is to learn how to use the blade of your foot to scrape the ground. This will give you a much greater surface area to sweep with and will provide a little more contact for the eventual throw. Work this drill at an easy pace to learn the balance and blade posture of your foot. Once comfortable, picture your foot as a scythe as you slide it across the mat; this is the action that you will need to finish with this throw.

DAY TWO:

FREQUENCY: 2-3 sets of 20 or 2x 5 minutes

For day two of your judo-style take-down practice, you will be practicing the ippon seoi nage, or one-armed shoulder throw. As with all throws, the key to the Seoi is to insert your hips deep underneath your opponent as you pull him off balance with the combined effort of your arms, hips, and leg explosion. To master this move, you should first start with this drill to learn the proper footwork and pivoting to get your hips in the sweet spot. It is also no accident that this movement is the perfect continuation from the above foot sweep. If you are already advanced with this move-ment, you should work this as a one-two combination with the foot sweep drill. For those that are starting out, focus on inserting your hips and piv-oting on your toes.

Foot Techniques

For my first day of foot sweep training, I practice the Kouchi Gari–styled attack. From a relaxed stance with bent knees, I step back with my right foot so that my legs are in a line. I make my left foot a blade by curling my foot toward the pinky toe side. Next, I sweep my foot in a semicircular arc, crossing the path of my right foot. Once finished with the sweeping motion, I step forward with my left foot and am ready to begin another repetition.

Ippon Seoinage

SHADOW IPPON SEOI

WEEK THREE: Judo Takedowns

I start in a square stance with my feet shoulder-width apart. I step forward with my right foot as my right hand grabs an imaginary sleeve or collar. Next, I step through with my left foot, all the while pulling with my right hand and scooping my left hand underneath. I pivot on my left foot until my body is facing the exact opposite position from where I started. My left arm is bent upward as if it is clamping down on an opponent's arm. I drop into a deep crouch, penetrating my hips under my would-be opponent. Finally, I throw my head downward to finish the takedown. From here, I stand up, grab with my other hand and prepare to drill the ippon seoi nage to the opposite side.

DAY TWO:

IPPON SEOI W/ ROLL

FREQUENCY: 2x 10 to each side or 5 minutes

Now that you are familiar with the basic entry mechanics of the ippon seoi, footwork and hip insertion, it is time for you to work on the throwing phase. My first three instructors, Careca, Oswaldo Alves, and Terere, always emphasized that throwing someone takes total effort and complete commitment. This drill is all about instilling a commitment into every throwing action. When you train to overthrow your opponent, as you will do when you shoulder-roll out of the ippon seoi, you also train your body so that the throw does not stop until you are both on the mat. As you practice, try to really whip yourself into the shoulder roll as if that extra "umph" is what you need to finish the takedown. Remember, the better your speed and explosiveness, the more likely your throw will be a success.

Ippon Seoinage Continued

For my second ippon seoi drill, I start in a square stance with my feet shoulder-width apart. I step forward with my right foot as my right hand grabs an imaginary sleeve or collar. Next, I step through with my left foot, all the while pulling with my right hand and scooping my left hand underneath. I pivot on my left foot until my body is facing the exact opposite position from where I started. My left arm is bent upward as if it is clamping down on an opponent's arm. I drop into a deep crouch, penetrating my hips under my would-be opponent. Finally, I throw my head downward to finish the takedown, forcing my body into a forward roll as I overcommit to the throw. I roll over my left shoulder, stand up, and prepare to throw my would-be opponent with the other arm.

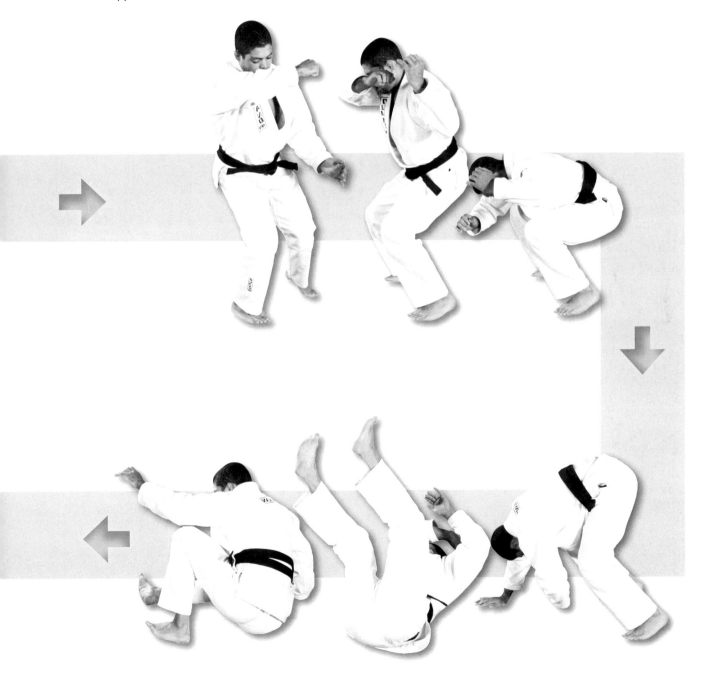

DAY THREE:

SEOI DROP

FREQUENCY: 5 sets of 20

To start off the third day of judo takedowns, you should work on the seoi drop. The seoi drop covers the same footwork and hip insertion as the ippon seoi nage, but this time you will keep both hands on your partner's arm to further elevate his shoulder. The key to this move is to immediately drop as low as possible as soon as you are in the typical Seoi stance and then to crawl back to the starting position. Once you have mastered this throw, it will be time to move on to the next step below.

FREQUENCY: 2 sets of 20 or 5-10 minutes

Our second drop Seoi Nage drill of the day has a slightly different emphasis from the first. Instead of only training your body to drop toward the mat, you will also be training yourself to penetrate deep underneath your opponent's hips. The deeper you go, the lighter your opponent will feel as you easily throw him over your shoulder for the takedown. Try to keep a pretty intense pace as you drop deep and your opponent leapfrogs. As soon as he recovers and turns after your first repetition, you should be gripping and attacking the next throw already.

Partner Seoinage Drills

I start by facing Marcel in a square stance with my feet shoulder-width apart. Marcel has his hands outstretched. I step forward with my right foot as my left hand deflects and grabs Marcel's right sleeve. Next, I step farther through with my right foot, all the while pulling with my left hand and punching my right hand into his triceps. I pivot on my left foot until my body is facing the exact opposite position from where I started. I drop into a deep crouch, penetrating my hips underneath Marcel. Finally, I throw my head downward and release my grips. I bear crawl out of the position, stand, and reposition myself for the second repetition. I should train this movement to both sides until I am comfortable.

SEOI W/ LEAPFROG

For this variation, I again start facing Marcel in a square stance with my feet shoulder-width apart. Marcel has his hands out-stretched. I step forward with my right foot as my left hand deflects and grabs Marcel's right sleeve. Next, I step further through with my right foot, all the while pulling with my left hand and punching my right hand into his triceps. I pivot on my left foot until my body is facing the opposite way. I drop into a deep crouch, penetrating my hips underneath Marcel. Finally, I throw my head downward and release my grips. I am so deep under Marcel that he has to leapfrog me to keep his balance. I come out the backdoor, Marcel will turn to face me, and we will start the second repetition.

DAY FOUR:

O-GOSHI

FREQUENCY: 2 x 5-10 minutes

Day four of our week on judo takedowns focuses on throwing, defense, and movement all at the same time. For the first hip throw exchange, you should work on the O-Goshi, or belt grip hip throw. As the attacker, you are concerned with getting the grip, inserting your hip, and bumping your partner off the mat. As the defender, your focus is to float over his hips as you jump to the front position, pummel your arm, and set up a throw of your own. The lesson to this throw is to move and always look for a way to inhibit or go around your opponent's hips.

FREQUENCY: 2x 5-10 minutes

The ippon seoi hip throw works just like the O-Goshi version, but this throw should be a little more familiar after yesterday's seoi nage session. Just like the previous drill, you should aim to lift your opponent's feet off the mat as he floats his hips to the other side. By float, I mean the ability to lighten the hips and ride the hip-throw movement to the other side. Think of it as a very relaxed jump that goes with the direction of the throw instead of fighting it. Practice this with your attention focused on your hip insertion if you are attacking and your hip relaxation and agility if you are defending. Your pace and intensity should be mellow.

Hip Throw Exchanges

I begin the drill facing Marcel with a mirrored grip. My right hand holds his collar and my left secures his right sleeve. To set up my throw, I release my collar grip, pummel my right hand under his arm, and grab his belt. I step in front of his hips and insert my hips to the outside of his right hip. Using my hips as a fulcrum, I bend Marcel slightly forward, lifting his heels off the mat. Instead of being thrown, Marcel lightens his hips and "floats over my right hip, landing to my front. From here, Marcel will pummel with his right hand, insert his hips, and try to lift my feet off the mat. Again, I float over his hip attack, landing to his front. We will continue in this fashion for the remainder of the time.

IPPON SEOI EXCHANGE

I begin the ippon seoi hip exchange drill by facing Marcel with a mirrored grip. My right hand holds his collar and my left secures his right sleeve. To set up my throw, I release my collar grip, swing my right arm under his right arm (clamping down for control), and step in front of his hips. As I bend Marcel forward for the shoulder throw, Marcel lightens his hips and floats over my right hip, landing to my front. From here, Marcel will clamp down on my right arm for the ippon seoi grip, insert his hips, and try to lift my feet off the mat. Again, I float over his attempted throw, landing to his front. We will continue in this fashion for the remainder of the time. It is also important that we switch hands at the halfway point so that we work both sides of the throw.

DAY FOUR:

UCHI MATA CAN-CAN

FREQUENCY: 4x the distance of the mat

Our final throwing drill for day four is the uchimata can-can. Just as with the single-leg takedown training, this will put all that time you spent in month two's single-leg hop drill to the test. While sparring or in competition, the purpose of the can-can, or hopping action, is to hop your opponent out of balance as he defends against the uchi-mata throw. This is especially effective if you are much smaller than your opponent. Likewise, the forward hopping action can buy you time as you try to defend against the sweep and come up with a possible defense. However, if you do try to hop as a defense, make sure that your opponent cannot pull on your sleeve. If he is able to pull on your sleeve, you are likely to get torqued into the throw, and you would not be the first victim to the uchimata can-can. Practice this down the length of the mat, making sure that both you and your partner are heading straight towards the end of the mat. For more advanced students with experience in judo, you can do can-can drills by switching from ouchi-gari to kouchi-gari as you hop down the length of the mat.

JUDO TAKEDOWNS: In Focus

Getting proficient at judo is a daunting task, but this is a sport that really takes drilling to heart. Before I ever trained jiu-jitsu, I was a student with my youngest brother at the Calasans Judo Academy under Prof. Calasans Camargo. I remember the classes were really fun and that we spent most of our time drilling throws instead of sparring. As a child, I didn't know any better, so I just did my repetitions. As I transitioned into jiu-jitsu, this had a profound impact on my training, because I was always comfortable with drilling and was never overly anxious to start sparring.

Later, I was invited to do some judo training with some of Brazil's greatest judoka, Carlos Honorato and Thiago Camilo. Again, it was no surprise that these champions did hundreds of repetitions for their throws every day. This is when I started asking myself, "What is more important, testing the movements in sparring or having faith that they will work based on their history of success?" Of course sparring would always be fun, but to master a throw or any technique, I learned that I should invest the hours into it to make sure that my body knows what it is going to test in sparring. Otherwise, I would only be testing mistakes, and takedown training is no place for sloppiness.

Hip Throw Exchanges Continued

Marcel and I start at the beginning of the mat with Marcel facing the end. I have him in a shoulder grip with my right hand while my left hand grips his sleeve at the elbow. Marcel is gripping with a standard collar and sleeve grip. To initiate the drill, I swing my left foot in an arc behind me. Then my right foot drives into Marcel's inner left thigh, taking him off balance. To regain his posture, Marcel has to hop forward. I will hop with him to keep him off balance. We do this from the beginning of the mat to the end. Once finished, I can either finish the throw or simply stop. From here, Marcel will take the shoulder grip, attack the uchimata can-can, and we will hop back to the beginning of the mat.

DAY FIVE:
THROW GAUNTLET

FREQUENCY: 2 sets of 20 or 2x 1-2 minutes

The last day of judo training is dedicated to three-man drills and the incredible benefits these could yield to your throwing abilities. The throw gauntlet is a particularly tough workout that I first learned at the white-belt level but really started using it while training with Terere and Telles at the TT Academy. I recall Terere constantly laughing and yelling for us to keep going faster and faster to maintain our heart rate. When getting ready for a tournament, I like to do this while focusing on only one or two throws—those will be the throws that I really get comfortable with for my matches. I usually choose complementary moves, but if you are still working on your throws, it is best that you just stick with a standard throw like the ippon seoi nage.

Three Man Drills

I start the throw gauntlet facing Marcel with both Kevin and Marcel on opposite sides of the mat (for the purpose of the book both are standing much closer than they would during drilling). Both of the throwing dummies should have their hands outstretched to assist in the throwing. Immediately, I sprint toward Marcel and attack him with the ippon seoi nage. As soon as I drop my hips down and lift his heels off the mat, I sprint to Kevin's side and execute another ippon seoi. Once finished, I will charge toward Marcel for my next repetition.

DAY FIVE:

THROW W/ PUSH UPS

FREQUENCY: 2 sets of 10-20 or 2x 1-2 minutes

The second three-man drill is a continuation of the one you just finished with the added upper-body exercise of the drop push-up. For the throw and push-up drill, I work my throwing technique, my cardiovascular system, and my upper-body strength. This workout will get your heart rate pumping—fast. Again, you should cycle out so that after your allotted time or set range, you replace one of the throwing dummies so that he can practice in the middle. Beginning to intermediate students should focus on the same throw every time, while more advanced students can play with different judo-style takedowns. Keep the pace of this very intense. After you have thrown and done your push-up, sprint to the other side and begin your next throw. If you have done this several times and your partners are good with their breakfalls, you can finish each throw to the mat for an even harder workout.

Three Man Drills Continued

I start the drill facing Kevin with both Kevin and Marcel on opposite sides of the mat (for the purpose of the book both are standing much closer than they would during drilling). Both of the throwing dummies should have their hands outstretched to assist in the throwing. Immediately, I sprint toward Kevin and attack him with the ippon seoi nage. As soon as I drop my hips down and lift his heels off the mat, I dive to the floor and immediately execute a push-up. Afterward, I sprint to Marcel's side and execute another ippon seoi. From here, I will continue to another push-up and then will sprint back for the next repetition. It is important that I stay explosive with my throws, strong with my push-ups, and fast with my sprinting to ensure a total body workout.

DAY FIVE:
Three Man Drills Continued
HUMAN BELT RESISTANCE THROWS

FREQUENCY: 2-3 sets of 10 or 1-2 minutes timed

The purpose of this throw is to increase the explosiveness of your throws without hammering your training partners into the mat over and over. By doing the human belt resistance drill, you actually get to use even more strength than is necessary to be successful with the standard throw. Remember how we overthrew our opponents with the ippon seoi roll? Now you get to over-explode into them for a similar benefit. Come competition time, if your opponent is able to withstand your first throw attempt, you can likely force the throw as you drive right through his defensive action. While you work this technique, be sure to relax coming out of the throw as you set up your follow-up. The intensity and explosiveness are only reserved for the lift. As a game, you can imagine yourself throwing both your partner and his assistant—I find that this helps build the fighting spirit because I am ready to throw anything!

I set up the human belt resistance throw drill with a left-hand inside collar grip on Marcel while Marcel grips my lapel with a right-hand outside grip; Kevin is holding Marcel's belt with his feet behind Marcel's to anchor him to the mat. In one explosive action, I execute the ippon seoi nage throw with the intention of throwing Marcel—hard! The weight of Kevin dragging against Marcel prevents him from being thrown. Instead of returning, I give an extra second of throwing force before I relax, bringing Marcel back to the mat. Now I am ready to return to the starting position and explode into my second repetition.

DAY ONE:
Jumping Guard

JUMP THE GUARD

FREQUENCY: 2-3 mat lengths

Any type of Brazilian Jiu-Jitsu stand-up training would be lacking without guard jumping training. You are practicing this last this month to ensure that you are comfortable with throwing before you learn to jump to the guard. This way, you can tell yourself mentally, "I am in control of this fight and I can choose if I want to get the takedown or jump guard for the sweep or submission." For this type of training, choose a partner who can safely receive your weight and is capable of standing in base. This is a great way to train, because it gives posture training for your partner while you get to work your core along with your guard attacking skills.

Marcel is standing in front of me and we have mirrored grips. Our right hands are each gripping the other's left lapel while our left hands grip each other's right elbows. Pulling on Marcel's sleeve grip, I jump my left leg over his right hip. My right leg follows the momentum of my left leg and jumps to the other side. I land in Marcel's lap and lock my legs. Marcel hunches slightly to accept my body weight, keeping his knees bent to prevent injury. Once finished, I will hop off Marcel and we can continue by having Marcel hop to the guard position unless I decide to continue jumping to the guard.

DAYS II & III: FLYING TRIANGLE

FREQUENCY: 2-3x0 10-20 repetitions

For days two and three of this week, you should focus entirely on the flying triangle. The reason I like to emphasize this movement over the flying armbar is because: (1) you will have to jump a lot higher to trap the arm with the flying armbar, (2) when you attack a flying triangle you trap the arm, making the transition to armbar very simple, and (3) you clear one of your opponent's defensive arms when you jump over it. Aside from the technical reasons, you should gain extra confidence with your guard jumping after learning this drill. I do suggest that you practice this move with an opponent who is strong with his standing posture and base and that you use a crash pad until you learn to accept the impact of falling to the mat on your shoulders. Keep up your focus; you are almost finished with month four!

For this drill, Marcel sets up by holding me with the standard collar and sleeve grip. I drop my arm to my side to make it easier for Marcel to clear it. Marcel begins his action by swinging his right leg over my arm. Immediately, he jumps his left leg high to follow the momentum of his right leg. Marcel lands in a triangle position with my right arm trapped between his legs. As Marcel's head falls back toward the mat, I bend my knees and keep him within my base so that I can hold his body weight. Once I have stabilized, Marcel sits up and then releases the position, ending in the original starting position. We can continue the drill by having Marcel repeat the flying triangle or we can take turns.

Flying Attacker

CLOSE UP

From this position, you can see just how exposed my right arm is for attack. Marcel's hips are beneath my arm and he is in the perfect spot to hyperextend my elbow with an armlock submission. Marcel keeps this in mind and has already locked my right shoulder with his left leg and knee. At this point, all Marcel has to do is lift his hips while extending my arm to affect my elbow joint. Pertaining to the triangle, Marcel is already pinching his knees together and closing off space so that he can quickly finish the submission once he hits the floor.

DAYS IV&V:
DOUBLE-LEG & GUARD PULL

FREQUENCY: 2 sets of 10-20 or 2 times 1-3 minutes

Just like last week, it is important that we close the last days of this week with a three-man throwing gauntlet. The purpose of this gauntlet is to combine throwing, taking the back, and pulling guard. This is to mentally reinforce that you are not just a thrower or a guard puller, you can do anything and you have the skill to choose whichever. With that being said, this is also an excellent conditioning drill, and it should be used in the months preceding a tournament to make sure that everybody is in top shape. For both novice and advanced students, be sure that you control your approach to the guard jump. If you do not check your speed, you will likely knock your training dummy over you as your momentum and hips crash into him. All students should sprint as fast as possible and have their partners stand as far away as possible for a harder cardio workout. To increase your reaction time, bring both your training dummies closer so that you have less time to prepare for your action.

Three Man Gauntlet

I start the drill facing Kevin with both Kevin and Marcel on opposite sides of the mat. Both of the throwing dummies should have their hands out-stretched to assist in the throwing. Immediately, I sprint toward Kevin and attack him with a double-leg takedown. Instead of throwing him, I duck under his right arm to take the back. As I take his back, I clasp my hands together for control. Immediately, I sprint to Marcel's side, check my speed, and then jump the guard. If this were a tournament or Marcel were in front of a crash pad, I could crash into him at full speed to knock him over. Afterward, I will release the guard and sprint back to Kevin to continue the drill.

MONTH FOUR: In Review

This month, you learned the importance of getting to the mat. Because competition jiu-jitsu does not start on the knees, it is incredibly important to feel comfortable starting a fight on your feet. We often handicap ourselves by starting most sparring rounds on our knees in class. Reserve some time to grapple from the feet as well to build confidence in this often familiar area. Once you are comfortable with moving on your feet, you should gain the confidence to dictate the course of the match, whether it is pulling guard or hitting the big throw. I have seen so many competitors train for a tournament and never once stand up to practice. This is a major disadvantage, and it shows on tournament day. It is just not practical to only fight from the knees. Throws are as big a part of the game as ground work so you must become comfortable on your feet if you want to be a champion.

Terere would often use his opponent's fear of the throw to pull guard right into a sweep or submission. This is also a great strategy to practice. The key is to be more comfortable on your feet than your opponent. From there, you can read him and make your next move. Sometimes, pulling the guard is the best way to get him on the ground. Other times, he will be trying to pull guard on you, and you will have to battle for a takedown! Either way, throwing and pulling guard skills are essential to the development of an attacking game.

While it is important to have good stand-up in jiu-jitsu competitions, at some point you will face an opponent with a judo or wrestling background. These two sports naturally have better takedowns than jiu-jitsu. I know this might frustrate some, but both these arts devote a greater amount of time to stand up grappling than most jiu-jitsu schools. Feel free to supplement 1-2 of your training sessions a week in judo or wrestling (depending on the competition you are entering). I have provided some good throwing drills in this month, but participating in an actual class aimed at takedowns only will get you even farther in your stand-up skills.

Personally, when it got close to competition time for me, I would make sure that I was spending more and more time with the Brazilian National Judo team. This time paid off with big throws and a more dominant top game. More than anything, I feel confident on my feet

WEEKEND WORK:

Find a gym with crash pads, wrestling mats, or a local beach, and practice finishing your throws to the ground with a knowledgeable assistant. If you can clear 50 throws in a session (both throwing and being thrown), you are going to be in good shape to take someone down and relax for stand up training.

and I am never afraid to go against a good judo player or wrestler, even at the highest level. Cross-training can be very helpful in getting you ready to compete; not only because it gets your stand up better, but also because it boosts your confidence, and that is a big part of winning a tournament!

My hard judo training pays off as I throw Rafael "Gordinho" Correa with a big morote seoi-nage during the 2008 Mundials. *(Photo: John Lamonica)*

MONTH FIVE:
Getting Out of Trouble

Without a doubt, Brazilian Jiu-Jitsu is based on self-defense and getting out of some sticky situations. What is amazing, though, is that jiu-jitsu athletes learn not only to gain some comfort in uncomfortable areas, but also to control them. Although every white belt has felt this defensive sensitivity from his instructor, it is a process built on experience and time on the mat. With that said, I think the art of escaping can and should be drilled. If you focus on the details of where to put your body and why you move the way you do, the rest is up to motor skills, so hit the mats and do those repetitions! We focus on getting out of trouble next because it is the direct result of a failed takedown or control. Plan for the worst and then shoot for the stars.

In week one, I focus your training on self-defense-style maneuvers. While they are appropriate for basic self-defense, they also apply to ground grappling. I believe it is very important for every student to have a well-rounded jiu-jitsu game. With these self-defense-style techniques, you can begin working to master every aspect of Brazilian Jiu-Jitsu. When I travel to different academies around the world, I am surprised at how many students are never even taught these techniques. These moves are the basic framework to old-school jiu-jitsu, and the details you pick up from them easily apply to many techniques when you get to the ground. Because they are purely leverage-based moves, drilling these techniques will help you in your physical understanding of how this martial art works.

Week two moves on to side control escapes. This is usually the next position to which a throw, guard pass, or sweep leads. Make sure you are extremely comfortable here. Everyone should spend a lot of time on the bottom of side control because it is a position that you will always need to know how to escape.

When drilling here, focus on your hands and elbows, keeping them inside the cross-face as a shell to protect against your opponent's control. Once ready, bring your hips and knees into your turtled-up game. Always remember—if you take away what your opponent needs to control or submit, you are back in control of the game, even if you are on the bottom. So when you drill, always hide your limbs and hips. This will prepare your body to begin doing it automatically when you get put in this position.

The goal of this week is to learn to fluidly escape the side control and its variations. Trust me, escaping is always the hardest part of a match. Do yourself a favor and master these escapes so that when the time comes, you won't meet your demise in the side control!

In week three, you will begin drilling escapes from knee-on-belly and the mount. Both of these are highly uncomfortable positions for the bottom guy, so you do not want to stay in them very long. Some coaching points for this week are to use your stiff arms where applicable, but never push your opponent off you. Your arms are only to hold your opponent in place while you escape your hips. When you extend your arms from the bottom position, even for a moment, you are opening yourself up to many submissions and attacks.

To be successful in this position, integrate your basic technical lift, bridge, and hip-escape movements with your new side control escapes. Once you do this, you will have a master escape plan that you can apply in any difficult situation.

Remember to drill many different escapes, but try to use similar movements. Link your basics! It is great to have one escape you do most often or you are the best with, but the body movements you learn this week are more important than any singular escape you will learn.

Finally, week four moves on to back and turtle escapes. The goal this week is to learn to sense back pressure and utilize the same basic movements you've been learning to get out of trouble. With back moves, you cannot rely on your hands because your arms are no longer between you and your opponent. Rely on your knowledge of the body and weight distribution. Leverage will come into play here, just like it did in the basic self-defense escape week. Also, never let your opponent flatten you out here. Always try to stay on one side of your hips or in a tight turtle, because once you are flat, your escape plan will be much more difficult.

When someone is on your back, you are at an extreme disadvantage, so learn to get out and keep your conditioning high so that you can continue the match. The more you drill the escapes, the more comfortable you will be in this position and the less energy you will expend.

By the end of this month, you will have an escape game plan for every disadvantageous position in jiu-jitsu. Drill these often to keep up on your game. Even if you feel like you dominate in your training and you don't get put in these situations often, you must learn them well because there will always be someone who can turn your game upside down. When you are training with your friends at the academy, try putting yourself in these positions to practice your escapes in closer to real-life situations. As always, repetition is your best friend with these drills so drill them often!

GAME PLAN:

As with everything this month, focus on getting to an early defense. If you are in sparring class and your opponent is about to pass your guard, prepare your defenses so that you can easily defend the position and escape. Developing this transition will endlessly frustrate your opponents regardless of rank or experience. If, instead, you focus only on late defense, you will undoubtedly get better at defending these tough situations, but you will also build a game that allows things to go too far. Remember, the best defense is early. A great submission artist can always force a submission if you have let the position get too precarious.

DAYS I&II:

SHOVEL LIFTS

FREQUENCY: 2x 10 or 2x 1-2 minutes

For week one of our escape training, you should first train some standing escapes. The shovel lift drill is an excellent self-defense escape move that teaches your body an important lesson about hip placement and leverage. As you step behind your attacker, you will load his weight onto your hips. Once you stand up, you will notice that you can easily lift him off the floor, even if he is much heavier than you. Aside from the technique itself, this is great practice for your standing base and lower-body strength.

DAYS III-V

FREQUENCY: 2 sets of 20 or 2x 3-5 minutes

The standing kimura escape drill is great way to learn how to use a submission to change positions. This movement is 100 percent technical, and you should feel your greatest improvements come in the form of improved footwork, foot placement, and kimura control. Practice this as a flow drill; do not try to rip off your partner's arm with the shoulder lock! You can work this at a slow to medium intensity; just make sure you keep moving constantly so that your body stays warm. For more challenge, ask your partner to grip harder and harder until you are capable of breaking his bodylock at 100 percent strength.

Hip Leverage

The shovel lift is set up with Marcel bodylocking me from behind. To start the drill, I clamp both my elbows down and then swing my right leg out and behind Marcel. As I do this, I reach down and grab both Marcel's legs behind the knee, which loads Marcel onto my hips. This is where the magic happens. With Marcel loaded onto my hips, I can easily lift him off the mat as I stand erect. Once finished, I return Marcel to the mat in front of me and grab him in a rear bodylock. He can now continue the drill with a shovel lift of his own.

Using the Kimura
STANDING KIMURA ESCAPE

WEEK ONE:
Standing Escapes

I set up the drill with Marcel holding me in a tight rear bodylock. To start the drill, I grab Marcel's right wrist with my left hand. My right hand then reaches over Marcel's left elbow and swims through to grab my own left wrist. With my figure-four lock set, I break Marcel's grip by torquing his arm away from his other grip. At the same time, I step my right foot to Marcel's front so that we are facing each other. Immediately, I step my left leg to the outside of Marcel's right side while slightly torquing his right arm. I continue by walking to Marcel's back. As I arrive to the back position, I release the figure-four lock and grab Marcel in a rear bodylock. Marcel can now continue the drill by executing a standing kimura escape of his own.

DAY ONE:
DEAD WEIGHT HIP ESCAPE

FREQUENCY: 5-10 minutes timed

To start off the week on side control hip escapes, you should first work the dead weight hip escapes. This is a mutually beneficial drill, as the bottom player gets to work on his escape movements without having to deal with the anchoring arms of his opponent. The top player gets to feel how his weight is manipulated and gets to teach his body how to adjust his weight and pressure to keep the top position without the luxury of hands. As a bottom player in this drill, you should be focused on lifting your opponent slightly with your bracing arms and then hip-escaping. This is a drill, so make sure your opponent's weight is constantly pressing into your chest as you try to lift and move. It is also very important that you develop the ability to lift and escape at the same time. This will allow you to escape from precarious positions without solely depending on your arm strength. As a workout, this drill does wonders on your pectoral muscles. Practice at medium intensity.

The dead weight hip escape drill is set up with Marcel leaning onto me while I am trapped under his side control. Marcel has both hands tucked into his belt and his feet more than shoulder-width apart for base. My hands are placed at his hip and shoulder with my elbows tucked in. For my first repetition, I lift Marcel upward with my arms, using my hips to give me a little boost if necessary. A fraction of a second later, I am already hip-escaping from Marcel. Marcel maintains his lean against my outstretched hands. I return to the starting position and Marcel leans back into the side control. I am ready for my second repetition.

The Hip Escape

FREQUENCY: 2x 10-20, each side

Whenever your opponent transitions to a modified scarf hold where he has one hand underneath your outside arm, he is leaving himself open to this easy armbar. Like all movements that are based on an opponent's reaction, you need to drill this enough so that you can feel the timing of when to execute the escape and submission combination. What I like about this position is that the first escape tells your opponent that he is about to lose the position. When he insists on keeping the position by pressuring back into you, he falls right into your armbar. Two things are key to this position: (1) using your grips as a brace to keep your opponent in place as you hip-escape away from him and (2) escaping your hips out so that you have the angle to swing your leg over his head and the room to insert your bottom knee as he stumbles into your armbar trap. This is a basic escape and submission combination that should be in everybody's repertoire.

We set up the drill with Marcel on top of the modified scarf hold. Marcel has his base switched and is controlling my body with his left underhook. My right arm is punching his near-side lapel into his chin while my left hand braces against his hips. To start the drill, I punch the collar into Marcel's chin to move his head away from me. Meanwhile, I escape my hips away from Marcel. Marcel reacts by pushing his head back toward me. As he does this, I utilize the gap created by my hip escape by sliding my left knee into the space under his left armpit. Immediately, I throw my right leg over his face, force Marcel to his back by kicking my leg downward, and finish the armbar submission. Having finished the submission, I release my legs and Marcel returns to the scarf hold for the second repetition.

DAY TWO:
BRIDGING ROLL OVER

FREQUENCY: 2x 3-5 minutes

While day one was dedicated to using hip escapes to get out of the side control, day two focuses on bridges and leg swings to change positions. Believe me, you will need both types of escapes when facing different opponents, so it is best that you get your body used to all of the possible escaping movements. To start the day, you should focus on the hip bump rollover, a technique that emphasizes getting underneath your opponent so that you have the leverage to roll him over with your bridging technique.

FREQUENCY: 2x 3-5 minutes

Now that you have had some time to drill the bridging option, it is time to work the swinging defense. The grip and sit up is an excellent escape drill because it uses two of my favorite jiu-jitsu principles–action and reaction. In fact, this simple drill utilizes that concept a few times in a very short move. For novice students, practice slowly and ask your partner to exaggerate his reactions until you can pick up on the timing. For more experienced students, have your partner put on the scarf hold at 100 percent and ask him to maintain the position at all cost. This will give you the resistance and reaction that you need while making sure that you can still execute the drill.

The Bridge & Swing

I start the drill on the bottom of Marcel's scarf hold position. With my right arm trapped, I decide to lock my hands together underneath both Marcel's arms. I make sure that my hips are glued to Marcel's; it is even better if I can get them slightly underneath him. In one explosive action, I bridge Marcel toward his head, bringing his feet off the mat. With his balance broken toward my head, I can easily turn to my left to roll him to the side. Once Marcel lands in the bottom position, I hug his head, secure his right arm, and switch my base so that I am in the scarf-hold position. From here, Marcel will continue the drill by locking his hands, getting his hips close to mine, and explosively bridging me to the other side.

GRIP & SIT UP

Once again, I begin on the bottom of Marcel's scarf-hold position with Marcel's left arm around my neck and his right arm trapping my left arm. I am grabbing Marcel's right shoulder with my right hand and my left hand cups his hip. To start the action and reaction, I pull Marcel's back to the mat. Marcel reacts by resisting the pull, leaning more intently into me. I use Marcel's momentum to swing my legs up to Marcel's head. Marcel does not like this, and he adjusts his body so that his weight does not collapse forward. I use this action and reaction to swing my legs to the mat, bringing Marcel to his back. I transition to the scarf hold and now it is Marcel's turn to reverse me.

DAY THREE:
HIP ESCAPE TO ROLL OUT

FREQUENCY: 1-2x 5-10 minutes

This is one of my favorite drills and is one that I learned from Oswaldo Alves. Like any good drill, this routine covers a lot of movement, positions, and jiu-jitsu transitions. In this position you have side control defense, the back position, a guard recovery, a guard pass, and the side control top. The key to this position is to move continuously throughout the entire drill instead of segmenting the movements by area. Remember, your goal is always to improve your fluidity and transitions, and this move provides an excellent opportunity to do so. Practice at a slow to medium pace and make sure you can do this with seamless transitions before moving on to tomorrow's drill.

The Hip Escape Flow

I start in the bottom of the side control position with Marcel on top. Marcel's left hand is blocking my face while his right hand cross-faces me. To start the drill, I underhook Marcel's left arm with my right. Immediately, I bridge to send his weight toward my head. As he shifts forward, I pull myself lower down Marcel's body. Using yesterday's drill, I swing my right leg and then kick it down to pull my body out from under him. I slip out to his back. Before I consolidate the back position, Marcel shoulder rolls over his left shoulder to escape. As his legs come over the top, I release his hips so I do not get sucked into his guard. I let Marcel's legs fall forward freely and I take the side control. From here, Marcel will continue the drill by initiating his escape and continuing through the transitions.

DAY FOUR:

ARM GUARD

FREQUENCY: 2x 3-5 minutes

This is a defense sensitivity drill that has some benefits for the top player as well. The goal of this exercise is to keep your hands inside your opponent's arms and armpits at all times as he transitions from the side control to the north-south and back. With your elbows and arms to the inside, you are always in a great position to limit your opponent's control and set up an escape of your own, therefore giving you inside control from an inferior position. For the top player, you get to work on your side to north-south transitions. I recommend that everybody start this technique very slowly until they are adjusted to the position. Even as you get better, you probably do not want the top player to go too fast. In this case, speed may open up too much space, and that could limit the quality of your training on the bottom.

WRONG POSITIONING

Whether you are sparring or drilling, you should never make it a habit to wrap your arms around your opponent's body from the bottom of the north-south. Although it may feel secure, it actually opens up your arms to armbars while exposing your head to chokes like the bread cutter and north-south guillotine. In a self-defense situation, this will not save you either. Holding your opponent like this leaves your head far too exposed to dangerous knee blows. Get used to hiding your arms instead and you will escape much easier while limiting your opponent's options.

FREQUENCY: 2x 3-5 minutes

Once you have mastered the arm guard movement, you are ready for the rollie-pollie. This is a technique that I learned from Leo Vieira, and I love it because it uses the legs in a similar way as the arms from the north-south arm guard. After drilling this, you will find that you have better control of your opponent, as he cannot find the space to drop his weight. The key is to lock your elbow to your knees as your opponent tries to drop his weight over you. This will create a nice platform that carries his weight over your body and not onto it. Like the previous drill, you should continue to shift your hands to the inside so that you are always frustrating his advances. As you improve with this shelling technique, you will notice that it is much easier to recover the guard position, and your guard and escapes will become much more difficult for your opponent.

North-South Defense

We start the drill with Marcel controlling the north-south position. Both my arms are tucked underneath his arms with my elbows close to my body. As I lift Marcel off me, he decides to transition to side control. During Marcel's transition, I track his left arm with my right arm so that he cannot cross-face me; my left arm and elbow must be securely tucked close to my body. Marcel feels a lack of control and transitions back to the north-south. While he does this, I hide both arms under his arms to retain inside control.

ROLLIE-POLLIE

I start with Marcel advancing into my side control. I have my left knee touching my left elbow, effectively blocking Marcel from achieving the side control. As Marcel leans his body over my own, I close my right elbow and knee so that both frames are supporting his weight. From here, Marcel transitions to the north-south and I keep my hands on the inside while keeping my elbows and knees together. As Marcel goes to my right side, I block his left arm cross-face with my right hand and then I close my right elbow to my right knee to sustain my shield. Marcel will continue the drill by going from north-south to side control for the duration of the drill.

DAY FIVE:

PENDULUM ESCAPE

FREQUENCY: 1-2x the distance of the mat

The pendulum escape is the first north-south escape that I learned in jiu-jitsu, and it just so happens that it can easily be converted into a drill. The main reason I made this into a drill was because I noticed that often students would pendulum once or twice and then give up. Use this movement to emphasize how easy it is to continually swing your hips away from your opponent. Since you have been working on so many hip movements and escapes, this move should come a lot easier to you. Work this at a slow to medium pace. Your hip swing does not need too much speed to be effective.

DAYS I & II

FREQUENCY: 2-3 sets of 20 or timed sets

The wall hip lift drill is an excellent way to use an inanimate object like a wall or a post to get great Brazilian Jiu-Jitsu hip training. While practicing this, you should see the wall as your opponent's body blocking you as it passes your guard. Then, you should use this hip-rocking action to get your hips elevated high enough so that you can switch directions. This simulates replacing the guard as your opponent gets the knee-on-belly. You rock your hips in front of your knee and you are back in the guard. Practice this movement by exaggerating your movement—going all the way to the other side. Believe me, you will never have an opponent as immovable as a wall, so take advantage of this unique training.

Making Space in North-South

We begin the drill with Marcel on top of the north-south position with my feet pointing to the end of the mat. Marcel has both my arms trapped and I am gripping him just below his shoulder blades. To start the drill, I keep my knees close together and swing my body to my right. As I swing back to center, I straighten my arms to get my body to move away from Marcel. He counters by stepping forward as I pendulum swing my body to the right, escaping my hips further. As I once again get to the middle, Marcel has to continue his advance before I get too far. I will continue this action of swinging my legs to escape my hips while Marcel follows me for the length of the mat. Again, remember to use your arms as a brace, preventing him from getting too close instead of just pushing him away.

Knee on Belly Recovery

WEEK THREE: KOB, Mount, Back EScapes

WALL HIP LIFTS

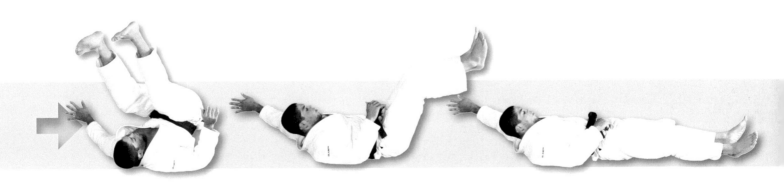

I start with my right side parallel to the wall and my right hand touching it. I rock both my legs upward so that my upper back is all that remains in contact with the floor. Using my upper back as a pivot point, I switch my hips to the other side so that my feet are now facing the opposite direction. I drop my feet to the mat and end parallel to the wall but in a reversed direction. Now I am ready to repeat the drill for the remainder of my workout. If I want to increase the difficulty of the workout, I will only use my hips and will go at a slower pace. If I want to increase the speed and bring more of my body into play, I can push off the wall with my hands to propel me to the other side.

DAYS I & II:
OPEN GUARD RECOVERY

FREQUENCY: 1-2x the distance of the mat

For week three, you will be combining knee-on-belly, mount, and back escapes. For the first two days, you will be working on this essential movement that combines a hip escape with a wall leg lift to realign the guard from the knee-on-belly position. While practicing, you should keep your elbows as close to your body as possible as you are stiff-arming your opponent's knees. You do not want to build the bad habit of opening up your elbows while pushing off. Remember, instead of pushing, your hands are always there to keep your opponent in the same place while you escape away. This is much more energy efficient both in drilling and sparring. As an experiment, you can try pushing with all your might to see how long you last—it won't be long! Practice this important drill at an easy pace. For advanced students, have your partner lean into you to mimic the pressure of grappling.

DAY THREE:

FREQUENCY: 3 sets of 10-20 or 2x 5 minutes

This drill is an excellent movement to develop explosiveness when getting out of the mount as well as submission awareness. Obviously, you also should be drilling the standard upa and elbow escape, but for now, I want you to have some fun by linking your bridging action with a foot lock attempt. Don't fret; later you will get to revisit both the upa and elbow escape in flow training. Instead, focus on three things: using your bridged hips to lift your part-ner off the mat, holding him there just long enough by stiff-arming his hips (not his belt), and pulling your hips into the cavity you have just created to recover the open guard and attack his foot. Practice at a medium pace and ask your partner to vary his intensity and resistance to your bridge. If you feel like he cannot be lifted, ask him to de-crease his pressure. Likewise, if he feels feather-light, ask him to drop a couple extra pounds of pressure into you.

Knee on Belly Recovery Continued

I start the drill with Marcel's right knee on my belly. I have both my hands on his closest knees and I have both my elbows tucked downward so that Marcel cannot trap my arm. To make space, I hip-escape away from Marcel while straightening my arms so that Marcel cannot easily advance back to the position. With space made, I insert my right foot on Marcel's hip to control a guard position. My left leg also follows to his right hip and I lift my hips off the mat. Now that my hips are elevated, I can pivot on my upper back to realign the guard with Marcel. Marcel can never pass my guard as long as our bodies are in the same line. From here, Marcel will pass to the other side knee-on-belly and we will continue the drill.

Mount to Guard Recovery
MOUNT ESCAPE TO GUARD

Marcel has me mounted with both hands posted forward on the mat. I have both my hands pressed into his hips as a brace. I swing both my legs upward to gain momentum. Slamming my feet to the mat next to my rear, I transfer that momentum from my legs into the mat and my hips as I thrust them upward in a bridging action. As Marcel's hips are lifted, I extend my arms into his hips to keep him momentarily hovering over me. When I drop my hips to the mat, I slide my left knee into the space I have created between our hips. My right leg then wraps around the outside of Marcel's left leg and I lock my right heel on his left hip. From here, I have trapped Marcel's foot, and it is ready to be attacked. I will release the hold, allow Marcel to remount, and we will continue the drill to the other side.

DAYS IV&V:

BACK ESCAPE MOVEMENT

FREQUENCY: 2-3x 5 minutes

This is another more unorthodox back escape, but again do not worry, you will drill the standard hip escape ad nauseam while helping your partner train his top transitions in the coming months. This is just to serve as a link between your jiu-jitsu basics and defenses while teaching your body the importance of hook removal and escape. If you can get rid of the hooks, you have a path out! For this movement, you will be using a sit-through technique to slide your leg through and reverse the position. Actually, this drill is quite fun and both you and your partner get to do the exact same routine. Try to feed off each other and move faster and faster for this timed drill.

DAYS I&II:

FREQUENCY: 3 sets of 8-10

Wrestling techniques will provide you with some of your best turtle escapes. In fact, whenever you are in the position and can touch your opponent's leg(s), he is technically at risk of you grabbing him, scooting your base underneath his hips, and then reversing him with a throw from the knees. In this movement, your goal is to increase your hip and leg strength while underneath the sprawl or turtle position. Focus on getting as deep as possible, pulling your opponent toward your rear to take the weight off his feet, and then arching back to lift him instead of shooting upward. Practice this at an easy pace at first, making sure you can feel all the leverage points throughout the drill. Once familiar, you can try to make the drill a little more explosive. As with all lifting techniques, you should use a partner whom you can safely lift.

Back Combination Drill

We set up the drill with Marcel on my back while I am facedown in an all-fours position. Using my left elbow against Marcel's left hook, I shove his hook off as I kick my left leg free. The kicking action opens up the hook for my elbow to remove it. Then, I bring my left knee in a sit-through action. My right hand arches upward along Marcel's right side until I am confident that I have cleared his right arm. I scoot my hips outside of Marcel's, place my right hand on the mat, and now I have an easy path to his back. I climb my left foot over to the mat and now Marcel is ready to repeat the drill to either side.

Sprawl to Power Double

TURTLE LIFT

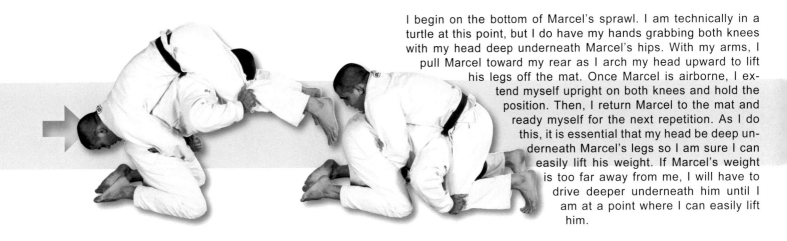

I begin on the bottom of Marcel's sprawl. I am technically in a turtle at this point, but I do have my hands grabbing both knees with my head deep underneath Marcel's hips. With my arms, I pull Marcel toward my rear as I arch my head upward to lift his legs off the mat. Once Marcel is airborne, I extend myself upright on both knees and hold the position. Then, I return Marcel to the mat and ready myself for the next repetition. As I do this, it is essential that my head be deep underneath Marcel's legs so I am sure I can easily lift his weight. If Marcel's weight is too far away from me, I will have to drive deeper underneath him until I am at a point where I can easily lift him.

DAYS I & II:

MASTER'S TURTLE LIFT

FREQUENCY: 2-3 sets of 6-10

This is an excellent power drill that builds on the previous technique. The purpose of the drill is to build explosiveness in your standard lift from the sprawl. Think about it, if you can lift your opponent clear off the mat, all the way into a standing position, then surely you can hit the reversal when both knees are bound to Earth. There is an important lesson in this drill—if you want to get good at something, you have to exceed your limits. Think of this as learning to punch through a target instead of punching the target itself. Practice this with slow controlled movements and be sure that you can safely lift your partner.

DAYS III & IV:

FREQUENCY: 3 sets of 20 or timed sets

For your first routine on both days four and five, you should focus on the sit-out drill. This is an incredibly useful drill that builds explosiveness and agility. I have seen the American champion Bill Cooper completely master this move and frustrate many opponents twice his size. However, if you want to master this, you will have to drill it often and hard. Your goal is to use a sit-through movement against your opponent's pressure to explode out of the sprawled position. Focus on opening up your partner's elbow as you do the sit-out—this will open up your path to freedom. When practicing, use increasing resistance with this move, building from a medium intensity when you are starting out to a high intensity as you add this movement to your arsenal.

Sprawl to Power Double Continued

Once more, I begin on the bottom of Marcel's sprawl. My hands are grabbing both knees and my head is deep underneath Marcel's hips. With my arms, I pull Marcel toward my rear as I arch my head upward to lift his legs off the mat. Once Marcel is airborne, I extend myself upright on both knees and then lift my left foot to the mat. Once stable, I push off my toes to bring my right foot underneath me. I stand and hold the position. Then I return to the mat, one knee at a time, and bring Marcel back to the starting position. It is important that I step one leg at a time and keep my knees over my feet. I do not want to risk knee injury by stepping up awkwardly. Be patient!

Sit-Outs

WEEK FOUR: Turtle Escapes

SIT-OUTS

I begin on the bottom of the sprawled position. Both of Marcel's hands are in front of my shoulders to block my take-down. To open up space for the reversal, I pull Marcel's left elbow away from his body and lift my right knee off the mat. This creates a large space under me and to my right. Immediately, I use a sit-through to slide my left leg underneath. I must explosively penetrate this leg all the way out from underneath Marcel. As I do so, I bury the back of my head into Marcel's ribs to drive him away. As Marcel presses into me, I continue my movement by turning on top of him and landing in the top of the sprawled position. From here, Marcel can continue the drill by doing his own sit-out as we continually trade positions.

DAYS III&IV:

SIT-OUT TURN

FREQUENCY: 2-3 sets of 15-20 or 2x 5 minutes

This is a great variation on the previous drill that will help both the top and bottom players simultaneously. In this drill, the bottom practitioner has the benefit of more sit-out training (there can never be enough) and the top player gets to work a defensive action where he scrambles to face his partner. Both players get an athletic benefit as they scramble for the attack and defense. Often scoffed at as nontechnical, scrambling is a reality in jiu-jitsu training, and you should train your body and mind to go after these moments. You can do this by simply asking your partner to really defend your sit-out to the back as you intently try to take his back off the reversal. You will build grappling attributes like you wouldn't believe!

DAY FIVE:

FREQUENCY: 3x 5 minutes

Brazilian Jiu-Jitsu is very much about feeling where your opponent's body is and noticing where his pressure isn't. These are unseen factors of the martial art and they need to be put into focus as much as possible. My old instructor and good friend, Eduardo Telles, would use this drill to expound on feeling pressure and then basing your reversal off your opponent's position. I thought it was great. The turtle sit-up technique is possible anytime your opponent controls your hips and gets his feet too close to your side without creating any middle-back pressure. To take advantage of this, simply grab his hips and then sit back, bowling your opponent toward his rear. Of course, you have to be worried about him scrambling to your back during sparring, so that is why I like to use this as a good flow drill for both people to learn about leverage and body placement through feeling. Practice this with low intensity.

Sit-Outs Continued

Once more, I begin on the bottom of the sprawled position. This time, both Marcel's hands are over my shoulders to assist with the drill. To open up space for the reversal, I shuck Marcel's right elbow away from his body and lift my left knee off the mat to create space. Immediately, I use a sit-through to shoot my right leg underneath my body as I penetrate my head to Marcel's right flank. As I do this, Marcel counters by circling his legs away from me and facing me head to head. Once we resettle, Marcel holds me again, and I will practice the move to the other side. As a variation, we could also trade off so that both of us get equal time working our sit-outs and the defense.

Feeling the Pressure

WEEK FOUR:
Turtle Escapes

TURTLE SIT-UP

To start the turtle sit-up training, I lean my weight onto Marcel's right side and back. Feeling that my legs are too far forward and that his hips are not locked, Marcel grabs around my waist with his right arm and simply sits back as if he were doing a turtle power lift. I easily fall backward because I have nothing to base on, and Marcel lands on top in side control. We will continue the drill with me on the bottom of the turtle position. It is important that I really feel Marcel make his mistake. I do this by asking him to move a little and then, when I feel his pressure on my lower back, I cup his hips and sit up to send him to the mat.

MONTH FIVE:
In Review

Escaping is both a worst case scenario and an inevitability. Hopefully, the drills this month have made you feel more confident in getting out of a sticky situation if need be. Escapes are one of the most important foundations of jiu-jitsu because at some point in your jiu-jitsu career, you will definitely be in a position that is less than favorable. If you train your escapes to a high level, you will never have to fear losing a position due to submission attacks.

In one of my first matches at black belt, I had my guard passed and my back taken immediately by Felipe Cranivata Simao. Instead of getting flustered and submitted, I relaxed and went back into my escape drills. I eventually escaped the back, passed his guard, took his back, and submitted him from the back position. I am so proud of this match because I was able to display the full spectrum of jiu-jitsu. Without a good foundation of escapes, I may have panicked here and lost to a submission. Because my competition training is so heavily drill-based, my body was moving to escape before I even had to think about it.

Remember, you can never drill too much! If you are training in class, and one of your friends keeps getting you in a bad position, turn back to this chapter and review certain escapes as you need them. The key is to drill, drill, drill!

WEEKEND WORK:

With a partner, work escapes into your positional sparring. Put 2 rounds of 15 minutes (with a five minute resting interval) on the timer and start from a dominated position. Your goal is simple, escape to either a neutral (guard) or dominant position. Your partner should actively try to keep you in a dominant position by transitioning and attacking submissions. Start over if you are either submitted or successfully escape. Try to do this routine every weekend - it is best if you could do it both Saturday and Sunday!

MONTH SIX:
Midterm Review - Putting It All Together

The goal of the Midterm month is to radically fix any of your errors or issues up until this point. To begin this intensive training month, I want you to categorize your drills and positions from one to four with one being your best positions and four being your worst. Then, work from the bottom of the pyramid up, training your category four positions for three weeks and your category three positions for one week. This means you will only be focusing on your two worst categories during this time. Each day of training needs to be intensive, mixing diet, positional sparring, calisthenics, and integrated drilling.

If you are having trouble identifying holes in your game, pull from identifiable situations during your class sparring time that are relevant to the first five months of this program. Below, I have provided some troublesome situations that you may have already faced with solutions and training routines. Keep the training dynamic. If your particular problem is not listed below, look through the book and create your own training routine.

Frequently Asked Questions:

Q: I am getting too tired from all of the drilling...
A: First and foremost you need to address your diet. Diet alone can provide huge gains in your energy levels. Pay special attention to pre and post workout meals. Next up, go back to your strength and conditioning month and focus on the weeks where you felt weakest. Once you feel better, dive into the jiu-jitsu specific months; it is important that you push yourself!
   Action: Revisit Chapters One and Two and return to the drills once the challenge is attainable.

Q: I never feel as if I can get close enough to throw/everytime I try to throw someone, I get pushed away...
A: Follow this gameplan: learn to grip fight and then work on your throwing entries. For fitness, make sure your lower back and core are strong. This will help with your durability during long nights of throw entries. By focusing on grip fighting, you will ensure that you can enter into a throw without being blocked in your attempt. This will eliminate a huge percentage of your missed attacks. Secondly, work on the rhythm of your throw by practicing a ton of throw entries, focusing on your favorite throws. Throwing takes a go-for-it attitude, speed, and explosiveness, so do your reps and then get back to stand up sparring. If you are still having trouble, handicap your training partner (making him grip in a certain fashion and avoid certain defenses) until you have your entrance nailed.
   Action: Revisit month four, week one: grip fighting and combine it with throw entry drills from later weeks.

Q: I have trouble finishing throws against stronger/more veteran opponents...
A: In this case, explosiveness is your friend and again, you will want to develop core, leg, and back strength. Don't make the mistake of depending only on your arms for finishing; the finishing muscles are mostly lower body. If you only have smaller training partners, work on three man uchikomi drills to build the explosiveness to throw through your opponents. Try to spend a couple of weeks in front of the crash pad and repeatedly throw your opponents onto the mat to build throwing endurance and finishing form. Finally, if you return to your stand up sparring and face a strong opponent that you cannot throw, change your strategy and work sacrifice throws and guard pulling. Remember the core concept of jiu-jitsu: go with the energy, not against it.
   Action: Use month two to get in shape, then drill throw entries from month four. Pay special attention to the three man uchikomi (pg 108) and then practice finishing the two person uchikomi on a crash pad.

Q: Every time I start from my feet, I get incredibly anxious...
A: Fear on the feet can most easily be assuaged by learning to fall. I promise that if you get comfortable falling 1,000 times, you will be far less fearful when training from the feet. Start with your breakfalls, then move to taking falls on the crash pad. Once you are confident in your falling skills, graduate to taking falls on the mats (make sure the flooring system is properly reinforced for judo or wrestling falls). Finally, as you gain confidence in this area, work on some physical training for speed and explosiveness for an athletic edge on your feet. Before you throw, you have to get used to falling - nerves are often associated with falling more than throwing!
   Action: Use month two drills for speed and explosiveness. Drill breakfalls (pg 48), handicap your partners during standup training by limiting their participation, and take a lot of falls on the crash pads to get acquainted with falling.

Frequently Asked Questions Continued:

Q: Whenever I try to pull guard in a competition, my opponent grabs my leg and gets takedown points...
A: Again, you are going to work on drills that get you faster and more explosive. Though it may seem counterintuitive, work on throw entries to learn to pull guard. Don't forget about grip fighting either. You need to have a good grip to pull guard successfully, otherwise, you are asking to get thrown or have your guard passed as you throw. Finally, to combat this specific scenario, shoot for a takedown first and then pull guard as your opponent defends your takedown attempt. This action/reaction is key to preventing the loss of easy points in a tournament setting.

   Action: Use month two drills to develop explosive/speed training. Then, review month four's week on grip fighting. Combine a favorite technique {such as the single leg} with a guard pull when your partner defends the throw.

Q: I can never escape when my opponent puts me in a tight cross-face from side control...
A: Before you focus on the cross-face, make sure you master the bridge and hip escape. Once these mechanics are solid, even an opponent with a good cross-face can get in trouble. Next, move to a preventative strategy by focusing on the arm guard drill. The number one best way to defend against the cross-face is to never end up in that position. Block the cross-face and your opponent cannot anchor his weight as easily while pressing the side control.

   Action: Practice bridging & hip escaping (pgs 58-64). Practice hip escaping with dead weight on top of you (pg 122). Drill the hip escape to roll out (pg 126) and arm guard (pg 128).

Q: I have trouble getting heavier opponents off me in all positions.
A: Aside from working on your fundamental escape drills from all positions, you need to remember one thing: the bridge is a force amplifier, you can lift a lot more weight with your hips and legs than you can with your arms alone. If your partner's weight is still an issue, try to handicap your training with a weighted vest to get used to dealing with the added pressure in training. Once you remove the vest, reap the benefits of your training!

   Action: Wear a weighted vest during your escape training to condition a stronger escape movement and wear it throughout positional sparring.

Q: Sometimes, my bridge doesn't budge my partner and my hip escapes go nowhere!
A: The bridge and hip escape should not be seen as solo movements on their own. Instead, look at them as closely related. Use your bridge to open up space for your hip escape and use the hip escape to move your hips into position for the perfect bridge. Whatever you do, keep attacking with these two and you will likely find a hole in your opponent's game to exploit.

   Action: Work your fundamentals in combination!

Q: Whenever I do your knee on belly escape, my opponent runs to North-South...
A: This is a very important way to look at jiu-jitsu. One successful technique often leads to a predictable transition. In this case, you can predict this transition and set up either a single or double leg takedown or the North-South escape as he comes around the corner. Think of this in all of your positions and you are on your way to becoming a technical nightmare on the mats!

   Action: Work hip escapes and knee-on-belly escapes (month five). Drill the single-leg takedown (pg 94) or arm guard (pg 128), and finish off your workout with north-south escapes.
      Note: Keep facing your opponent and you can easily catch the leg for a single leg - if he beats you to the punch go right into your north-south pendulum to make space for you to go to your knees and escape again

Q: My turtle sweeps and reversals are not working against my upper classmates...
A: Technique is great and should always be held above everything else, but I also want you to condition yourself to scramble and work out of tough situations. In this case, wrestling skills will pay off in spades. Take positive movements from wrestling like lifts, switches, and sit outs to change position in transition.

   Action: Incorporate more wrestling movements to keep your opponent at bay. When he reacts or goes into a scramble, you can recover guard or reverse.
Try this sequence: Ball push-ups (pg 20) > turtle bottom drills (pg 135) > takedown drills (month four) > wrestling positional sparring

Q: Is it better to drill submission or position defense?
A: Personally, I make sure I have the knowledge of how to escape submissions, but remember, once a good opponent has a submission in tight, you are very late. It is best to get used to avoiding the submission with good posture and great positional escapes than depending on difficult submission escapes. Just like the cross-face defense, your best bet is to be preventative, not late to the party!

MONTH SEVEN:
En Guarde - Passing & Feeling the Guard

This month, we move our focus to passing the guard. Instead of thinking of passing as individual techniques, you should look at it as interrelated categories of passing techniques. It is much more important that your body knows a couple of around-the-leg, under-the-leg, and over/through-the-legs (acrobatic or not) passes than to have an encyclopedia of every pass in your arsenal. Much of your passing success in sparring and competition will come from your ability to flow between passing categories when met with a wall.

While learning the drills this month, keep in mind that there are two types of passers: those that break through the wall when they are met with resistance and those that walk around/jump over it. You should have both in your game. You need to teach yourself to feel when your weight and pressure can dissolve a defense (only if you can do so while using weight, not power), but you also should not continue driving forward if there is an easier path to your goal—this is the path of least resistance, and it is the path of jiu-jitsu. Once you learn to combine these categories of passing, then there will not be a guard in existence that you cannot pass.

Be sure to focus on lines of defense in the same way that a standup person looks at a sprawl. For a wrestler, the first line of defense against a takedown is the hands, then the elbows, then the head, then the chest, and finally the hips. For the guard player, it starts with the feet, then the shins and knees, then the knee line, and then the hips. Neutralize each variable and you should neutralize the guard as well as the recovery.

The first week of the month focuses on around-the-legs passes. I purposely put this one first because the torreando and its variations were the first passes with which I was successful. I like to stay far from my opponents because it minimizes their control over my body and keeps me safe from their potential attacks. You'll find that your opponent often feels naked as he chases you for control. If you don't allow him to grab a hold of you like he wants, you remain in control.

To be successful with around-the-legs passes, you must be quick on your feet and be able to control your opponent's hips. Remember, it is your foot speed and hip control versus his hip escape and back mobility. Often enough, you can outrun your opponent's defenses. These passes are excellent at building athleticism and agility, so you must drill them often to make sure your endurance is good enough to last in a real match.

Focusing on posture and range as I pass the formidable guard of Rafael Lovato Jr, during my 2008 World Title run. *(Photo: John Lamonica)*

In week two, you will learn to refine around-the-legs passes. This week, focus on more advanced concepts, like eliminating the hooks, hip switching, and hip control to pass. You will also learn to approach different types of guards and how to pass them around the legs.

Be sure to use the same concepts from last week. For example, keep your hips far from your opponent as you get past his knee-line defense. Just like last week, be sure to drill these moves repeatedly because of the amount of agility and footwork it takes to be successful.

Week three introduces under-the-legs passes. The drills this week focus on controlling your opponent's hips and stacking him to get to his side. This style of passing uses more pressure and weight. Always remember to stay on your toes when passing, especially here because it puts more pressure on your opponent as you dig your toes into the mat.

Remember to be open-minded when using these passes. If your opponent has too strong of a block, switch up your game plan and try an over- or around-the-legs pass. Utilize your around-the-legs passing skills to get to the side once your opponent is stacked, and develop a strong shot to the under-the-leg position. The wrestling skills you picked up in month three should help you here.

In week four, I add acrobatic passing to your game plan. These types of passes help you to develop spontaneity in your jiu-jitsu passing. Think of acrobatic passes as a way to channel the game. If you try to cartwheel or somersault the guard, plan on passing as your opponent tries to catch up to your movement. This is how you really link acrobatic passes to around- and under-the-legs passes. This week you cover passes that go over the legs.

Not only do the drills you covered in month two help your acrobatic game, your acrobatic passing drills help to build your strength and balance as well. As you work on these drills, you'll notice your agility improving, especially with your sweep defense and scrambling skills.

This month you will learn all you need to know to get better at guard passing. Drill all these types of passes over and over to see great results. As you move from week to week, you will notice your footwork and agility making leaps and bounds!

GAME PLAN:

When many people start to pass the guard, they focus solely on their arms. Often, they use their arms to get rid of tricky leg grips, to push the feet, or to grab the head and lock in the position. What they are missing is the most essential movement to great passing: foot work. Keep your lower extremities in mind while you pass to become an excellent guard passer. You will use your legs, knees, and feet to remove hooks, drive weight onto your opponent, move the hips, and transition around the guard. As with dancing, master the footwork and bring a greater level of functionality to your passing game.

DAY ONE:
MONKEY WALKING

FREQUENCY: 2-3x the distance of the mat

For your first day of around-the-legs guard passing, you should focus on the side-to-side movement that is key to getting around the guard quickly. To be successful with this drill, focus on really exaggerating your hand placement on the mat. The more you "turn your hands over" the easier it will be for your hips and legs to follow you. Think of your hands as what will coil up the spring that is your hips and legs. The more coil, the more extreme the movement. In the case of guard passing, the further you get to the side, the better your chance of passing to side control or the north-south. Practice along the length of the mat and try to stay at the same level throuhout.

DAYS II&III:

FREQUENCY: 3 sets of 20

The hand-to-floor torreando (bull fighter) drill is the two-person application of the side-to-side movement drill. This time, instead of having both hands on the mat, place one hand on your partner's knee and use your hand on the floor to pivot from side to side. As with the previous drill, it is crucial that you learn to whip your legs from side to side as you become more comfortable with the movement. Make sure you are relaxed while practicing so that your hips and body can easily flow to each side. Also, you have two days to practice this, so make sure you really try to perfect the movement. This technique is the building block for quite a few of my favorite guard passing drills. Practice this at a medium to intense pace, depending on your skill level.

Learning to Pivot w/ the Hands

For the monkey walking drill, I start facing the end of the mat. I lean down and put both hands in front of me. Pivoting on my hands, I jump my legs to the right side, taking my hands off the mat as I land. Next, I place my hands in front of me, but turn them so that my right hand is near my body and my left hand is far. Both hands should be pointing in the direction I would like to land. I jump to the other side and once again remove my hands from the mat. I will continue this drill until I arrive at the end of the mat. While practicing, I really need to emphasize hand placement to coil up my hips. Once my hands are on the mat, I let the setup whip my body to where it needs to be.

Partner Hand Pivot Drills
HAND-TO-FLOOR TORREANDO

WEEK ONE: Around the Legs Passes

For the hand-to-floor torreando, I have both my hands on Marcel's knees with my legs on his left side. To pass, I drop my right hand between Marcel's legs, turning my fingers upward to face Marcel's head. This torques my body and I unload this pressure by jumping my legs to Marcel's right side. From the right side, I now switch my grips by putting my right hand on the knee and my left hand on the floor. Once more, I jump my hips to the other side, landing in the starting position. I will continue doing this movement from side to side until I have finished off my set.

DAY FOUR:
TORREANDO TO KNEE-ON-BELLY

FREQUENCY: 3 sets of 20

The torreando to knee-on-belly is usually one of the first around-the-leg passes that a student learns, and it is also one of the best when it comes to drilling. Personally, I loved this movement so much that it was my dominant pass all through white and blue belt. There are many little things that make this drill a passing powerhouse: driving your hips forward to bend your partner's knees, using your stiff-arms and hips to release the feet from your hips, and the famous cross-step that brings your leg directly to the knee-on-belly position. This movement is really a thing of beauty. It is direct and highly applicable from drilling right into class or competition. Remember, this is a highly technical sequence, so make sure you drill every piece correctly before picking up the speed.

DAY FIVE:

FREQUENCY: 2 sets of 20 or 2x 1-5 minutes

To finish the week on around-the-legs passing drills, I like to use the previous movement to set up the armbar. In this situation, you want to build a lightning fast transition from the pass to the attack, so your partner will help you by keeping his arm exposed throughout the training. This is basic stimulus training. Although it may seem unrealistic to your armbar development, it is actually very intuitive. If you do enough repetitions this way, your body will automatically respond to an exposed arm by taking it and finishing with the well-rehearsed submission. Practice this with intensity toward attacking the arm, but do not throw your hips into the final submission so you can save your partner's arm throughout the repetitions.

The Torreando Pass

The torreando to knee-on-belly drill starts with me in Marcel's open guard. Marcel has both his feet on my hips and I am holding both his pant legs on top of his shins. To bend Marcel's knees, I thrust my hips forward and keep my arms stiff. To release Marcel's feet from my hips, I shoot my hips backward while stiff-arming with both arms. This creates a gap between us, and I quickly take advantage of this space by cross-stepping my right foot to Marcel's right hip; my hands steer Marcel's legs away from this side as I move toward it. I drop my right knee on Marcel's abdomen while retaining my grips on his shins. Once finished, I return to the starting position. I will execute passes to both sides until I have finished the set.

Attacking Off the Torreando

WEEK ONE: Around the Legs Passes

TORREANDO TO ARMBAR

Once again, Marcel has both his feet on my hips and I am holding both his pant legs on top of his shins; Marcel stretches his right arm upward for me to attack. I bend Marcel's knees toward his body by thrusting my hips forward. To release Marcel's feet from my hips, I shoot my hips backward while stiff-arming with both arms. I then cross-step my right foot to Marcel's right hip and immediately drop my right knee into Marcel's right armpit to secure the arm. Continuously, I grab his exposed right arm with my left, swing my rear (left) leg over his head, and fall back into the armbar position. Once finished, I return to the starting point to start my next repetition.

FREQUENCY: 3 sets of 20

Week two is dedicated to mastering the around-the-legs style of passing. This week you will build on last week's fundamental around-the-leg movement with new grips, strategies, and variations. The first move of the week is this hip and knee pin drill. The key to this drill is leaning all of your weight onto your opponent's hips to immobilize his movement and sidestepping to help bring the foot to the floor. Practice this drill at a medium pace and ask for constant feedback regarding your hip pressure.

FREQUENCY: 2 sets of 20 or 2x 1-5 minutes

The knee pin to armbar drill is a drill that is in the same vein as the torreando to armbar drill. Basically, I love to attack immediately after or during a guard pass. This way, my partner does not have time to think or set up his defense as I devise some offense. With that said, you can only master these types of spur-of-the-moment reactions through constant drilling. Usually your window of opportunity is pretty small and you will need timing and confidence if you are going to be pulling these off in class or at your next competition. As with all of these armbars off the pass, ask your partner to keep his hand posted for you to attack. For more advanced students, you can have your partner pull his arm back earlier to increase your reaction speed to grab and finish with the armbar.

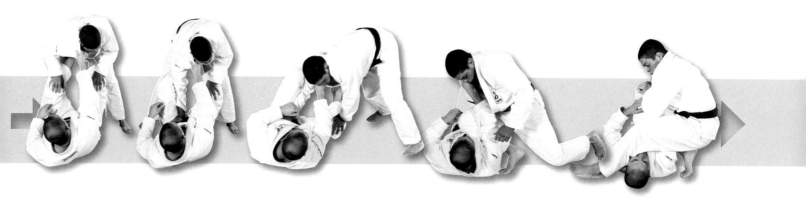

The Hip & Knee Pin Torreando

We begin the hip and knee pin within Marcel's open guard. Marcel has both feet on my hips and his right hand is on my collar. Because his right hand has the collar, I put my right hand on his hip and my left hand on his knee. I step my feet to create distance between my hips and his feet and I lean my body weight into Marcel's body. Next, I sidestep to Marcel's right side, bringing his right knee to the mat. Once the knee hits the floor, I step forward to the knee-on-belly position. After I retreat to the starting position, Marcel reaches with his left hand to grab my collar and I will repeat the drill to the other side. It is vital that I always drill going away from Marcel's arm. I never want to build a habit of going into a possible choke!

KNEE PIN TO ARMBAR

I initiate the knee pin to armbar within Marcel's open guard. Marcel has both feet on my hips and his right hand is on my collar. Because his right hand has the collar, I put my right hand on his hip and my left hand on his knee. I step my feet to create distance between my hips and his feet and I lean my body weight into Marcel's body. Next, I sidestep to Marcel's right side, bringing his right knee to the mat. Once the knee hits the floor, I cross-step my left knee under Marcel's armpit. Marcel keeps his right arm in my armpit, so I can attack it. I oblige by grabbing his arm with my left hand, swinging my leg over his head, and sitting back into a nice armbar. As I finish, I stand back into Marcel's guard 'and repeat to the other side.

FREQUENCY: 3x 3-5 minutes

Before you start drilling different around-the-legs passes against the butterfly or hooks guard, it is even more important that you first drill hook removal. The feet, or hooks in this case, should always be the first things you address to pass the guard. If your opponent can use his hooks to stick to you, there is no pass. Therefore, it is really important for you to practice this drill until you are comfortable so you can take your partner or opponent out of his comfort zone. The best thing about the hooks drill is that it often opens up an easy knee slide pass as you pop out of your opponent's control. Practice this with varying resistance from your opponent so that you can use the right amount of pressure to release the hook.

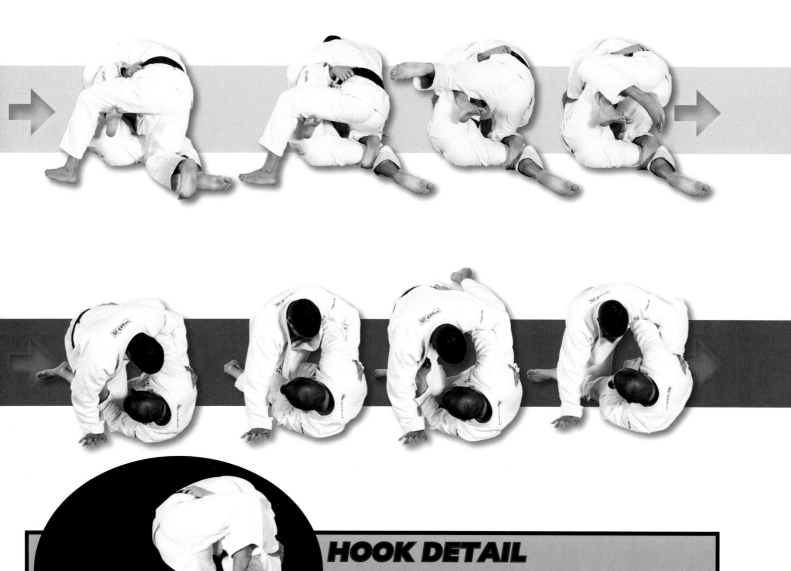

HOOK DETAIL

As you unhook your foot, you need to make sure it circles under-neath your partner's. This is the exact same concept as keeping your feet underneath your opponent's knees while locking down the mount position. Likewise, if your foot is underneath your op-ponent's, he cannot possibly get his hook back. As for the leg that slices over the thigh, make sure that you hook your foot so your opponent cannot escape his leg back to either stand up, sweep, or recover. Once your knee slides over, that leg is now yours!

Eliminating the Hooks

I start the drill inside Marcel's hooks guard. He has his right hook under my left thigh and he underhooks my left arm with his right. First, I slide my right knee over Marcel's left thigh and base my hand in front of me on the mat. My left hand pushes down on Marcel's left hip to anchor him to the mat. I do not want Marcel to lift me! Next, I circle my left foot clockwise to free it from the hook. Once liberated, I drop my left foot on the mat between Marcel's knees and stand my right foot outside of Marcel's guard. Obviously, I am now in a great position to cut my knee through for a guard pass. Instead, I let Marcel recover the hooks guard and I will continue the drill to the other side.

DAY FOUR:
THE TERERE PASS

FREQUENCY: 2-3x 3-5 minutes

Day four of our Master week on around-the-legs passing focuses on switching your hips to get around the guard. I cannot tell you how many times my old master, Fernando "Terere," passed my guard with this. He was so quick with this move that I felt like I never had a chance. Terere would practice this over and over while the rest of us sparred and the results were obvious in his championship medals and lightning-fast guard passes. While practicing, focus on a few key details: getting your head lower than your partner's to control the pass, wheeling his shoulder to the floor close to you and his legs away, grabbing his far leg, and exaggerating your hip switch. Once comfortable, you should practice this with speed and utter commitment.

Switching the Hips to Pass

For the Terere pass, I set up inside Marcel's butterfly guard. Marcel controls my body with an underhook under my armpit. To alleviate Marcel's control, I grab deep over his shoulder with my underhooked arm and circle my head below Marcel's chin. As I do this, I grab his outside pant leg with my free hand. From here I do two things at once. I fall to my left hip and pull Marcel's upper back to the mat. As I pull Marcel's body down, I also steer his legs away with my pant grip. This creates a wheel-like motion and it makes it so that I do not have to fall as far from Marcel to pass his guard. Once passed, I come back to my knees, Marcel recovers the guard, and we continue the drill. Whenever I practice this drill, I make sure that I throw my leg backward as I fall to my hip. This ensures I have base as I fall back and that I have sufficient space to clear his legs.

DAY FIVE:
CHINSTRAP PASS

FREQUENCY: 2-3x 3-5 minutes

To finish off the week you will work on a great pass that was taught to me by Leo Vieira. This movement works really well as a combination with the previous movement or whenever your opponent insists on keeping his head underneath yours. Instead of fighting to circle your head under, you put him in a chinstrap, block his hips, and pass. This puts him in a "twister"-like position where his neck is turning away from his hips, making it very easy to pass his guard. His hips and side control will open up like you wouldn't believe! While drilling, make sure you have both warmed up your necks, backs, and hips and be careful to save your partner's neck while drilling! As for tempo, drill this at an easier pace; you do not want to injure each other while pulling on the chin.

Controlling the Chin & Hips to Pass

Here again, I set up the chinstrap passing drill from within Marcel's butterfly guard. This time, Marcel will keep his head low. To commence the drill, I put Marcel in a headlock with my left arm, grabbing his chin with my left hand. From here, I do two things at once to open up Marcel's side: I turn his chin toward the outside and I place my right hand on the mat close to Marcel's left inner knee. Immediately, I arch my rear off the mat, bringing my knees off the floor. This creates space for Marcel's legs to get out from underneath me. Still turning Marcel's neck and blocking his legs, I pass Marcel's guard. Once I release the position, Marcel recovers the butterfly guard and I will immediately pass to the other side. It is important that I only use speed in starting my pass the moment Marcel arrives in the guard. This creates guard pass timing and will always take your partners and opponents out of rhythm when you are rolling live.

DAYS I & II:
SINGLE UNDERHOOK DRILL

FREQUENCY: 3 sets of 20 or 2x 5 minutes

After two weeks of around-the-leg passing, I like to start the first couple of days of under-the-leg passing with a move that bridges both categories. The single underhook drill realistically mimics what happens when you are going for an underhook pass and your opponent defends the pass. Instead of insisting on the first pass, you change gears and utilize your around-the-leg movement to get to the open side. While practicing, be sure to press your shoulder into the leg that you are underneath before you jump to the other side. You do not want to just jump from side to side without this contact. Practice this at medium-high to high intensity.

Under the Leg Mobility

I set up the single underhook drill by having Marcel lift his left leg straight up with his right leg on the floor. I approach on Marcel's left side and slide my head and right shoulder underneath Marcel's stretched leg. My right hand is posted on the floor to serve as a pivot point and my left hand is checking his knee. Marcel pushes into my body with his leg to provide a little realism to the drill. Feeling his pressure, I go with his momentum and jump my legs to the other side as if I were doing the hand-to-floor torreando drill. Having arrived on Marcel's right side, Marcel drops his left foot to the floor, lifts his right, and we continue the drill to the other side. Remember, as with all under-the-leg drills, it is imperative that I press some of my weight into Marcel's leg as I do this. The more advanced you are with this movement, the more weight you should drop. Just make sure that you find a happy medium between pressure and mobility.

DAYS I & II:
DUCK-THROUGH PASS

FREQUENCY: 3 sets of 20 or 2x 5 minutes

This is an amazing drill for developing the attributes and movement for under-the-leg passing. In this drill, you will pull your opponent's knee down to change the angle of his lifted leg. When the leg follows, pass under the leg and then turn the corner to his side control. This concept of passing under the leg with your head out from between both legs is an important one. When your head is on the outside of his legs, you do not have to worry as much about triangle chokes or armbars. Think of this as passing from side to side and make sure to keep pressure on his upright leg as you make your transitions. As with the previous drill, work on your rhythm until you can do this at full speed at a high level of intensity. Make this move a workout.

Under the Leg Mobility Continued

I approach on Marcel's left side. Marcel has his right leg stretched upward and his right knee bent with his foot on the floor. Starting the drill, I push Marcel's left knee to the mat with my right hand. This brings Marcel's right leg a little closer. With my right hand still on his knee to prevent his hip movement, I drive my right shoulder into Marcel's leg and step my left hand outside his right hip. I pivot on both hands to swing my legs around to Marcel's right side. The swinging of my body further pushes Marcel's leg away from me as I arrive on his side. Marcel continues the drill by dropping his right foot to the floor and lifting his left leg to the sky. I drop his knee to the mat, pressure into his leg, and continue the drill to the other side.

WEEK THREE: Under the Legs Passes

DAY THREE:
THE DUCK-THROUGH SLIDE

FREQUENCY: 3 sets of 20

This is an excellent drill that helps with an intermediary transition in guard passing. I consider this a plan B pass because it usually happens in sparring when you have already passed and your opponent manages to free his outside leg and then throw it over your head to block your path to his side control. Next time this happens you will not hesitate to pass because your body will easily realize what is happening. The keys to this movement are trapping your partner's bottom leg so that your leg does not get caught as you try to pass along with consistent shoulder pressure into his leg. By keeping his bottom leg stretched, your shoulder pressing into his leg should do wonders for your partner's flexibility as well.

Under the Leg Plan B

I approach on Marcel's right side. Marcel has his right leg stretched on the mat and his left stretched upward. Starting the drill, I push down on Marcel's right knee with my right hand. My left arm then grabs Marcel's left leg just under the knee for control. Next, I slide my left shin over Marcel's right thigh. With my shin pinning his bottom leg and my toes blocking his escape, I can bring my right leg over his right foot as my shoulder pressures into the back of his leg. I turn the corner and arrive on Marcel's side. Marcel continues the drill by bringing his left foot to the floor and then lifting his right leg. I can now continue the drill to the other side. As I practice the drill I make sure that I do not get overly anxious to pass, it is very important that I trap Marcel's leg to the mat so I can safely pass over his leg. Otherwise, Marcel is likely to trap my leg and impede my progress. Therefore, you should ask your partner to "hook" your rear leg (the one that passes last) if you fail to trap his leg with your shin and hook.

DAY FOUR:
THE OVER-AND-UNDER PASS

FREQUENCY: 3 sets of 3-5 minutes

The over- and under-the-leg guard pass is a staple in Brazilian Jiu-Jitsu. I remember as a white belt watching guys like Nino Schembri use this move with a lot of success in competition, and I knew I had to master it one day. The key to feeling confident with this drill is in how you grip the legs, tripod-base, and move from side to side. This drill focuses on two passes: an under-the-leg pass and one that goes around (or slightly over) the legs. While practicing, your partner should put weight into his stacked leg and use his arms against your hips to stop your progress. Your job is to keep the pressure on and move from side to side as smoothly and quickly as possible and do so without losing your balance or releasing the legs. Keep in mind, this drill will exhaust your opponent who gets to lie in a stacked position and withstand your pressure throughout. Practice this at a medium-high to high level of intensity.

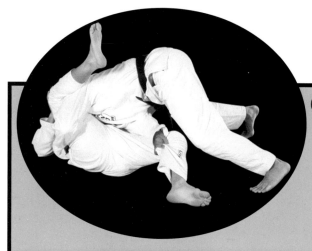

GRIP DETAIL

When gripping the bottom leg, I like to grip slightly below the knee with a knuckles down grip. This way, I can use my fist to punch the leg into the ground. I do not want this leg to move around or be off the floor. By grounding it, I limit his mobility while making it easier for me to keep my base. To keep the leg pinned, I stiff-arm the leg and use my body weight to immobilize the limb. Whatever you do, don't let your opponent have control over his leg!

Combining Over & Under the Leg Passes

I begin the guard passing drill in the over-and-under position. My right arm is underneath Marcel's left leg and my left arm is pinning his right leg to the floor. While in this position, I keep my hips high with my weight driving forward into Marcel's hips and abdomen. My legs are spread wide so that I am in a strong base. I do not want to get tipped over while passing! Once comfortable with the starting position, I walk my body over to Marcel's right side. Marcel stops my progress by stiff-arming my left hip. This is my signal. I immediately walk to the other side, finishing on Marcel's left side. Once more, Marcel stiff-arms me to stop my progress. My stacking pressure should bother him a little bit here. I continue the drill by passing from side to side, changing the side every time Marcel blocks my hips. While practicing, I make sure that my pressure is solid and that Marcel is uncomfortable throughout. This drill should help with both my mobility and my weight distribution over my opponent.

DAY FIVE:
THE LEO VIEIRA TRAP

FREQUENCY: 3 sets of 3-5 minutes

The first time I saw this technique was while training with Leo Vieira. He would do it all the time, and it works incredibly well off the action and reaction principle. As you push your opponent's legs forward, he will usually resist by pushing back. This is when you cross his legs in front of you, trap them with your shoulder and body weight, and pass. This movement also works great for drilling. Instead of completing the pass as I learned it, I work on what I think is the most important phase, trapping the leg to expose my opponent's back and side. Work this with a medium-high to high intensity to ensure that you also get a tough workout.

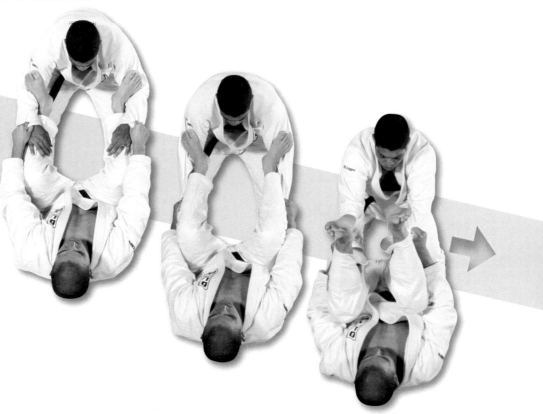

I start the drill inside Marcel's spider guard. Both of his feet are controlling my biceps as he controls both my sleeves. First thing, I have to get rid of Marcel's control, so I circle my hands underneath Marcel's legs and grab his pants at the calf level with a knuckle-down grip. Next, I stiff-arm my arms forward to force Marcel to roll back. Marcel does not want to be rolled to his back, so he resists by pushing forward with his legs. This is when I use his momentum against him. I pull both his legs to my right side. I trap his legs between my right knee and pin them in place with my right shoulder. Marcel's back is exposed and I could take his back or pass to side control if we were in a sparring situation. Marcel defends by rolling his legs and hips back to a square position. Once again, I go with his momentum as I bring his legs to the other side. We will continue to do this at a fast pace for the duration of the time to complete the drill.

Turning the Hips

DAY ONE:
HEADSTAND PASS

FREQUENCY: 3 sets of 10-20 to each side

For your first day of over-the-leg or acrobatic guard passing, you should work on this basic headstand pass. The idea behind the maneuver is simple; your body always needs to be in alignment. So, if you put your head on the same side as your body, you will be coiled up. Use this energy to jump over the guard for realignment. For the drill, just work back and forth with your head on the same side. Focus on elevating your hips and legs to vertical as if you were trying to minimize the power of his hooks. This should be practiced at an easy pace and should be a great application to the gymnastic movements you did in Month Two.

DAYS II&III:

FREQUENCY: 2 sets of 20

The first drill of days two and three is a variation on the previous day's work. This time, instead of keeping your head stationary, you will move your head to the same side as your body to retorque your hips. Not only does this -spring-load your hips, but it also prepares you for the next drill of the day. As you practice, keep the top of your head on the mat! You do not want to risk a neck injury by looking upward. In addition, try to feel your weight pressing into your opponent's abdomen as you jump from side to side. This is what your arm and shoulder are for—to distribute your weight over your opponent's core! Practice this at a relaxed pace and work on a seamless transition from side to side.

Headstand Basics

I start the headstand pass within Marcel's flattened butterfly guard. Both my hands are in front of his hips and my left arm is hugging his midsection. My head is pinned to Marcel's left hip and the top of my head is on the mat. To pass to the other side, I jump my legs from Marcel's left side to the vertical position above him to his right side. Once on his right, my body is realigned. To continue, I jump back to the vertical and to the left, or coiled, side (because my head and legs are on the same side). I will continue the drill by jumping from side to side to finish the set.

Mastering the Headstand

WEEK FOUR: Acrobatic Passing

SWITCHING HEADSTAND PASS

I start the switching headstand pass drill within Marcel's flattened butterfly guard in the same configuration as the previous drill. I jump my legs from Marcel's left side to the vertical position above him to his right side. Once on his right, my body is realigned. To continue, I switch my head to Marcel's right side to torque my hips and then jump to the other side to realign my body. I will continue to switch my head and jump from side to side until I finish my set.

DAYS II & III:
HIP ESCAPE HEADSTAND PASS

FREQUENCY: 2-3x the distance of the mat

The hip escape to headstand pass drill realistically replicates a common sparring scenario and it is the fruition of the work you put into the previous two drills. This time, your opponent is going to work his hip escape technique while you get to build your acrobatic passing skills. For this movement, your opponent will physically push your head off axis as he hip-escapes so that your legs are on the same side as your head. As you know from the last two drills, this coils up your hips and you should jump over to the other side. This is a dynamic movement and is one of my favorite drills because both partners are doing a proper movement. The partner on the bottom slips away by hip-escaping and pushing the head to the leg side and the person on top gets to pass off his defense!

Mastering the Headstand Continued

I start the drill on Marcel's right side as if I have just passed his legs and need to transition to side control. Marcel defends by escaping his hips away from me and pushing my head further toward his right, putting my head and legs on the same side as Marcel's body. I counter by putting the top of my head onto the mat, pushing Marcel's left knee to the mat so he cannot catch me in the guard, and jumping to his other side to realign my body. This forces Marcel to turn to face me, hip-escape away while pushing my head to the same side as my legs. Again, I drive his knees to the mat and jump my legs to the other side. We will continue like this for the distance of the mat.

DAYS IV & V:
CARTWHEEL & SPIN RECOVERY

FREQUENCY: 2-3 sets of 20

The star, or cartwheel, pass is one of my favorite techniques and this is not only because of the pass itself. What I like about this movement is that the pass often causes a good player to adjust or chase you to avoid having his guard passed. This reaction is predictable, so I like to use this movement to make my opponent follow me; when he does, I am ready to pass in another direction or with another form of guard passing. For this drill, both partners get to use good jiu-jitsu movement. The passer focuses on whipping his legs around to the back as fast as possible while the bottom player gets to use an inverted north-south recovery technique. Try to keep the pace fast with the cartwheeling, just make sure your legs and hips are high enough off the ground to avoid a possible hook.

The Star

I begin the drill facing Marcel in the guard with control of both legs. With my hands underneath Marcel's feet, I try to throw his legs forward to force him to roll backward. Marcel resists and I let his feet fall to the mat. As Marcel's body follows his legs to a sitting position, I place my right hand on the mat to the left of Marcel's legs and my left hand on his shoulders. Then, I cartwheel over Marcel, making sure that my legs have the elevation to clear his head. I use the round-off style of cartwheel to land behind Marcel. Marcel counters by falling to his back, grabbing both my ankles, pulling his crossed feet to my hips, and spinning to recover the guard. We finish in the original starting position (albeit 180 degrees apart) and I am ready to start the second repetition of the drill.

MONTH SEVEN:
In Review

While it is great to learn all the drills this month, to become a proficient guard passer, you do not need a thousand guard passes. Instead, just focus on mastering one or two passes over, under, and around the guard. This way, you will be able to use combinations of simple techniques to get past even the most daunting guard player. Sure, drill everything! Then narrow down your favorites and become an expert at them.

This month, never forget that you are submission artist, even when you are drilling a guard pass that does not include a submission. Keep your mind open to where your opponent is overexposing himself so that you can later react faster when you incorporate submissions into your passing game.

Remember, a good guard passer stays on his toes. Just as a boxer and judoka stay on their toes, so should you! This will increase your mobility and forward pressure when passing. Also, as a passer, the relationship between your hands and your opponent's knees is important. The general rule of thumb is to always keep your hands, arms, and shoulders to the inside of your opponent's knees while passing. The more inside you are, the less control your opponent has over you.

One last tip: Guard passing and later, top transitions, depend on a dance like choreography, so work on your footwork to increase your speed! Footwork is one of the major building blocks to creating a strong passing game so drill often and keep moving those feet!

WEEKEND WORK:

At the end of each week, you should work that particular guard pass into your positional sparring. Once again, 2-3 rounds of 15 minutes should get you in much better passing shape. If you are swept, submitted, or are successful in your guard pass, start over until the timer has hit zero! If you are unsuccessful in your pass attempts or your training partner is at too high of a level, feel free to handicap him by asking him to grab his belt and using just his legs or by holding a pair of tennis balls.

MONTH EIGHT:
Staying Dominant -
Top Transitions

The focus this month is transitioning between dominant top positions. The goal of drilling the top is not to learn to hold your opponent; instead, it is to learn how to use both your opponent's and your own reactions to either advance your position, retreat to a safe dominant top position, or move to the submission. I never like to stay in one position for too long when I am training. It is a good idea to move between top positions to stay dominant and confuse your opponent so he doesn't know what you will do next.

This month, each week is organized by the origin of the transition. If the move starts in the side control and the transition is to the mount, the move is classified as a side control transition. This should help you get a better understanding for the sometimes confusing web of jiu-jitsu positions.

The first week is focused on side control drills. Your first goal is to learn to transition from one side of the side control to the other. This around-the-head movement will occur over and over in jiu-jitsu, whether it is with the side control, turtle, or knee-on-belly. Be sure to pay attention to your hands when transitioning from one side to the other. It will help you teach your body how to stay in base on top while protecting you from your opponent's recovery.

Keeping aggressive on the back during a black belt match. *(Photo: John Lamonica)*

The next step this week is to learn to transition into different dominant positions. You need this skill to advance the position both when your opponent is not defending and when he is using a proper side control defense. Drill these types of moves often because it is important to know how to move from different top positions seamlessly to keep the game progressing. I have seen too many competitors who pass the guard and just stay on top of side control until the match ends. Sure, they win with three points, but the game isn't exciting and they never open up enough to get to another position that is even more dominant. Remember, the more dominant the position, the better chance for a submission!

Finally, this week you should think of side control as your base camp. You can retreat to it from any position, and likewise, continue to transition to any other dominant position to continue the match. As with all the drills in this book, repetition will help you to develop a fluid style in side control that is open to transitioning and staying dominant on top.

Week two moves on to knee-on-belly drills. I base a lot of my knee-on-belly transitions on Fernando "Margarida" Pontes, who used the position with the most dominance during the early 2000s. He could choke, maintain, armbar, and transition in and out of it with ease. His opponents were obviously not pleased, and his dominance on top inspired me to get my top game up to par.

Your goal this week is to develop knee-on-belly control as your opponent tries to buck you off, all the while working to expose your opponent, or rather, to influence him to expose himself, to submissions. In the case of knee-on-belly, you are most likely to progress to the mount or retreat to side control, though progressing to the back is also a possibility.

By its nature, the knee on belly can feel precarious so focus your drills on keeping your opponent threatened and under the pressure of your knee. This will cause him to react and will make him far more predictable.

The third week of the month is centered on mount transitions. Your first goal is learning to keep the mount by only using your legs. This should teach your body how to hide your feet from the half guard and make your transitioning life much easier once you reintegrate your arms.

Staying on the mount has everything to do with your ability to transition between the mount and the seated mount. Once in the mounted position, you also need to master the transition to the armbar. This is not because it is the highest percentage or the most "basic." Rather, you should master it because it makes you move to a different angle, and you have to use your legs and hips differently to sustain your top pressure.

While training this week, keep the half mount in mind. It will come into play often, especially as you learn to hide your foot from your opponent's escape. The great news is that this position offers a nice transition to the back position.

The back is the focus of week four. Your goals this week are to develop control when you do not have the hooks, to teach your body how to retain the back when your opponent defends, and to dominate the turtle position through transitions. This is a great week to revisit and expand upon your back defense techniques. Remember, your opponent's hands and defense are in front of him. Use this to your advantage and glue yourself to his most exposed body part—his back!

This month you will become a top transition master. Be sure to drill all types of transitions so you can move fluidly and beautifully when you are on top of your opponent. The top game in jiu-jitsu should be dominant, and after this month you will be well on your way to becoming an assertive top guy!

DAY ONE:
HIPS & BALL MOVEMENT
FREQUENCY: 5-10 minutes timed

Week one of our top transition training will focus on the side control position. Learning to transition while in the side control is often difficult unless you have learned how to move your hips and maintain your balance while on them. This is one of my favorite drills and it is one of which my good friend Marcel Louzado is an absolute master. More important, I have also felt Marcel's pressure as he has rolled his hips all over me while sparring, and I can say this from experience, when someone has developed this mobility and balance, it makes the life of the person on the bottom quite miserable. Once this week of training is over, continue practicing this as a pre-class warm-up. While practicing, hold each position to really feel how you equalize your balance. You can go as slow or as fast you want between positions, but I recommend changing it up so that you can do it both slow and controlled and with speed.

DAY TWO:

FREQUENCY: 2 timed sets of 5-10 minutes

Now that you have had a chance to reacquaint your body with hip balance and movement, it is time to put it to the test with some side control switching transitions. Day two is dedicated to two things: developing a quick transition time from side control to side control and teaching your body to react as your opponent tries to escape the bottom position. The key to this is your ability to switch your hips, move on your toes, and use the proper handwork to set up the pinning technique. The first drill of the day is an arm-wrap technique that comes directly from the pages of wrestling. This is a great escape when you have the time to read your opponent's intentions. It is vital that you use the quarter nelson technique to trap the arm, opening up a path to his other side. Upon arrival, you will feel that the quarter nelson easily becomes a tight cross-facing pin. Practice this at a controlled pace—if you cannot execute this move with precision, you are going too fast! Work on a smooth transition and then add speed as you get used to the footwork.

Developing Side Control Movement

Marcel starts the drill by sitting on the Swiss ball with both hands outstretched. Slowly, he rolls onto his right hip. Marcel must keep as much of his right leg and hip in contact with the ball as possible while stabilizing his balance with his right hand. Immediately, Marcel uses his hips to roll the ball back to the starting position and then continue to his left hip. Once Marcel has found his balance he will adjust his speed as he goes from side to side, always making sure to hold the position at either hip.

Side Control to Side Control Transitions
QUARTER NELSON TRANSITION

I begin in the side control position; I am trapping Marcel's head with a cross-face with my left arm. To escape, Marcel swims his left arm underneath my right to make an underhook, gaining some control of my body. Immediately, I posture up to make space for my right arm to swim around his left arm, making an overhook. I continue to overhook his arm, feeding my right hand all the way behind Marcel's head to trap his arm and open up his back. From here, I walk around Marcel's head to his back, landing on my hip in the side control position. I keep Marcel's left hand trapped with my hips and thigh as I secure the cross-face position with my right hand. The drill will continue as Marcel underhooks with his right arm, forcing me to escape once more to the other side.

DAY TWO:
ARM CONTROL TRANSITION

FREQUENCY: 2 timed sets of 5-10 minutes

In the previous drill, you had the positioning and time to wrap your opponent's arm with a quarter nelson grip as he tried to swim his arm to set up his escape. This drill goes one step further in that it teaches your body how to react when your opponent is more explosive and agile in his escape. The key to this movement is still securing that underhooking arm to open up the path to the back and the other side. While drilling, it is equally important to develop some speed while dealing with your partner's move. You do not want him to get to his knees, so you should drill this move until you are comfortable doing a few things at once: securing his arm, pressing into his body to slow him down, and smoothly transitioning to his back.

I begin in the side control position. I am trapping Marcel's head with a cross-face with my left arm. This time, to escape, Marcel explosively swims his left arm underneath my right to make an underhook, gaining some control of my body and pushing me slightly away. Immediately, I pressure into Marcel and press my right hand into his hip to slow him down from getting to his knees. Then, I swing my left hand over his body to secure his left arm. With his arm secured, I drive my left elbow into Marcel's side to further inhibit his progress. From here, I walk around Marcel's head to his back side, landing on my hip in the side control position. I keep Marcel on his right side by pressing my chest into his left elbow. After I release the pressure, Marcel returns to his back and we will repeat the drill to the other side.

DAY THREE:
THE KNEE CUT TRANSITION

FREQUENCY: 2 timed sets of 5-10 minutes

Where day two of side control drills focused on transitions around the head, day three emphasizes transitions that cut over the body. For your first drill, you should start with this nice arm triangle attack. Aside from honing your submission skills, this drill also ingrains a very important concept in jiu-jitsu: when your opponent turns to face you, don't stay there! In this case, as your opponent faces you, finish with the head and arm choke or arm triangle. The key to this drill is trapping your opponent's arm with your head and arm while using your hand on his hip to anchor him to the mat. You should practice this movement at a slow pace, working on controlling his head and arm throughout the transition. For more advanced students, try to have your partner trap your feet as you go from side to side. Once trapped, you can either continue with the pass (while holding his head) or reset the position until you are comfortable that your opponent cannot secure your legs.

Advanced Side Control Transitions

I start on Marcel's right side in a loose side control position. My left forearm is blocking Marcel's right arm and my head is elevated. To initiate, Marcel bridges into me while shooting his left arm in front of my head toward the mat. I react by hugging his head and arm with my left arm, neck, head, and shoulder. As I do this, I press down on his hip with my right hand. With pressure on his bridging hip, I replace my right hand with my inside, or in this case, left, knee. I slide my knee all the way across his abdomen, following it with my right leg. I land on Marcel's left side in an arm triangle position. I release the choke, allowing Marcel to reset the starting position, and we will continue the drill to the other side. Detail: It is important that I lead with my inside leg as I cut across his chest. This way, if Marcel traps a leg it will be my rear leg and I can easily free this by kicking it open with my inside leg or using the power of my hips driving to side control to slide my leg free.

DAY THREE:
KNEE SMASH PASS

FREQUENCY: 2 timed sets of 5-10 minutes

The knee smash pass is a marvelous continuation of our side control drills that cut across the body, and it is a drill that I practiced for years while training with Terere. In fact, this is one of the movements that he is an absolute master of, and once my body learned to move this way, I was able to completely change my game. As far as move classification, this movement is somewhere in the middle; it is almost a guard pass (it definitely is if the opponent gets his knees in front of you), and it is almost a side control transition. This drill should do wonders for your timing, as it did mine. Focus on pinching your opponent's knees together as he turns into you and immediately cross-step to the other side. Do not hesitate—just go. When it comes time for sparring, your opponent should always feel confused and frustrated as you constantly hop to his back and he tries to escape. Practice this until the knee smash and cross-through are instantaneous.

Advanced Side Control Transitions Cont.

I start on Marcel's right side. Marcel is flat on the mat in a side control–like position. To initiate the drill, Marcel turns onto his right hip. As he does so, I cup his left knee with my right hand and use his momentum to push his knees together. Without releasing his knee, I cross my inside (left) leg over his left knee. Once my foot has crossed the knee, I release my right hand's pressure and step my left foot to the mat. Having crossed Marcel's body, I finish on his left side and I am ready for his second hip escape.

DAY FOUR:
KNEE-ON-BELLY POP-UP

FREQUENCY: 2-3 sets of 20-30 to each side

As you get to day four of side control drills, it is important to look into another important transition, the knee-on-belly. So far, we have focused on transitions around the head and over the legs, and now it is time to master transitioning to the knee-on-belly position. This first drill is the most basic drill for knee-on-belly. It is also one of the most important. I drilled this a lot with my old instructor Careca, and I did well with this position from white to purple belt. As you do your repetitions, think of the movement in the same way as a surfer jumping up to his feet. You really want to pop up to the knee-on-belly position and keep the pressure on! Practice this movement often until your transition is seamless.

FREQUENCY: 2-3 sets of 20-30

Day four's side control to knee-on-belly transition training continues with my favorite prop, the Swiss ball. Although nothing can quite replicate the feeling of a live partner, the Swiss ball does offer some benefits. First of all, you have no need for a partner and you can train this anywhere you can bring the ball. Secondly, you will use a lot of stabilizer muscles in your chest, arms, and legs as you jump to and stabilize the position. While the previous drill works on smoothing out your transitions, this one provides similar benefits along with gains in strength and balance. Remember, as you try to become a champion, you not only want to have smooth movements, but the strength to progress the match as you would like.

Transitioning to Knee-on-Belly

For the knee-on-belly pop-up drill, I start on Marcel's right side with my right hand gripping his left hip. I arch my back as I prepare for my push-off. In one motion, I push up off of Marcel's left hip while I jump my hips upward and slide my knee across Marcel's abdomen, making sure my toes are off the mat. Once I have achieved the knee-on-belly, I return to side control for my second repetition. Practice both sides equally.

KNEE-ON-BELLY BALL MOVEMENT

Marcel sets up the drill by facing the Swiss ball with both hands on it. To initiate the movement, he sprawls onto the ball, spreading his legs wide. From here, Marcel pops up to the left knee on belly position, making sure that he never removes his hands from the ball. Marcel then sprawls back and immediately jumps to the right side knee on belly. Again Marcel sprawls back and is ready to continue the drill to the left side. He will continue alternating left to right until he has finished his repetitions.

DAY FOUR:
KNEE-ON-BELLY RETREAT

FREQUENCY: 2x 3-5 minutes each side

Now that you are getting familiar with transitioning to the knee-on-belly from side control, it is also time to make your body familiar with collapsing back to side control when your opponent escapes. Although you usually want to follow or ride your opponent while in the knee-on-belly, it is just as important that you have a plan B when he escapes too far. This drill emphasizes the importance of keeping small gains and retreating to a favorable position instead of insisting on something that may lead to your opponent's escape. In this situation, if you try to follow your opponent, you may walk right into a single-leg reversal. Learn to collapse your weight and go with your opponent's energy—right into a strong side control position. Ask your partner to provide a strong hip escape as you practice!

DAY FIVE:

FREQUENCY: I set of 20-30 to each side

For the final day of our week on transitions from side control, it is important that you work your movement in and out of the mount position. This is a drill made famous by Oswaldo Alves that I still do to this day. It is a simple hip warm-up, but there is butter knife movement hidden in this basic drill. The butter knife refers to your ability to smear your hips onto your opponent in order to transition to new positions without making space, just like a knife smearing jam on bread. Key to this movement is the exaggeration of your base switch as you come off the mount, your chest-to-chest pressure to keep from falling off, and the use of your hips to drive your body over your opponent. Try to warm up with this move anytime you train your top transitions.

Transitioning to Knee-on-Belly Cont.

Just like the knee-on-belly pop-up, I start on Marcel's right side with my right hand gripping his left hip. In one motion, I push up off Marcel's left hip while I jump my hips upward and slide my knee across Marcel's abdomen, making sure my toes are off the mat. Marcel defends by pushing my knee off him as he hip escapes to his left, forcing my right foot to the mat in the process. Instead of chasing Marcel with the knee-on-belly, I collapse my right hip to Marcel's lower torso in a sprawl motion. From here, I reacquire the side control position and am ready for my second repetition.

Transitioning to Mount

FAST MOUNT

I set up the drill in the side control position on Marcel's right side; I have a tight cross-face with a grip under the left arm, and my base is switched with my right leg toward Marcel's head. To start the drill, I swing my leg over Marcel to mount, making sure to feel my hips drive through—I keep the chest-to-chest pressure constant. Once my right knee hits the mat, I switch my base so that my left leg swings toward Marcel's head. From here, I drive my hips back over Marcel, remount, and end with my leg scorpioned back in the original starting position.

DAY FIVE:
MOUNT FLOW

FREQUENCY: 2-3 sets of 3-5 minutes

This is the most dynamic drill that I know from the mount, and I really have to thank Fernando "Terere" for teaching this one to me. I love it because it has everything: a mount transition as your opponent tries to bridge into you, an exposed arm to attack as you mount, another possible attack as you step over, and a transition back to side control. Once you master this movement, your top game transitions are truly formidable. The key to this drill is in two movements: switching your hips so that you can step over one leg, and collapsing your weight onto your hip so that you can step over with the second leg. If you are having trouble with this movement, I suggest practicing the crumbling hip drill until you are comfortable. Remember, without the crumbling hip, your leg will be too heavy to lift and the angle will be wrong.

Transitioning to Mount Continued

I begin in the side control position on Marcel's left side. I have my hips switched so that my right leg is close to Marcel's hip. Marcel creates the action by bridging into me as he underhooks my left arm with his right. Instead of falling back, I take advantage of the opening under his right arm and step over him into a mount position while holding his arm, leaving Marcel open to a possible arm attack. At this point, my right knee and left foot are on the floor. While keeping Marcel's arm trapped, I collapse my hips to the left to take the weight off my right leg. Now, I can easily step my right leg over Marcel's head, leaving Marcel open to a second possible arm attack. From here, I slide on my left hip to side control (facing his legs) and I await Marcel's next bridge move. I will continue the transition from side to side for the duration of the drill.

DAY ONE:

KNEE-ON-BALL

FREQUENCY: 3-5 minute warm-up

Where week one of our top transitions was focused on movements originating from side control, week two continues with some excellent drills for moving in and out of the knee-on-belly position. To start off, you should focus once more on developing your knee-on-belly balance. Although this Swiss ball drill is not focused solely on the knee-on-belly position, it provides such great knee balance that it is always a great starting point for knee on belly transition training. Your goal here is to develop an easy movement onto both knees as you suck your legs underneath your body to "knee mount" the ball. From there, take the time to sit back into the knee-on-belly position and then return to the starting spot. Practice this movement as slowly as possible. If you can do this continuously at a slow pace, that is even better. You should feel your lower leg and core muscles burning after a prolonged warm-up.

FREQUENCY: 2x 3-5 minutes

Circle the ball is an excellent drill that I learned while training with Marcel Louzado. This movement mimics a stepping over and following motion that is very important to knee-on-belly maintenance. While you are practicing, make sure that you support your weight on the ball and then commit to a large jump with your knee-on-belly. As with the previous drill, this movement also has crossover benefits for guard passing, even though you will be spending most of your time with your knee on the ball. Practice this movement at a slower pace; there is no need for explosive training because the focus should be on balance and mobility as you move yourself "around the world." One last thing, always practice all knee-on-belly drills to both sides, so after you finish a revolution, switch legs!

Developing Knee-on-Belly Balance

Marcel is starting the drill seated on the Swiss ball. First, he brings his left leg toward his body as he rotates slightly toward his left hip. This allows him to pull his left leg underneath his right as he rolls to the "knee mount" position. After stabilizing, Marcel drops his right foot toward the mat and uses his hips and ball to rotate his left leg through to the front. Once in the starting position, Marcel will continue the drill to the other side.

CIRCLE THE BALL

Marcel starts with his left foot on the Swiss ball. He extends his leg to move the ball forward and then he moves his foot to the right while bending at the knee to get to the knee-on-belly position. This early phase is great for one-legged balance. Next, Marcel puts both hands on the ball and jumps his right leg out from behind him (due to the ball movement) to a forward position. This brings Marcel to the other side. From here, Marcel turns to face the opposite direction and jumps his right leg back to the start. After catching his balance, Marcel stands upright and extends his left leg in the starting position. From here, he can continue the drill until it is time for him to switch legs.

DAY TWO:
SIDE-TO-SIDE KNEE-ON-BELLY
FREQUENCY: 2-3 sets of 20

Day two of our knee-on-belly transition training focuses on mastering your transitions against a complacent partner. The first drill is the side-to-side knee-on-belly drill, which is an over-the-body transition. The goal here is to develop a rapid-fire knee-on-belly switch. Although often scoffed at as too flashy, this movement has a great sparring and competition application when your opponent is trying to move his hips away while keeping his elbows tight to defend against chokes and arm attacks. Beyond this, the side-to-side knee-on-belly drill offers a chance to use a great knee-pivoting movement to release one foot from the knee-on-belly as another takes its place. It is this same movement that will be crucial for taking the mount and hiding the feet while in side control or the mount to prevent your opponent from putting you into the half guard. So, keep in mind and remember, sometimes the most flashy movements have very important benefits for your jiu-jitsu. The important thing is to keep learning new body movements—this is the real fundamental of Brazilian Jiu-Jitsu.

FREQUENCY: 2 sets of 20

While the last drill focused on an over-the-body knee-on-belly movement, the following focuses on an around-the-head path. This movement needs to be learned here because it is crucial for advancement to hip-escape defense as well as the spinning armbar. Your focus here should be on leaning your weight into your opponent's chest. As for mobility, turning your near-side elbow out so that your arm does not impede your progress around the head and coordinating your footwork so that you can easily make the transition from side to side should help you move more easily. There is a great lesson here: the opening of your elbows not only affects attack and defense but also your mobility from side to side. Start your practice at a slow pace and build to a medium speed. With regard to faster speeds, remember, you should be able to stop at any point and be in base. If you cannot, you need to slow down your repetitions until you can keep the pressure on your opponent throughout the cycle.

Knee-on-Belly & Transitions

I set up the drill from the left knee-on-belly position; I will keep both my hands on Marcel throughout the drill to keep my base. I start the drill by bringing my right knee to Marcel's left hip. From here, I will switch position by pivoting on my knees and circling both my feet so that they point to Marcel's right side instead of his left. This movement needs to happen above the hipline to ensure that Marcel cannot push my feet into his half guard. I finish in the right knee-on-belly position, and I am ready to continue the drill to the other side.

KNEE-ON-BELLY PIN TRANSITION

I set up the drill from the left knee-on-belly position, with both my hands pressing into Marcel's arms. To start the drill, I switch my grips so that my left hand holds Marcel's left hand with my fingers pointed toward his feet and my right hand also presses into his right with my fingers in the same direction. I step my right leg closer to Marcel's head, take my left foot off his belly, and walk around his head. Because my elbows can open as I turn, I can freely move to Marcel's right side. I end in the right side knee-on-belly, and I am already in position to transition back to the other side knee-on-belly. While practicing, make sure to keep your weight driving into your opponent. This is not only imperative to switching with the knee-on-belly, but also in guard passing.

DAY THREE:
KNEE-ON-BELLY STEP-AROUND

FREQUENCY: 3x 3-5 minutes

For day three of our knee-on-belly transition training, it is important that you incorporate realistic defensive movement from your partner so that you can build on your skills from yesterday. In the knee-on-belly transition drill, you will combine the previous drill with a resisting partner who will hip-escape while pushing off your knees. Instead of collapsing back to side control as you did in week one, you should now focus on circling his head toward his exposed back. In the same fashion as the side control, whenever your opponent turns to face you, you should always have an option to circle toward his back. Practice this drill at medium intensity, paying close attention once again to footwork and using your hands to pressure your partner.

DAY FOUR:

FREQUENCY: 3x 5 minutes

So far, this week of knee-on-belly transition training has focused on knee-on-belly balance, or riding the knee-on-belly, and movement from one side to the other. For your fourth day of training, you will focus on transitioning into and out of the cowboy mount position. This is where your day-one Swiss ball training will come in very handy as you transition from one knee to two knees and then to the cowboy mount position. I like to drill this technique in order to include dynamic body movement into my training regimen. Also, I use this mount to set up triangle chokes and armbars as I move into it, and Americana locks as I flow out. Be mindful while practicing this drill. The transition from the mount to the knee-on-belly is just as important as the transition to the mount itself. Keep pressure on your opponent throughout the drill!

Knee-on-Belly vs. Escape

I set up the drill from the left knee-on-belly position, with both my hands pressing into Marcel's shoulder and right hip. To start the drill, Marcel pushes off my knees as he escapes his hips away from me. I react by stepping over Marcel's head with my right leg and then whipping my left leg around afterward. Marcel returns to the flat back position, and I slide my right knee into the knee-on-belly position. Next, Marcel will escape again and I will transition back to his left side to finish the repetition.

Knee-on-Belly to Mount
KNEE-ON-BELLY TO COWBOY MOUNT

I set up the drill from the left knee-on-belly position, with both my hands pressing into Marcel's shoulder and right hip. To start the drill, I put my right knee on Marcel's chest above his arm. Next, I turn toward his legs and whip my left leg around until I land in a cowboy mount position. Instead of stopping, I continue by sliding my right leg off the mount and posting my left foot away from his hips. I place my hands on Marcel's torso for support and slide my right knee onto his body to finish the transition. Now I am ready to spin back to the other side to finish the repetition. While drilling, I must keep pressure on Marcel throughout to ensure he stays on the bottom position.

DAY FIVE:
KNEE-ON-BELLY TO ARMBAR

FREQUENCY: 3 sets of 20 each side

For your final day of knee-on-belly training, it is important to connect submissions to the previous techniques of movement and balance. Although you can make any knee-on-belly submission a drill, I prefer to use the armbar for my individual game. The basic knee-on-belly to armbar should be your first option because it is your most direct armbar from the position. Therefore, you should drill this movement often on day five. The key to this position is sliding your knee under your partner's armpit to secure his arm for the submission. Get used to executing this movement with a higher intensity. It is vital that you forcefully go after his arm so that in a real fight your opponent will feel overwhelmed by the attack. However, start slowly and build your intensity until your movement is smooth and clean so you do not forgo control.

FREQUENCY: 2-3x 5 minutes

The spinning armbar drill from knee-on-belly is all about teaching your body to identify holes and then attack them. In this case, your partner will put his hand on your knee as if to push it away. This opens up space between his body and elbow, and you will take advantage of this by securing his elbow and spinning into a tight armbar position. The spin itself should be comfortable by now, especially after your knee-on-belly vs. hip-escape training. The key to this position is pulling his elbow tight to your body and pinching your knee tight to his armpit as you spin through to secure a nooselike armbar. Practice this at a medium to medium-high speed. This is an awesome position because even if you bungle the transition, you always have the kimura, back, and side control to continue your attacks.

Knee-on-Belly Attacks

I start in the knee-on-belly position with my left knee on Marcel's abdomen. I grab the end of Marcel's sleeve with my right arm and pull up on his sleeve as I push down on his chest with my left hand. This opens Marcel's arm for the attack while helping me to maintain my balance. Immediately, I slide my left shin into Marcel's left armpit, lean slightly to my left, and swing my right leg over for the armbar. I do not need to crank the submission. Instead, I swing my leg back out and stand back up to the knee-on-belly position. I will repeat the same side until it is time to switch.

KNEE-ON-BELLY TO SPINNING ARMBAR

I'm starting the drill from the knee-on-belly position with Marcel pushing my left knee with his right hand. This opens up his left elbow, and I quickly swim my left hand into the hole, cupping his right triceps with my left hand. With the arm secured, I control Marcel's posture by lifting his arm to my chest and pulling him to his left side. As he gets lifted, I am already stepping over his head with my right leg and spinning to face his feet and then body. My right knee slides in under Marcel's right armpit, and I secure the armbar while pinching my knees together. I do not finish the position. Instead, I swing my left leg off Marcel's head and finish with the knee-on-belly position on Marcel's right side. I will continue the drill by repeating the attack back to the starting position.

DAYS I&II:
MOUNT CONTROL

FREQUENCY: 2-3x 5 minutes

For the first two days of your mount transition training, you should focus on one very fundamental movement in Brazilian Jiu-Jitsu. This is the mount control drill. The purpose of this drill is to transition from the mount to a seated mount when your opponent hip-escapes. The reason why this is so important? If you do not make the transition, your opponent can easily trap your lower leg in the half guard. Therefore, it is crucial that you learn to hide your feet from his escape while retaining control over his body. Practice this movement from side to side, using pressure (both arms forward) to slow down your partner's turn. This way, you can predict his movement and feel the proper timing to switch to the seated mount.

DAYS III&IV:

FREQUENCY: 3 sets of 20 or 2x 5 minutes

After two days of training the mount to seated mount position, it is time to work some submissions from the mount for the next two days. I like to focus more of my mount submission drills on the armbar because there is a lot of movement and position change with this attack. While practicing, you should focus on securing your opponent's elbow to your chest, pressing down on his chest for base, and shifting your weight so that you can easily swing your leg over his head. Also, try to get a good rhythm as you rock your legs back to the mounted position—this will increase your speed and help with your overall timing. Finally, you should work this at a controlled pace. Be sure that you do not explode into the finish every time; you will want to save your partner's arm so that he can last through many repetitions.

Mount Transitions

I begin the drill in the mount position with both hands forward on top of Marcel. I keep my weight pressing slightly into Marcel so that he has to use some effort to get to his side. Marcel turns to his left side. As I feel him moving, I release my right leg, placing my foot on the mat in front of his hips. As I do this, I quickly slide my left knee up to Marcel's head to block his back from returning to the mat. I stay on my left toes to keep pressure and retain my agility. Once I have established the position, I release the pressure and Marcel returns to the mounted position. Now, we can repeat the drill to the other side.

Mount Attacks

MOUNTED ARMBAR

WEEK THREE:
Mount Drills

I begin in the mounted position. Marcel offers his right arm and I secure it by grabbing toward his right elbow/triceps with my right hand. With both hands, I pull his elbow to my body. In a movement similar to the previous drill, I turn to a perpendicular angle and press down on Marcel's left shoulder for base. Instantly, I swing my left leg over Marcel's head and fall back into the armbar. Although I straighten his arm, I release the submission before I bridge my hips into it—this saves Marcel from a sore arm later in the workout. With the arm released, I swing my legs up off Marcel toward his right side. I put my left foot on the mat next to his hip and then step my right leg over to reassume the mount. From here, I can either continue with the same arm or attack the other side. Either way, I need to practice attacking both arms equally.

DAYS III & IV:
ARMBAR SWITCH

FREQUENCY: 2-3x 5 minutes

Sometimes your opponent will manage to escape his elbow from an armbar and you need to have a plan B that is better than falling to your back and accepting the loss of the top position. This is why you should practice the mount armbar switch drill. As your opponent defends his arm and then pulls the elbow free, he often does so at the cost of exposing his outside arm. Attacking this elbow and using your hand to push your body to the other side of the mount are essential to your success with this drill. You can practice this at an easy pace, but make sure that you add enough resistance to the first armbar attack so that your partner will really try to escape his inside elbow while exposing his outside arm.

DAY FIVE:

FREQUENCY: 2x 3-5 minutes

Although mainly a half guard drill, you should use the half mount hip switch to wrap up your week of mount transition training. With regard to the half mount, it is a fact of life that you need to be ready when your opponent traps your foot and tries to recover the half-guard. The goal of this drill is to feel your opponent turning toward you and then react by switching to the other side. As with all my movements and drills, I always go to the other side that my opponent is facing—in other words, I always go to his back. I go to where his defense is not set up. Practice this drill with a focus on continual transitions without stopping. Make this a cardio workout at medium to medium-high intensity. Once mastered, your back-taking and passing skills off the half mount should improve drastically.

Mount Attacks Continued

I begin in the armbar position on Marcel's left side. To initiate the drill, I swim my right hand underneath Marcel's left arm to attack it and free my left hand to grab his right elbow. Marcel slightly escapes his elbow, so I release his arm and post my right hand on the mat for base. While pulling Marcel's right elbow toward my body, I push off the mat, propelling my body into an S-mount position. I swim my left hand under Marcel's left arm and fall back into the armbar position on Marcel's right side. Marcel pulls his elbow again, so I release his arm, cup behind his elbow with my right hand and base with my left hand on the mat. From here, I will continue the drill from side to side. While practicing, I must always base with my forward hand, so that I can push myself to the other side. If I base with the rear hand, I will face his legs and I will not be able to swing over to the mount.

Half Mount Movement
HALF MOUNT HIP SWITCH

WEEK THREE: Mount Drills

I begin in the half guard as if Marcel has just transitioned there from my mount. I bait Marcel to turn into me by giving him space between our bodies. As Marcel turns into me, I put both my hands on the mat for base and then kick my right leg to the other side of the half guard. Once again, this forces Marcel to react by turning into me. As he does so, I step over to the half mount. Marcel continues the drill by facing me once more, and I will continue by switching from side to side to expose Marcel's back.

DAY ONE:
TURTLE PRESSURE

FREQUENCY: 2-3x 5 minutes

To start off day one of the back transition week, you should first focus on your mobility to get to the back from a turtle top or sprawled position. In this drill, you will work an around-the-world-type movement where you walk all the way around your partner, making sure to keep the pressure on throughout the move. Focus on keeping your hips pressed into him and be wary of where your legs are in relation to his arms. At first, just practice the below movement, and once you are familiar with the footwork, have your partner try to grab your legs so that you can step up the realism of your training as you sprawl your legs away from him.

FREQUENCY: 2-3x 3-5 minutes

This is one of my favorite drills for top-game mobility, and I have actually used it a couple of times in competition; the last time was at the 2008 Mundials. As a drill, I like it because it focuses on approaches to jiu-jitsu. Just as you should have passes over the legs, around the legs, and under the legs, you also need to have different angles of approach around the turtle position. This time, instead of going around the body, you will be going over it. When it comes to sparring, this movement is not all flash. It really works great to confuse your opponent. If he tries to face you, you cross right over his back to the back position. This can be very frustrating for him, as he always feels as if he is too late in his offense. I trained this movement a lot with Ricardo Vieira, and I know from experience how overwhelming it can feel.

Turtle Movement

I begin the turtle pressure drill on top of Marcel's turtle position. My left hip is leaning into Marcel's right flank and I have cupped his left hip with my right arm. I transition from my left hip to both hips pressing into Marcel as I step my right leg toward his head. As I do this, I grab his hips with both my arms. From here, I shuffle my legs so that my right leg is now on the other side of his head. I keep pressing my hips into Marcel throughout the movement. To finish, I turn onto my right hip, consolidate the left side of Marcel's turtle, and grab his right hip with my right arm. I can now continue the drill to the other side.

HUMAN BALL

I begin the drill by facing Marcel's turtle position. Instead of running around his body, as I did in the previous position, I will go over his body to the back. I place both hands on Marcel's shoulders, dropping my weight into my arms so that he feels some pressure. I step my right foot outside of Marcel's left arm to make grabbing the single-leg more difficult, and then I slide my left leg over Marcel's back as if I were doing a baseball slide. As my hips pull through to the other side, I turn to face Marcel and put downward pressure on his hips and rear to control his back. Once finished, I stand back up and place both my hands on Marcel's hips; now I will repeat again to the front. For more advanced training, I will ask Marcel to try to face me or grab the single-leg as I continually cross over to his back.

DAYS II&III:
LEO VIEIRA BACK ATTACK

FREQUENCY: 2 sets of 10-15

This is a back-taking move made famous by Leo Vieira that I have reworked into a very fun drill. The purpose is to work your back flexibility and upper-body strength for the forward turtle flip. Besides making a great drill, it will keep your opponent from rolling into your lap so you can develop the option to pull yourself back to his turtle to insert your hooks. For the student on the bottom, this is great for developing your base while turtled. It will take a lot of strength and stability to resist the roll, and this training is usually fun and productive toward controlling the back without the hooks. Practice this at an easy pace—it does not need to be done explosively.

FREQUENCY: 2x 5 minutes

The second drill for days two and three focuses on keeping the back position when your opponent tries to escape. This is an excellent movement to foster sensitivity, grip strength, and back control. The most important factor will be your ability to glue your chest to your opponent's upper back. With your upper torsos bonded together, it will be easy for you to escape your hips, go to the north-south position behind him, and then pull him back to the control position. As you practice, guide his body where you want using your grips and chest-to-back pressure. You can practice this at an easy pace, or if you are more advanced, you can have your partner really try to escape as you go through the sequence below.

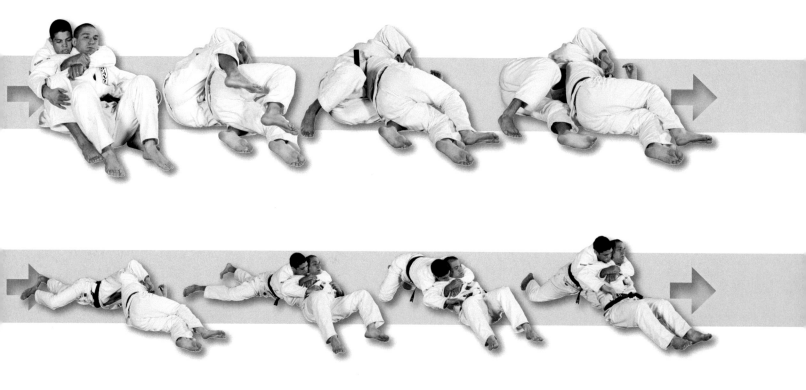

Controlling Without Hooks

I begin on the back side of Marcel's turtle position. I have both my hands locked underneath both of Marcel's armpits. Ready for action, I drive my weight forward until the top of my head (not my forehead) hits the mat to the left of Marcel's head. Immediately, I stand my legs upward as if I were executing a headstand. Once upright, I allow my legs to fall to Marcel's front right—that is, to the side opposite to the one my head is on. I land in a wrestler's bridge. To return, I jump my feet off the mat and I pull my body back to the starting position. Once in the starting position, I drive my head to the right side of Marcel's head as I start my next repetition. This time, my legs will go to the left side to prevent any type of neck injury. Any time I make a roll, I ensure that my neck is safe by keeping it out of trouble and throwing my legs over the other side.

THE BACKPACK

I set up the drill on Marcel's back without the hooks. I have an over-and-under grip with my right arm underneath his armpit. Marcel triggers the drill by falling to his left side to escape. Instead of trying to fight Marcel's weight and pull him on top of me, I opt to hip-escape to realign my body with his. I keep control of Marcel with my grips and chest as I hip-escape until we are close to being on the same line. At this point, I scoop my left leg underneath my right to come up to my knees. This puts Marcel and me on the same line. To retake his back, I step up to my foot, lifting Marcel's back off the mat. Then, I simply sit back into the back position as I pull Marcel on top of me. From here, Marcel will execute another escape, and we will continue the drill for the remainder of the time.

DAY FOUR

BACK CONTROL MOVEMENT

FREQUENCY: 3-4x 3-5 minutes

For your fourth day of back transition training, you will focus on keeping the back position when someone escapes past your hooks. This is a great continuation of the last back control drill, but there is a big difference. Instead of escaping to a stomach-down position, you will now push your opponent over as he escapes; this will open up room to reinsert your leg and retake the hook. The key is in how you slide your knee up the back. This will turn into a hook once you pull him back on top of you! Practice this at a slow to medium pace and ask your partner to progressively increase resistance for more realistic drilling.

DAY FIVE:

FREQUENCY: 3-4x 5 minutes

As with most transitions, I love to make sure I not only drill movement but also submissions in movement. As with the mounted position, I also like to make sure that my back submission drills include a lot of body movement so that I know I am maximizing my skills to flow from one area to another. This is why, once again, you will be working with the armbar from the back. This can be a very sneaky position, and it often catches an opponent by surprise when he is only thinking of defending his neck from the choke. Practice this at a medium speed and focus on controlling your partner's entire body with your figure-four grip.

Maintaining the Back

I start the back movement drill on Marcel's back with both hooks in. Once again, I have an over-and-under grip with my right hand under his armpit for body control. Marcel initiates the drill by knocking my left hook off his body while he falls to his left side. As Marcel fights to put his back on the mat, I maintain my upper-body control over him. Then, I push off the mat with my left foot to turn Marcel onto his left side. I slide my left knee high up his back and then sit to my rear (I do not fall back) and fall to my right side so that my hook is on the bottom. I put my left hook in and Marcel repeats the movement to this side. We will continue this drill from side to side for the duration of the time.

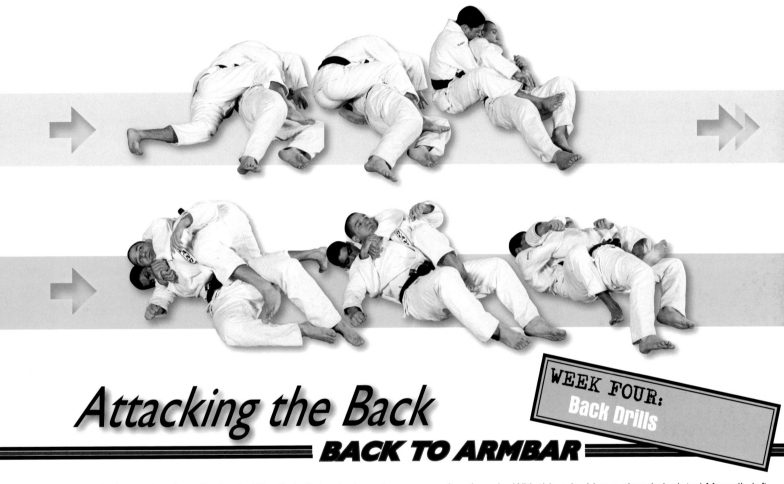

Attacking the Back
BACK TO ARMBAR

I begin the armbar from the back drill with both hooks in and an over-and-under grip. With this grip, I have already isolated Marcel's left arm. I reach over with my right hand and grab his wrist. Then, I feed my left hand under his elbow to grab my own wrist, forming a figure-four lock. Once here, I push the grip into Marcel and swing my body to a perpendicular angle. This allows my left leg to form a belt-line grip on Marcel while my right leg swings over the top and down onto his head. I push Marcel's body down with my leg pressure against his upper head, and we land in the armbar position. Immediately, I release the submission by lifting my right leg up, and Marcel drives into me. I accept his position by taking his back again. Then, I switch grips and start drilling the move to the other side.

MONTH EIGHT:
In Review

This month, you learned that transitioning happens anytime you move from one position to another. This can happen as a result of your opponent's action or escape attempt, your own attempt to move to a more dominant position, as well as any submission where positional change may occur (like an armbar).

As a general rule, whenever your opponent turns into you from side control, his back is exposed! Learn to slow your opponent down with your body weight and then use your footwork to traverse to his back! The key this month is not only drilling the techniques, but also to begin seeing the openings for transitions. This will help you astronomically in tournament because you will see your opponent's options before he does! Once you get a good foundation of transitions, they will become a natural part of your jiu-jitsu game. You won't have to think, "Okay, my opponent is showing me his back to escape the side mount, now I will transition to the back." Instead, you'll just be on his back in a split second! I really believe drilling makes basic movements become second nature to you.

Remember, your opponent's arms are very important for transitioning. While sparring, you can use your tight positioning to force your opponent to make a mistake. When he exposes his arms to escape or overcompensates... attack! Do not be afraid to use a little pressure in your drills, this will add a layer of realism to your partner's defensive actions.

WEEKEND WORK:

For each week of training, side control, knee-on-belly, the mount, and back, spend the weekend working on maintaing the top position and transitioning to the other dominant positions against a fully resisting partner. Use the same 2-3 rounds of 15 minutes, staying on top throughout the session. While training, focus on getting back to your original position (if you start in knee on belly and end up on side control, transition back to knee on belly) and only stop if your opponent escapes or if you get the submission.

MONTH NINE: The Wet Noodle - Guard Part I

This month and next, I have set up a drill routine for the guard. This month, in particular, you will work on some basic guard movements, your closed guard, the butterfly guard, and maintaining the guard. Just like last month, the drills will focus on transitions more than technical instructions for specific moves.

The key to transitioning on the bottom is, once again, hip movement. The more flexibility the better, especially in your hips and lower back. When it comes to the guard, flexibility really boosts your ability to frustrate and find comfort in the position. Once in the guard, it is vital that you drill guard defense, or retention, submissions, and reversals. If you feel like you have developed a very strong defensive guard, then it is time to add some submissions and sweeps. Likewise, if you only have a good closed guard arsenal of submissions, it is also time for you to open up that guard and defend the pass.

When working with the guard it is important to drill sweeps, submissions, and retention. Once you are ready, link them all together. Jiu-jitsu is not made up of independent moves. We are lucky in that our techniques blend together, and they should. Make your bottom game just as continuous and free flowing as your top has become.

Personally, I anchor my bottom game off the threat of submission. Fernando "Terere" made the biggest impact on my guard game. Because of his training methods, I use submissions to make retention easier and hit the sweep. Whenever I am successful with the retention or my opponent defends a sweep, I immediately like to attack a submission. Others may choose to do the same with sweeps. Either way, develop your game personally, but use all three categories to achieve what you aim for.

In week one, you will begin to develop your guard by practicing basic guard movements. It is important to develop your hip mobility so that you can easily change sides and angles of attack. This ties back to month three, when you learned how to move your hips. Heavy hips equate to immobility. Keep them light and flexible. You do not want to be stuck in one place because your hips don't move correctly.

When your back is flat on the mat, it is important to get used to lifting your lower back up. You will get a bigger speed boost by pivoting on your upper back than if you play lazily with your whole back on the floor. You must also learn to follow your opponent by using your feet as a guide and your hooks to "hitch a ride." Use smart drills that boost your Brazilian Jiu-Jitsu guard IQ as well as your sensitivity.

Week two introduces drills specifically for the closed guard. Last week was a collection of basic movements, and this week focuses on simple submissions. Drill these submissions until you cannot move. I've heard of students drilling a move 1,000 times, and I think this is the right idea. The more you practice these movements, the easier it will be for your body to perform them under pressure. When you practice closed guard submissions, ask your partner to offer progressive resistance. A thousand armbars with some resistance are worth far more than the same number against a limp fish.

This week, the reason we focus on simple submissions is because they chain together so easily. As you add new moves and drills, ask yourself how easily they fit into your other drill routines. If you can alter a move to make it fit—use it. If not, then it will be hard to adapt to your specific game.

When I am fighting in a tournament, my goal for every match is to end in a submission. Training simple submissions repeatedly makes for better success in competition. From drilling a lot, my confidence is high and I think to myself, "I will finish this guy." Remember, the goal of the closed guard is not only to control your opponent's posture, but also to submit him. Make your closed guard a submission playground.

In week three, you will be drilling the butterfly guard. In general, the goal of the butterfly guard is usually to reverse/sweep. This should be an aggressive guard because you have less contact than you do with the closed guard. You must continue moving and using hip escapes to stay ahead of your opponent.

To avoid being passed, you should focus on the range. When your opponent closes the range to flatten you, use the drills from this chapter to get back to an upright position. If your opponent runs away, grab the single-leg.

As you will learn this week, it is important to develop your hook strength, sit-up skills, forward drive, and arm drags to master the attacking and defensive aspects of this guard.

It does not matter how many attacks and sweeps you have if you cannot control from the guard. In week four, you begin to prepare yourself to stop the pass so that you can do what you want to do. All the submissions and sweeps in the world won't help you if you can't keep your opponent in your guard long enough to attack him.

Again, focus on range. Have options for when you are early, at the midpoint, and late in your pass defense. Obviously, the earlier you defend, the better, and the less amount of energy you will have to expend.

While drilling this week, focus on mastering early defense sensitivity and awareness and late defense work ethic and tenacity. Your goal is never to tire during late defense. This will take some time to develop, but keep practicing until you get it right!

Once you start getting it, link sweeps and submissions to your guard retention and your guard will be a misery for anyone.

WEEK ONE: Basic Guard Movements

DAY ONE:

HIP-UPS

FREQUENCY: 3-5 sets of 20

For your first day of basic guard movement, start with an exercise that is integral to developing a strong armbar and triangle, the hip-up. The hip-up is basically a bridge without the use of your feet on the mat. Instead, you will rely on your abdominal muscles to get your lower back, rear, and legs high off the mat. As you practice, try to hip-up from side to side to simulate arm and triangle attacks. Make sure you try to explode into every repetition and that your rear never touches the mat.

FREQUENCY: 3-5 sets of 20

This is a basic drill that is practiced in almost every school in the world. However, it being commonplace does not mean that it should be ignored in your training. The triangle drill does several things that are great for benefiting your triangle movement. You get to go from side to side, mimicking the angle change needed to attack the triangle. Your hips shoot upward, simulating the finishing phase of the attack. Finally, there is also the classic triangle lock and squeeze, which has become emblematic of Brazilian Jiu-Jitsu. Practice this as if you are really trying to finish someone and don't just "go through the paces" while practicing this. Every repetition needs to count.

Lifting the Hips

My back is flat on the mat, my arms are at a forty-five-degree angle away from my body, and I am ready to do my first hip-up. As I roll my knees toward my chest, I use my back, hips, and abdominals to explosively lift my legs off the mat and toward my left side. From here, I move my hips from side to side while keeping my rear off the mat. My abdominals should be tight throughout the drill, and I need to always use explosive motions to launch my hips into the air.

SOLO TRIANGLES

Once again, I start from a flat back position with my hands out at a forty-five-degree angle. I rock my legs toward my chest and explode them upward as if I were executing a hip-up. This time, as I reach the apex of my hip-up, I triangle my legs with my right ankle locking under my left knee. I close the triangle, and my feet descend toward the mat. Before my feet touch the floor, I again launch them upward to execute my second repetition to my right side. I will continue this from side to side until the set is over.

DAY TWO:
FOLLOW THE LEADER

FREQUENCY: 2x 3-5 minutes

The hip-up is an incredibly useful movement, and I am dedicated to applying useful movements to as many drills and as many areas of jiu-jitsu as possible. This was a basic drill from one of my first days in Brazilian Jiu-Jitsu, and I still do it whenever I revisit the guard or need to work on my guard retention. In this situation, you will practice the same movement as before to keep your partner in front of your legs. If your partner is always in front of you, at least he is not next to you in side control or on top of you in the mount. Use the same movement from yesterday to move your hips into alignment with your partner whenever he circles around you. For the top player, move at an easy pace until the bottom player is comfortable with following. As you pick up the pace, the workout becomes increasingly tougher for the student on the bottom!

Following Your Partner

I start with Marcel facing my guard. I am on my back with my knees tucked toward my chest. As Marcel circles to the right, I track his movement by putting my hands on the mat and using my arms and abdominals to lift my hips off the mat and swing them to the right. After I face Marcel, he continues his movement and I continue to follow by swinging my hips back to the square position. We will continue in this chasing drill until the time has elapsed. To make the drill more difficult, Marcel can rapidly change directions (he moves either clockwise or counterclockwise), or he can pick up the pace of his circling.

DAY TWO:

HOOK & FOLLOW

FREQUENCY: 2-3x 3-5 minutes

Your ability to use your hooks effectively will not only allow you to sweep your opponent with ease, but also hitch a ride when your opponent is trying to pass the guard. Use this guard sensitivity drill to learn how to use your hooks to ride your opponent wherever he goes. Basically, you will be hooking the inside of his leg and then using your partner's movement to move you as well. Focus on keeping your hips off the mat while you do this. If you anchor your rear to the mat, you will move more like a deadweight than a feather. In this case, you want to go with his momentum instead of fighting it. Practice this at an easy to medium speed. If you are more advanced, ask your partner to change directions mid cycle to catch you by surprise.

DAY THREE:

FREQUENCY: 2-3 sets of 20

The wall movement drill is a great way to open up your hips, gain a lot of mobility, and help your spider guard and inverted recoveries. It is absolutely crucial that you learn to speed up your hips while you train. To do this, you should keep your weight on your shoulder, which will be your pivot point, while your top leg pulls your hips to the other side. Now, when you bring this movement to sparring, don't just throw your leg over the top as if that is enough. Throw your leg, and then walk (or, technically, pull) your hips to the other side.

Following Your Partner Continued

I start with Marcel standing in my open guard. I place my right hook behind Marcel's left knee and my left foot on Marcel's hip while raising my hips off the mat for mobility. I always keep two points of contact with my legs on my opponent at all times. With my hook in, Marcel moves counterclockwise, and my hook pulls my body along with him. At this point, Marcel can continue to walk in the same direction or he can stop and go the other way so that I can work changing my hooks and riding to the other side.

Wall Practice

WALL RECOVERY

WEEK ONE:
Basic Guard Movement

I start with my back on the floor and my feet on the wall. My legs should be bent to ninety degrees. Immediately, I bring my right leg under my left as I swing my hips away from the mat. From this side position, I step my left leg far in front of me. Next, I pull my hips through to my feet, go to my back, and then turn to my left side. To turn, I should use my left foot on the wall as a pivot point so that I can turn onto my other side and get my right leg over to the top. From here, I will make my next step and continue the drill.

DAY FOUR:

HIP CIRCLES

FREQUENCY: 2 sets of 20

This is an excellent warm-up drill to loosen those hips and learn to pendulum your legs. This pendulum, or swinging motion, is very important for both guard attacks and reversals. As your leg makes a wide arcing motion, your hips and other leg will automatically follow the weight of your swinging foot. The first time I practiced this movement was under the great instructor, Oswaldo Alves, and I have continued to use this drill ever since. It is a great warm-up and stretch, but most important, it is jiu-jitsu relevant. Practice this at an easy pace, paying special attention to the swing of your top leg; make sure you are opening up your hips more and more with every repetition.

DAY FIVE:

FREQUENCY: 2 sets of 20

For your last day of basic movement training, you should work on your inverted guard movement. This drill is a type of sideways shoulder roll that works great for stretching the upper and lower back, creating the necessary flexibility for all types of inversion. Try to focus on this movement here because we will revisit this movement later this month with the inverted recovery to triangle and next month as we go deeper into inverted drills. As with yesterday's drill, practice at a relaxed pace. You should try to be as free of tension as possible to help loosen up those muscles!

Hip & Back Mobility

I set up the hip circle drill in a seated position. As I lean to my right side, I pull my left leg back in a hurdler's stretch position. Staying on my left hip, I swing my left leg in a low-to-high clockwise arc; I try to paint as large of a circle with my leg as possible. As my top leg reaches the peak of the circle, my right leg follows it in an arc of its own. My left leg finishes on the floor and my right (following) leg swings through to a hurdler's stretch. From here, I lean forward and then continue to the other side. I must make sure that every circle is bigger than the last—this will open up my hips more and more, greatly increasing my flexibility.

Getting Used to Inversion
INVERTED GUARD MOVEMENT

WEEK ONE:
Basic Guard Movement

I set up the inverted guard movement from the seated position. As I fall toward my left side, I tuck my left hand behind my back to open up my shoulder. My left shoulder hits the mat and I tuck my chin toward my chest. At this point, I roll all the way onto both shoulders. To get back to my upright position, I bring my feet toward my right side to help me carry my momentum in that way. I tuck my right hand behind my body so that it is out of the way and I sit up to a seated position. Now, I can either continue in the same direction for the length of the mat or return back to the original starting position.

DAY ONE:

ARMBAR

FREQUENCY: 2-3 sets of 20

Today is going to be a very hard workout if you have never focused on closed guard drills before. The goal of day one of closed guard training is to work on both your closed guard submissions and the conditioning necessary to be successful with them. For the first closed guard attack drill you should work on the basic armbar. Make sure that you utilize the hip circle movement as you pendulum your feet from side to side. Let your hips follow your foot to get into position and practice with speed and snap. Every armbar should feel as if it "snaps" or locks into the submission. Aside from the positive impact on our jiu-jitsu, this is great for a ferocious abdominal workout as well.

FREQUENCY: 2-3 sets of 20

Your second drill on day one is the arm push triangle drill. This is a fast action movement that utilizes surprise and explosiveness to catch your opponent off guard. Similar to the armbar drill, this technique not only helps your jiu-jitsu, but also gives a great conditioning workout. Remember, the difference between a successful triangle and a missed submission is often measured in milliseconds, so drill this technique long after this month is over. Focus on speed while mastering the quick push and pull.

Basic Attacks

For armbar drilling, I start with Marcel inside my closed guard. First, I will attack his right arm. I cross grip his elbow with my right hand and hold his left shoulder with my left hand. I open my legs, bringing my head close to Marcel's left knee. From this perpendicular angle, I can easily swing my left leg over Marcel's head for the armbar. To continue, I pendulum swing my left leg in a counterclockwise arc. As I do this, my head follows the momentum of my left foot and I end on Marcel's right side. I switch my left hand to control behind his left elbow/triceps. I throw my right leg over his head, and finish the armbar. From here, I will swing my right leg in a clockwise arc, my head will follow, and I will continue the drill by armbarring to the other side. I repeat submissions until I have finished my set.

ARM PUSH TRIANGLE

I begin with Marcel inside my closed guard. I have control over both his sleeves. In a blink of an eye, I open my legs and shoot Marcel's left hand to his body while I pull on his right arm. Just as quickly, I close my guard over his left arm. Next, I lock the triangle choke by pulling Marcel's right hand to my right hip as I cinch my right ankle under my left knee. Following the triangle, I bring Marcel back into my closed guard so that I can continue my attack to the other side.

DAY ONE:
KNEE-INSIDE OMOPLATA

FREQUENCY: 2-3 sets of 20

The knee-inside omoplata is a favorite drill of mine because it combines guard defense with one of my strongest submissions. For guard defense, you will get to feel how to make space with your feet on your opponent's hips and control his forward pressure with your shin on his chest. With the submission, you will learn to kick your leg through to the omoplata. As you practice, make sure that you always have one knee inside so that you can handle his weight while the other leg attacks. This can be drilled at an easy to fast intensity—easy for skill acquisition and intense for competition rhythm.

DAY TWO:

FREQUENCY: 3-4 sets of 20

Day two of closed guard training emphasizes sitting up to attack. For the first exercise, you will focus on the hip bump sweep, which is basically a sit-up and bridging action to roll or reverse your opponent toward his rear corner. For the drill, you will not finish the sweep, but you will explosively sit up, keep your rear hand based behind you to maintain attacking posture, and clinch your opponent's elbow. The only thing left is to bridge, and this will be much easier than the often-tough abdominal workout of the sit-up. Beginners should practice by starting with their hands over their heads to generate momentum, whipping them forward while sitting up. All students should pause at the apex of the move to feel stable in the attacking position. For more advanced students, you can have your partner drive forward a little to test your position. If you can resist his drive with your based-out arm, you can definitely hit the sweep or one of the submission combinations that this position is known for. Once finished with the month, you can work this into your exercise or warm-up routine by substituting this for standard sit-ups.

Basic Attacks Continued

Once again, I start with Marcel in my closed guard. I have grips on both his sleeves, and I will not release them for the duration of the exercise. I kick off my action by sliding both my knees between Marcel's arms; my feet are planted on his hips. This creates a frame where Marcel can no longer press his weight into me. Keeping my left leg inside, I kick my right leg to the outside of Marcel's arm. As I do this, I use my left foot on his hip to pivot to a more perpendicular angle with him. My head scoots closer to his left knee. From this angle, I punch Marcel's left hand toward my hip while I swing my leg in front of his face to lock the omoplata. Finished with my first attack, I release the hold and return to the starting position so that I can omoplata Marcel to the other side.

Sit-Up Attacks

HIP BUMP SWEEP

As with all closed guard attacks, I begin with Marcel inside my closed guard. To attack, I rapidly sit-up to my left hand and reach over Marcel's right shoulder with my arm. Both my feet are on the mat for support, and I secure his right elbow with my right hand, gluing his arm and shoulder to my body for control. I finish the action phase by bridging slightly into Marcel as if I were going to roll him toward his rear left side. Once finished, I return to the starting position and prepare to attack the other side.

KIMURA

FREQUENCY: 2-3 sets of 20

The kimura and hip bump sweep are related techniques. Both use the same classic sit-up to threaten the opponent's base and both could be used interchangeably. The difference between them lies in your bottom hand, not the hand that crosses the shoulder. By grabbing your partner's wrist and going over his shoulder to grab a figure four lock, you cannot drive your body as deeply into him as you could in the last drill when you reached over his shoulder and posted your hand on the mat. This is because you are only upright to the elbow level, and this changes your attacks. Though you can still go for the previous sweep from here, you are much better off focusing on the kimura submission or a possible guillotine choke or back-taking move off the defense. Practice this move to see how quickly you can secure the hold!

DAY THREE:

FREQUENCY: 2-3x 1-5 minutes

The guard jump and roll is a great way to build on your guard jumping skills and sweeping skills at the same time. Terere always told me the best time to sweep someone is right after you get to the guard, and that is the same whether you get there from the ground or the feet. I agree, and what better way to introduce yourself to the position than by combining it with a drill you are used to? In this situation, the shoulder roll represents a possible sweep, where the roll sets up a single-leg takedown or, simply enough, a transition back to the feet if the sweep fails for any reason.

Sit-Up Attacks Continued

Once more, I begin with Marcel in my closed guard. I grab his right wrist with my left hand and then sit up to his right side. My right arm reaches over his shoulder and secures my left wrist to lock the figure four-hold. From here, I have the leverage to torque his arm free for a kimura submission. Instead, I continue the drill by returning to my back, grabbing his left wrist and figure-four locking his left arm. I will continue these back-and-forth repetitions until I finish my set.

Intro to the Shoulder Roll
GUARD JUMP & ROLL

WEEK TWO:
Closed Guard

Facing Marcel from the standing position, I start the drill by jumping to the closed guard as drilled in month three. As soon as I land in the position, I fall back and hook his leg with my left arm. My right arm then pushes off the mat and I use this to boost my right leg free. As my leg comes around, I roll over my left shoulder and fall close to Marcel's right side. From here, I do a master's lift to stand up. Now, I am ready to jump guard again and to drill the technique to the other side.

DAY FOUR:
CLOSED GUARD SHOULDER ROLL

FREQUENCY: 2 sets of 20

Your fourth day of closed guard training expands on the standing shoulder roll practice you did on day three. This time, you will commit to the exact same rolling movement, but this time your opponent will remain on his knees and you will use a standard shoulder roll to return to the starting position. This open guard shoulder roll is the basis of many closed, inverted, and cross guard sweeps, so make sure you can easily roll and then return all the way back to guard before you move on to the second move of the day. If you are having the problem of rolling away from your opponent as you return, make sure to roll over your inside shoulder and use your bottom leg as an anchor to your partner's body. This way, the arc of your top leg coming through will bring you to the guard instead of away from your partner.

FREQUENCY: 2-3 sets of 20

You may have noticed that your opponent's arm was rather exposed as you did the previous drill. This drill is going to take advantage of that with my favorite guard submission, the omoplata. For this drill, you are going to use a cross-grip on your opponent's sleeve to control his arm while the swinging of your hips does the rest of the attack for you. The setup is nearly identical to the previous move, but to make sure you drill with a sense of reality, really throw your hips into the roll to your knees and then throw your hips into the return roll to omoplata. This should keep him off balance and illustrate the power behind your core.

Shoulder Roll Series

From the closed guard, I swim my right arm underneath Marcel's left leg. I unlock my guard and pendulum my left leg in a long clockwise arc. As I get perpendicular, I roll over my right shoulder, using my left hand on the mat to help push my hips through. I land on all fours next to Marcel's left side. I return by rolling over my right (inside) shoulder while using my right arm and leg to anchor myself to his body. My left leg returns in a long counterclockwise arc, and I pull myself to the closed guard. Now, I am ready to continue the drill to the other side.

OMOPLATA SHOULDER ROLL

From the closed guard, I swim my right arm underneath Marcel's left leg while my left hand cross grips his sleeve from control. I unlock my guard and pendulum my left leg in a long arc clockwise until I roll over my right shoulder. As I land on all fours next to Marcel's left side, I drive into Marcel's arm with my hips, forcing him to momentarily check his balance. This is my signal. I immediately roll back over my right shoulder and swing my legs down in line with my body instead of turning to go back to the guard. The force of my legs drives Marcel down to the mat and we end in the omoplata position. From here, I will open my legs and go back to the closed guard. Now, I will drill the move to the other side.

DAY FOUR:
TRIANGLE SHOULDER ROLL

FREQUENCY: 2-3 sets of 20

This is the final shoulder roll technique for this week and it is the culmination of both the shoulder roll and the shoulder roll to omoplata drills. This time, you will combine the explosiveness and grips of the previous technique with the return path of the shoulder roll to land in the triangle position. Master this along with the omoplata attack and you will have a great one-two combination sequence with which to overwhelm your opponents. This movement works because your opponent's uncontrolled arm is not in play. Make sure you return over his shoulder so that you can land in the triangle.

DAY FIVE:

FREQUENCY: 2-3x 5 minutes

If there is any drilling sequence that I would consider the most important for the closed guard, this one is it. This is the master attack series, and it makes up the majority of the major submissions from the position. I like this routine because your partner's defense easily feeds into the next submission. Although many people have practiced with this drill, I don't know how many have really considered how often they have hit the triangle from the armbar escape or the omoplata off the triangle defense. This movement is incredibly fundamental, so much so that I have probably won most of my matches from closed guard using a submission chain from this series. This is an absolute essential!

Shoulder Roll Series Continued

Similar to the omoplata shoulder roll, I swim my right arm underneath Marcel's left leg and my left hand cross grips his sleeve from the closed guard. I unlock my guard and go for the shoulder roll drill. Again, I throw my hips into the movement to get Marcel off balance. Then, I return to the closed guard, using my right arm and leg to help hook me into the position. As my left leg comes around from the all-fours position, I clamp it down on top of Marcel's shoulder and then lock up the triangle choke. I will then release the choke, return to the closed guard, and practice the movement to the other side.

Flow Attack

MASTER ATTACKER

I begin in the closed guard gripping Marcel's right arm to set up the armbar. I put my left foot on his hip and go for the attack. Once I lock in the armbar, Marcel pulls his arm out, leaving him open for the triangle, and I bring my leg around and lock in the submission. To defend, Marcel hugs his left arm around my right hip. This saves him from the choke, but makes it easy for me to transition to the omoplata. From here, Marcel powers into me to defend the position, landing him once again in the triangle. This time, Marcel tries to underhook pass around to my right side, exposing his arm for the finishing armbar. Finished with the drill, I will go back to closed guard and start again. It is more important to flow and use control between submissions than to use a lot of intensity.

DAY ONE:

BUTTERFLY SIT-UP

FREQUENCY: 2-3x 3-5 minutes

The butterfly sit-up drill focuses on sitting up from a nearly flattened butterfly position. This position can occur due to a pass attempt, posture control, or failed sweep. The important thing is that you develop the tendency to always sit up from here. This gives your legs a lot more power, as they are assisted by your body weight and movement to hit the sweeps that the position is famous for. While practicing, focus on breaking the blade of your forearm into your partner's throat. He will not want to continue pressing into you because of choking discomfort. For a more advanced-level workout, ask your partner to really pin you to the mat.

DAY TWO:

BUTTERFLY GUARD: In Focus

When it comes to the butterfly guard, there is no one better than Fernando "Terere" Augusto. Not only was he a master of using it for simple sweeps, but he would also use grips and controls that were really unorthodox for the time. The secret to Terere's butterfly guard was in his understanding of attack and movement. He realized that this guard had to be offensive, and he developed offensive options from every stage of the guard. When his opponent ran, he would follow to the single-leg guard. If his opponent pressed into him, he would use his rocking motion to again make distance and hit the sweep. If his opponent stayed, well, he couldn't, and those who waited got swept or submitted. If the time came where Terere felt he had to move to another guard, he was open-minded. He would always move into the spider, closed, and half guards, but would always return at a moment's notice to hit his basic butterfly sweeps.

As a guard player, you should work on a few things to instantly increase the efficiency of your butterfly guard. First, learn to use your arm as a frame and your hip-escape movement to sit to the upright position. Second, discover the rocking chair or the use of your hooks to rock your opponent from on top of you to your front. Build your quadriceps muscles and hamstrings so that you have the power to lift his body. This power matters with the hooks. Finally, always attack from this position. Do not let your opponent get comfortable, and never allow his weight to pin your hips to the mat.

Getting the Butterfly

I start the butterfly sit-up drill from a semi-flattened butterfly guard. My right shoulder is on the mat and I have both hooks, but Marcel is pressing me into the floor. I change the situation by sliding my left forearm across his throat, bracing my hand against his left shoulder. Next, I punch my forearm into his trachea to get him to allow me some space. As he complies, I sit up to my right forearm, move my hips away from him, and finish in a square butterfly guard. From here, Marcel will put his head below my chin and drive me back to a semi-flattened position. I make sure that I land on my side to retain offense.

Developing Your Hooks

BUTTERFLY LIFT

FREQUENCY: 3-5 sets of 20

For your second day of butterfly guard training, you should start by giving your legs a position-specific workout. Simply stated, your only goal with this drill is to lift your partner as high off the mat as you possibly can and then repeat. Be careful though, this is not usually the sweeping movement. Usually, the butterfly sweep, as it is commonly called, is a side-to-side motion, and often enough a good opponent will easily defend the sweep if you try to do it overhead. Overhead butterfly sweeps often cost too much strength for sparring, but they are great for physical training and leg stamina. Once you are comfortable with this movement, you are ready to introduce a sparring application with the next technique.

I start the butterfly lift drill with Marcel based out on top of my flattened butterfly guard. I have both arms underhooking his armpits with my hands clasped together. Marcel will keep his forearms on the mat for the duration of the drill. Using my hooks and quadriceps, I lift Marcel as high as possible. Marcel bases with his forearms. I return Marcel to the mat and I am ready for my second repetition. I should mix up my repetitions so that some are slow with continuous muscle tension and others are explosive.

DAY TWO:
BUTTERFLY KICK-OUT

FREQUENCY: 2-3x the distance of the mat

Now that you have warmed up with butterfly lifts, it's time to expand on that move to make it more jiu-jitsu specific. The butterfly kick-out uses the same lifting technique, but this time you will have the assistance of momentum to help you get your opponent off the floor and then send him away from you. Again, this is a great workout, but this movement also works very well to open up your opponent for straight armlocks and sweeps. If you apply the same motion to a head and arm choke, this technique turns into a nightmare submission. Focus on launching your partner away from you as you come back to the seated position. This is where you will find your attacking range!

FREQUENCY: 2x 5 minutes

This drill bridges the gap between the butterfly lift and the footlock submission. The reason I have you doing this drill is to get you to look at the butterfly guard differently from just the traditional sweep or the common attacks. From this end position, you have a range of sweeps, half guards, x-guards, and back-taking possibilities, so I am sure you will get a lot out of this drill. While drilling, try to kick your leg through, just as you did in last week's omoplata drill. This will put you into position to lock up the leg and threaten with the attack. For your partner on top, this is an excellent drill to work his passing mobility and balance.

Developing Your Hooks Continued

I start the butterfly kick-out drill with Marcel in my butterfly guard. I have both arms underhooking his armpits with my hands clasped together. To start the drill, I rock backward and then, using my hooks and quadriceps, I lift Marcel as high as possible. Marcel bases with his hands on the mat. As Marcel returns, I ride his weight to the seated position, but kick him further away from me as I stabilize. To continue, I scoot my hips back underneath Marcel for leverage, and I will fall back for my second kick-out. I will continue like this for the length of the mat.

BUTTERFLY LIFT & TRAP

I start the butterfly lift and trap drill with Marcel in my butterfly guard. I have both arms underhooking his armpits with my hands clasped together. To start the drill, I rock backwards and then, using my hooks and quadriceps, I lift Marcel as high as possible. At the peak of my lift, I kick my right leg through and force Marcel to land on the side of my left leg. Using a counterclockwise movement, I lock my right foot onto Marcel's left hip, trapping his left foot in the possible ankle lock. I drop my right shoulder to the mat to simulate a lock and then release the hold. Marcel and I return to the starting position so I can continue the drill to the other side.

DAY THREE:
SIT-UP DRILL

FREQUENCY: 2x 20 minutes or 2x 3-5 min

Day three focuses on mobility from the butterfly guard. In particular, it focuses on moving to a single-leg guard and circling around a kneeling opponent. For this drill, you will focus on moving from a butterfly guard to a seated single-leg position. This is my go-to attack whenever my opponent tries to run away from my butterfly guard hooks. When drilling, continue from the single-leg position all the way to a standing leg pick. This will link the position with your offense and it should help you to avoid one of my cardinal sins of grappling—waiting for your opponent to set up his counter.

FREQUENCY: 2-3x 3-5 minutes

The scoot-around drill is one of my favorite drills for teaching anybody at any level to take the back. The idea here is to use your hip-switching abilities to continually rotate around your partner, traveling all the way around his back until you return to the front. Aside from taking the back, this drill also helps with your arm-drag skills because now you have an anchor in your partner's body for you to pull against. I cannot reiterate this enough—the guard should never be lazy, so develop your zeal for movement now and give yourself an attacking butterfly!

Butterfly Mobility

I start in a down guard position with Marcel in front of me. Marcel will keep the same position throughout the drill. I sit up to my right elbow and then to my right hand. At the same time, I grab his right leg with my left arm and hug my head tight to his quadriceps. With this position, I can easily do a master's lift to get to my feet and then pick his right ankle with my left hand, simulating the takedown. Finished, I return to the position, making sure that I hug his leg until I am all the way back to my starting spot. For my next repetition, I will sit up and attack his other leg.

SCOOT-AROUND

I start in a butterfly guard position with my right leg on the outside of Marcel's knees and my left leg on the inside. My right arm is under Marcel's left armpit and my left arm is posted on the mat. As I pull with my right arm, I switch my hips to the left side. From here, I readjust my left arm and repeat until I clear my head under his armpit and take his back. I continue this motion until I clear under Marcel's other arm and return to the starting position. Next, I will repeat the drill to the other side.

DAY FOUR:
SAME-SIDE ARM DRAG

FREQUENCY: 3 sets of 20 or 2x 5 minutes

The same-side arm drag is an excellent way to deflect your opponent to the mat. I like to practice this off my opponent's attempt to pass, and you should drill this the same way. As soon as your opponent grabs your legs, cup his triceps, make a big hip switch, and go! The key to this movement is the side-to-side hip escape that you learned in your third month of training. As with all arm drag motions, you should always drag your opponent to where you were, not to where you are! Combining your drag pull with your hips is the path to mastery!

FREQUENCY: 2-3x 5 minutes

The tug and push is an excellent drill that I learned while training with the guys at Master team. All of the good guys like Terere, Demian Maia, Comprido, and Leo Vieira would do this move. Basically, this is an excellent drill for keeping your opponent at an attacking range while setting up the arm drag off his torreando pass attempt. This is also a drill that completely mirrors what happens in sparring, and I recommend you have your partner actively try to pass your guard with the torreando after you are comfortable with the motion. The key is to do a same-side arm drag while blocking the arm on the side that your partner wishes to pass. This puts your partner's body out of line and makes it easier to set up the reversal.

Pass Prevention

I start in the butterfly guard with Marcel standing in front of me. Marcel grabs both my pant legs to pass my guard with the torreando. Before he can pass, I cup my left hand behind his right triceps as I post my right hand on the mat for base. In one motion, I do a side-to-side hip escape to the left while pulling or arm dragging Marcel down to the mat. Marcel breaks his fall by posting his hand in front of him and then turns to face me. As he turns, I am already grabbing his left triceps for the next same-side arm drag. I will continue changing from side to side for the duration of the drill.

TUG AND PUSH

Once again, we start in the butterfly guard with Marcel standing to pass with the torreando. He is gripping both my pant legs. As Marcel steps over toward my left side to pass, I block that direction by pushing into his right biceps with my left hand. At the same time, I arm drag Marcel's left arm to my midsection with my right hand. Marcel loses balance and I am in a great position to reverse him. Instead, Marcel resets the position and I will do the tug and push to the other side.

DAY FIVE:
SIDE-TO-SIDE ARM DRAG

FREQUENCY: 3-4 sets of 20 or 2-3x 2-5 minutes

The side-to-side arm drag is one of the highest percentage and useful reversals from the butterfly guard. It should be very familiar to you after practicing the same-side arm drag. In fact, it uses the exact same concept of pulling your opponent to where you were as you hip-escape away from him. The only difference is that you will use a cross-grip arm drag instead of using the same side as before. As a benefit, you will have a little more power to pull from in this drag, and this movement also works well against torreando passes. The only minus is that sometimes you can pull your opponent to your back if you are not careful.

DAY ONE:

FREQUENCY: 2x 5 minutes.

Along with submissions and sweeps, guard maintenance makes up the third facet of a complete guard game. You must be able to retain or maintain the position to have prolonged success here. The rocking chair is an excellent way to retain the guard, and it works really well as a first line of defense, or early defense. These maintenance techniques work a lot easier than later defenses. The rocking motion of this technique keeps your feet between you and your opponent. It is a lot faster than hip escaping to follow or shuffling your hips. Think of this as acting like a weighted ball that always ends upright. You are going to be the weighted ball and you are always going to bob up in the butterfly guard.

The Arm Drag

For the side-to-side arm drag drill, I start with Marcel on his knees in my butterfly guard. He is holding both my knees, and I am cross-gripping his left triceps with my left arm. I step my right leg out wide and post my right arm away from my body. Rapidly, I lift my hips with my right hand and both legs as I pull Marcel hard to the mat in front of him. As I do this, I escape my hips away from Marcel and then reach up with my right hand to his back. Marcel reacts by turning to face me and I counter by cross-gripping Marcel's right arm so that I can arm drag him to the other side. We will continue like this for the duration of the drill.

Long Distance Guard Maintenance

ROCKING CHAIR

I start in a downed guard with Marcel standing in front of me. As Marcel starts to walk in a clockwise path to my right, I sit up. As he continues in the same direction, I will keep falling back, so that my head is going away from my opponent, and sitting up again, so we are back in the same line. This rocking chair motion helps keep me from being too late in my guard defense.

DAY TWO:
LEG THROW TO GUARD RECOVERY

FREQUENCY: 3 sets of 20 or 2 sets of 3-5 minutes

Oftentimes, your opponent will try to throw your legs from the contact range. At this point, your whole side is available for the taking and you must react very quickly to resolve this situation. This is where this guard recovery drill comes in handy. Every time your legs get thrown, you will step your outside leg onto your partner's hip and then realign your guard. This exercise is a continuation of the wall movement drill, and it is easy to practice. Ask your partner to really throw your leg out of the way as if he is passing your guard. This will create a sense of urgency in your recovery and should help with your timing.

DAY THREE:

FREQUENCY: 2 sets of 20 or 2 sets of 3-5 minutes

For your third day of guard maintenance, focus on mid-range defense. In this case, you are late to your defense and your opponent is passing, but you still have hip mobility to help you through. For this particular situation, you will do an inverted roll to defend a very common guard pass. The key to this movement is your ability to loop your top leg under your partner's armpit and hide your head for the roll. Once you do your inverted roll, your path always takes you to the triangle choke. Make this your first option off defensive rolls and you should see your submission percentage increase.

Contact Range Recovery

We start the drill with Marcel inside my open guard. Marcel is standing and has both his hands on my feet. In one forceful motion, he throws both my feet off to his left side, opening up my right side for the guard pass. I react immediately by stepping my right (outside) leg onto his hip and then use this foot on his hip as a pivot point to pull my left leg and hip back to a square position. I end with both feet on his hips and Marcel continues the drill by throwing my legs again off to his right. I will recover guard once more, and we will trade leg throws and recoveries for the duration of the drill.

Middle Range Defense
RECOVERY TO TRIANGLE

I start the drill with Marcel passing my guard. He has his right arm on my knee and his left hand on my collar. He has jumped past my legs, and I have to react. First, I block his path by looping my left leg over his right arm until I can hook under his armpit with my left foot. While I do this, I hook my left hand under Marcel's left armpit. Using this under the arm grip, I hide my head underneath Marcel's arm. If I do not do this, Marcel can stop my roll with the cross-face. I initiate the roll by pushing off the mat with my right foot to propel myself onto my right and then left shoulder. I use my left foot as an anchor point and spin my right leg in a clockwise motion until I am almost square with Marcel. As my leg comes around, I lock my leg over Marcel's left arm in the triangle position. Afterward, I release the choke and Marcel will immediately pass to the other side to keep the drill in motion.

DAY THREE:
SIT-UP HIP ESCAPE

FREQUENCY: 2 sets of 20 or 2x the distance of the mat

Whenever you sit in the butterfly guard, you have to expect to have your opponent try to pass toward your back side. This makes sense because all your defenses, from your hands to your arms and knees, are in front of you. Armed with that knowledge, you have to prepare for the eventuality that your opponent will try to get to this difficult-to-defend spot. This is where all your hip-escape variations from month three will come into play. There is one thing that you must not do from this position—fall to your back to defend. As you fall, your opponent will pass the guard, so use this drill often to get used to getting away from your opponent without going to your back. It will take time to get used to, but it is essential.

Middle Range Defense Continued

I begin with Marcel on his knees facing me in my butterfly guard. My right leg is forward, so Marcel knows he can pass over my knee to take my back. As Marcel passes, I know I have to react. I keep my left hand posted on the mat and grab his right shoulder with my right hand. At this point, I will not let Marcel advance any farther. I stiff-arm Marcel with my right arm and hip-escape to my rear-left corner. I go this way so that Marcel does not have an angle to pass, putting my hips even farther from him. Once far enough, Marcel faces me, I pick a side, and Marcel will jump over my guard toward my back side. I switch my grips and prepare for the pass. We will continue this drill until we have finished our set or we reach the end of the mat.

WEEK FOUR: Guard Maintenance
DAY FOUR:
BICEPS BLOCK & HIP ESCAPE

FREQUENCY: 3-4 sets of 20

Whenever your opponent tries to hop over your butterfly or any other guard for that matter, you only have a few moments to escape before he anchors his weight to you. This is why you need to drill the biceps blocking escapes. They will buy you a little more time to escape because your opponent cannot lock down a head-control position. This moment of uncertainty is all that you need to hip-escape and reconfigure the guard. However, you cannot just wait, holding his biceps, because eventually your opponent will drop his weight and adjust against your biceps control. Instead, use this drill to work on developing your timing to go from the blocked biceps to the hip escape.

FREQUENCY: 3-4 sets of 20

Whenever you do the previous escaping movement you also leave your opponent exposed for the triangle choke. This time, after you have blocked the biceps and hip-escaped away, I want you to slide your leg through and over his trapped arm. This leaves you in position to finish off a beautiful triangle choke transition that is one of my absolute favorites. This is probably one of the most common submissions that Terere caught me with when I first came to his academy in São Paulo. While practicing, make sure that you really drive your opponent's biceps into his body so you have room to slide your leg over his arm for the triangle trap.

Blocking the Biceps

Marcel starts the drill by jumping over my butterfly guard. Before he can consolidate the side control, I block his left biceps with my right arm while I slide my left forearm in front of his trachea as a frame. This blocks Marcel from holding me in side control and buys me a couple of seconds. I push my left foot off the mat and hip escape away to make some space between us. I immediately slide my right knee into that space and do not stop until I have slid my knee all the way back to the guard. We continue the drill when Marcel passes the guard to the other side.

PASS BLOCK TO TRIANGLE

Again, Marcel starts the drill by jumping over my butterfly guard. Before he can consolidate the side control, I block his left biceps with my right arm while I slide my left forearm in front of his trachea as a frame. This time, I really pin Marcel's left arm to his body. As I hip-escape, I take advantage of Marcel's trapped right arm by lifting my left leg onto his back. Then, I slide my right leg into the space created by my hip escape, making sure to pass my leg over his left arm. I quickly lock the triangle from the square submission and easily submit Marcel with his right arm securely trapped. We will then reset the position and repeat to the other side.

DAY FIVE:
DOUBLE UNDERHOOK ROLL OUT

FREQUENCY: 2-3 sets of 20

Even though you would rather defend the pass early, sometimes the guard passer is so good that you have no choice but to fight against his pass late. Keep this in mind; late passes are by nature more frantic because you are not in control and you are close to losing the guard. In this case, you will work a rollout technique that I have all my white belts do. The trick here is not just to roll your hips, but to back roll and then pull your body away from your opponent so that you can sit to the guard. This will keep you from getting squashed underneath him and should help with your timing to get out of hairy situations with the double underhooks pass.

FREQUENCY: 2-3 sets of 20

This time you have to deal with a savvy opponent who not only passes over your guard, but also manages to get some weight over you. Practice this drill so that you do not fret in this situation and are able to bump your opponent into the guard before the three seconds have elapsed (it takes three seconds to be awarded side control or passing points). The key to this position is your ability to make space by bridging and not just pushing your opponent's head haphazardly. You must push at the top of his head instead of his neck. The top of his head is the end of your lever, not the neck or lower head. Follow this sequence: Get your hand in place, bridge, drop your hips, pass his head as a gap opens between your bodies, and hip-escape to recover. Although it sounds complicated, you will be putting this together in this drill chain in no time.

Late Defense

We start in the guard position with my feet on Marcel's hips. Marcel goes for the pass by underhooking both my legs and pulling them high onto his shoulders. As Marcel lifts my hips to pass, I let my legs fall over my right shoulder. I am sure to rotate my arms over by pointing the tops of my hands to the floor so that I can come up on a takedown if I choose. As I back roll out, I grab Marcel with my right underhook, step my right leg between his legs, and then sit back into the guard. From here, Marcel and I will reset the position and continue the drill.

HEAD PUSHING ESCAPE

Marcel starts the drill by jumping over my guard and pressing into my lower abdomen. I circle my right hand to the outside, pressing my hand into the upper-left side of his head. Immediately I bridge, keeping a slight pushing tension as I do so. I drop fast and push hard on his head, clearing it to my left side. With Marcel's feet and head on the same side as my body, I can easily realign the guard. From here, Marcel will pass to the other side and we will continue the drill.

MONTH NINE: *In Review*

This chapter is dedicated to the most basic elements of guard playing. The key is combining your basic body movements to control, defend, and attack from the guard. Although the guard is a defensive masterpiece, you must keep it in your mind that you are an attacker and in particular, a submission specialist. Whether you are defending against a guard pass, breaking down the posture, or taking a quick breath, your opponent should always feel threatened by your guard submissions. Having a dangerous guard will open up many more opportunities because your opponent will fear every grip you make.

Just as a boxer has his 1-2 punch and 1-2-3 combinations, so should the guard player. Learn to understand which attacks and sweeps are complementary and build your drilling and game plan around them. Just like passing, it is great to know all the options, but become an expert in just a few! Once you find the best combinations for your game, stick to them and drill them until you become incredibly confident with them. Not only will your good combos work on classmates who are less experienced than you, they will also begin working on the classmates who are much more experienced. The trick is to start drilling your moves on the less experienced, and then work your way up to the harder opponents. This goes for all your drills - not just your guard!

Finally, remember the closed guard should always be an attacking position. Make sure you drill returning to the closed guard from every position. It can be your home base for many types of sweeps, submissions, and transitions to other guards.

WEEKEND WORK:

The weekend work will take on 2 elements. For the first element of every session, you should open with the 10 extra minutes of the Submission Transition Flow Attack from closed guard. This is one of the best attack drills in jiu-jitsu and you need to master the links between these submissions. Afterward, train 1 round of 15 minutes from the closed guard and 1 round of 15 minutes from the butterfly guard. In the closed guard situation, you can only open your legs to attack and you must start over if your opponent opens your guard or you get the submission. For the butterfly guard you must sweep or submit while your partner must pass the guard.

MONTH TEN:
The Wet Noodle - Guard Part II

Because the guard is far too complicated for just one month of training, it is also featured in month ten. This month, you will be focusing on essential guard movements, the spider guard, different open guards, and how to train the open guard. There are so many different types of control, that you really must drill all the different guards to gain some level of comfort with each. Of course, many famous competitors use certain guards more often than others and excel at them, but to really succeed at a high level, you must still be proficient in everything.

One of the most influential instructors I've had in regards to the open guard is Ricardo Vieira. When I roll with him, he moves fluidly between different open guards and is always attacking a sweep or submission. His game feels like an invisible man—he is gone and moving into something new before I even realize he was there to begin with. I developed the drills in this month to try to emulate his guard and get my open guard on his level. I feel that to even come close, you must practice specific movements over and over to get your body familiar with the open guard.

Once you are familiar with the different guards and how they move, transitioning will become a lot easier. Often enough, transitioning is a matter of changing your grips, foot placement, and angle when your opponent changes his pass from one type of guard to another. Combine this month's routines with those in month nine for a more complete set of bottom skills.

The first week will focus on essential guard movement. Like the first week last month, this week is all about getting your body used to performing certain movements that will help with your guard work. It also focuses especially on inverted guard movements, like inserting a leg between your opponent's legs to maintain the position. You will also develop a sensitivity for inserting your foot combined with inverting or spinning on your shoulders.

I like to use inverted movements as a form of recovery, to link between guards, and to set up attacks. Some will like to hang out in the inverted position, and this is okay for a while, but I prefer to use a more active guard.

As with other areas of jiu-jitsu training, I drill to move from the bottom and top. While on the bottom, I continuously move and attack until I get an advantage, reverse, or submit. The drills you will practice this week will teach you to do the same.

In week two, you will move on to the spider guard. The goal this week is to teach your body to defend, maintain, and attack from the spider guard position. As you will notice, the drills this week do not focus on holding the position. You must drill so that your hips are constantly moving. Although the spider guard looks like a battle of grips and foot pressure, it is really a battle of hip movement.

I cannot reiterate this enough: If you hang out in any guard too long without movement or attack, you will get your guard passed. Keep moving and always have your mind set on attacking.

Using my guard mobility to "slip out the backdoor" during my open weight fight with Roger Gracie in the 2008 Mundials.

An attacking spider guard is one of the most dominant and frustrating open guards in jiu-jitsu. There is a lot of control here, with plenty of submission opportunities. I learned this guard from watching Terere, and you can see Terere's imprint on all his former students' guards. For example, look at Rubens "Cobrinha" Charles. His spider guard is beautiful, and I think he owes a lot of that to his training at TT.

Terere was a big advocate of drilling, and he helped mold my training so that I wouldn't stop until I got something. Before a tournament, he would help me create a strategy, and for the weeks before a competition, I would only drill the elements of that strategy. Then, at the tournament, I would be completely confident with my movements and beat my opponents with the exact moves I had been drilling. At TT, I realized the real importance of drilling, and my training method has not changed since.

After training open guard elements and then the spider guard, week three moves into a mixed curriculum of open guards. This week, the goal is to learn how to use the De La Riva guard and x-guard in transition. You'll notice that I am not teaching you complete techniques in these guards. It is more important that you learn to transition in these guards, and then the techniques you know will fall into play.

Movement is the most important thing to drill in these guards. With the movements, you will learn to adapt to any situation because you will be used to moving in and out of the position instead of locking onto the guard for dear life. Just remember, your end point is not the guard or the reversal; it is the submission. Use every movement in jiu-jitsu as a transition to your ultimate goal—your opponent tapping out.

The last week of the month, you will train the open guard. Although we have mostly focused on repetition-based drilling, this week's routine involves actual training, but not like you might think. Instead of grabbing a partner and testing out all your new moves on him in a full-fledged sparring match, you will have limits on your training in order to remain focused on the guard. It is vital that you adapt these types of limited drills to your guard game, but also remember that these limitation training methods are not exclusively for the guard, and you can use them to get better in all aspects of jiu-jitsu. Every time you handicap yourself in training, you get to focus on isolating what you want to work. Handicap your legs to work your arms. Handicap your grips to foster more movement, and so on.

After you finish month ten, you will be well on your way to becoming an open guard ace! Now take these newfound training methods and apply them to your developing repertoire and you will begin to see results in all aspects of your game.

DAY ONE:
INVERTED MOVEMENT TO SPLITS

FREQUENCY: 1-2 sets of 20 or 1x 5 minutes

The goal this week is once again to work on some of your inverted movements from last month while adding some new skills that should help you transition into and out of the inverted position. The inverted movement to splits is a great example of taking a drill from last month and adding a stretch to further help loosen the guard. Practice this instead of just back roll stretches if you really want to get your legs, hips, and back more flexible for inverted training. Drill at an easy pace, and as with all flexibility-based movements, practice after you have lightly warmed up with a jog or some basic calisthenics.

DAY TWO:

FREQUENCY: 2-3 sets of 20

The north-south recovery is one of the first inverted guard recoveries that you learn when you start Brazilian Jiu-Jitsu, and it also makes a great drill. For this technique, it is important that after you cross your feet on your opponent's hips, you use your hooks as a pivot point to transition back to the guard. Also, be sure to unwind your body so that your head follows the leg closest to you, not the top leg. If you unwind toward the top leg, your legs will be intertwined and this is not where you want to be! Although this is purely a drill, it does have a very good application in an inverted recovery from the bottom of the north-south position.

Beginning Inversion

I set up the inverted movement to splits from the seated position. As I fall toward my left side, I tuck my left hand behind my back to open up my shoulder. My left shoulder hits the mat, and I tuck my chin toward my chest. At this point, I roll all the way onto both shoulders. To get back to my upright position, I bring my feet toward my right side to help me carry my momentum in that way. I tuck my right hand behind my body so that it is out of the way and I sit onto my right hip and leg. My left leg swings back into a hurdler's stretch and I hold the stretch. Afterward, I will roll back to the starting side finishing in an opposite-side hurdler's stretch. I will continue this way for the duration of the drill.

Basic Inverted Recovery
NORTH-SOUTH RECOVERY

I start on my back, holding Marcel's ankles. Using my grips on his legs, I pull my feet toward his hips. Before my feet get to him, I cross my legs so that my left (close) leg is on his right hip and my right (far) leg is on his left. Next, I unwind in the direction of the bottom leg. Using my feet as pivot points, I pull my head out on Marcel's right side and rotate on my upper back until our bodies are realigned in the open guard. Marcel will continue the drill by walking around to the other-side north-south, where I will once again grab his ankles and repeat the recovery for the remainder of the exercise.

DAY THREE:

HOOK & ROLL

FREQUENCY: 3 sets of 20

This drill should feel incredibly familiar because you just practiced a few of its variations during last month's week on the closed guard. This time, you are revisiting the movement in preparation for some inversion training. The entry shoulder roll is very similar to the roll used for the hook and spin later this week, so really try to get some solid repetition training now so that your neck, back, and shoulders are a little more limber come day five. Practice with less explosiveness than in previous shoulder rolls.

DAY FOUR:

FREQUENCY: 1-3x 5 minutes

The clock movement drill is one of the best guard exercises I learned from Terere. This drill will teach you an important concept when playing with inverted techniques as well as the open guard in general. Whenever an opponent is passing, I like to get one foot between his legs. This is better than trying to put your feet on his hips because your feet can always be batted away. If you have a foot hooked between his legs, you have connection with your opponent, and you can follow his movement. While drilling this technique, try to keep your upper back in the same position and only use your legs, lower hips, and back to follow. Your partner can either go around a full 360 degrees, or reverse every 180 degrees.

Loosening the Back w/Sweeps

From the open guard, I swim my right arm underneath Marcel's left leg. I unlock my guard and pendulum my left leg in a long clockwise arc. As I get perpendicular, I roll over my right shoulder, using my left hand on the mat to help push my hips through. I land on all fours next to Marcel's left side. I return by rolling over my right (inside) shoulder while using my right arm and leg to anchor myself to his body. My left leg returns in a long counterclockwise arc, and I pull myself to the open guard. Now, I am ready to continue the drill to the other side.

Relaxed Inversion

CLOCK MOVEMENT

WEEK ONE: Essential Guard Movement

I'm in the open guard position with Marcel standing. Marcel will circle my body, making sure that he is always close enough for my legs to make contact with him. I keep my right leg hooked between his legs and allow Marcel to pull me to an inverted position as he walks around. My leg rides his motion. When he gets to the halfway point, I switch legs and Marcel continues his path around my body until we are back at the starting point. I must only use my body from my lower back down to my feet to follow.

DAY FIVE:

HALF SPIN

FREQUENCY: 2 sets of 20 or 2x 3-5 minutes

The half spin is without a doubt my favorite drill for guard inversion, and I spent many hours on this at the former TT Academy. I really love the rhythm you get from this drill as you flow from side to side and effortlessly transfer your legs and transition. The movement reminds me of break dancing for jiu-jitsu and I mean this as the highest of compliments. As far as jiu-jitsu application, you can see this drill imprinted all over the games of some of the former TT students, such as the Mendes brothers, Cobrinha, and the Langhi brothers. They all have shown great ability to use this movement to sneak to the back, and you can too!

FREQUENCY: 2x 3-5 minutes

The around the world spin is a continuation of the previous drill, and it does a couple of things that the previous drill just cannot do. First of all, you get a better flow to your drill because you never stop and you can go in the same direction for several revolutions. This helps break up the seams of your jiu-jitsu, and I want your jiu-jitsu to be seamless. Secondly, you get to invert toward your opponent's back and not just his front. This greatly helps your ability to take the back from the De La Riva and single-leg guards, which has been made evident by recent wins of Rafael and Guilherme Mendes, who, in my opinion, probably have the best back transitions from the De La Riva guard in jiu-jitsu.

Hook & Spin Inversions

I start in a single-leg guard with both legs around Marcel's right leg. Marcel is standing and he will keep the same position throughout the drill. As I roll onto my right shoulder, I swim the top of my right hand under my left leg so that it is hooking the outside of Marcel's right leg. I roll onto both shoulders to invert and slide my left leg between Marcel's legs as I remove my right leg. Next, I swim my left hand next to Marcel's left foot and swing my right leg in a clockwise arc to recover the single-leg guard. The momentum of my leg takes me to my rear and I end holding Marcel's leg in single leg guard, ready for my next repetition.

AROUND THE WORLD SPIN

Again, I start in a single-leg guard with both legs around Marcel's right leg. This time, I roll onto my left shoulder and swim the top of my left hand under my right leg so that it is hooking the outside of Marcel's right leg. I roll onto both shoulders to invert and slide my right leg between Marcel's legs as I remove my left leg. Next, I swim my left hand next to Marcel's left foot and swing my right in a clockwise arc to recover the single-leg guard. The momentum carries me all the way to Marcel's side, but I do not stop. I continue to roll again to Marcel's front side as I hook and spin all the way around Marcel's body. I will do this for the remainder of the time.

DAY ONE:

FOOT CIRCLES

FREQUENCY: 1 set of 5 minutes

The first two-thirds of day one of spider guard training focuses on circling your feet to eliminate your opponent's control. For the first drill, you will start in a standard open guard, but you need to realize that this movement is best understood in this situation before it is bridged into the spider guard itself. The keys to this drill will be (1) your ability to limit your opponent's pressure by keeping his body weight off your hips with your knee and foot on his hip and (2) your hip mobility, which is far more useful to your hook circling than knee ligament flexibility. Practice this one at a slower pace if you are a beginner, but don't be afraid to ratchet up the intensity as you get better. Higher-level practitioners should have their partner really try to underhook and penetrate with every underhook.

FREQUENCY: 2-3x 3-5 minutes

The previous movement is great for learning the basics of circling your feet to retain the open guard, and the following drill will take your motor skills a step further. For this drill, your partner is going to get even more control over your hips, shutting down the previous move. Instead of giving up, you should work to escape your hips, loosen his grip on your leg, and recommit yourself to the previous leg circle. You really have to feel this technique so that your body understands what it means to "make a better angle." Often enough, this is what divides good spider and open guards from the rest.

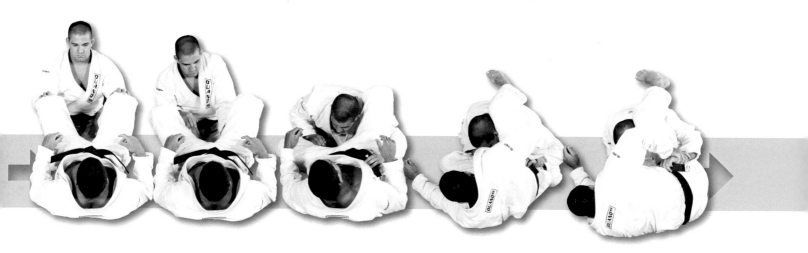

Keeping the Spider Guard

Marcel begins the drill in a kneeling posture within my open guard. Both my feet are on his hips. As Marcel swims his left arm underneath my right leg for an under-the-leg pass, I keep my left foot on his hip with my left knee pointed into his chest as I circle my right foot counterclockwise to escape it back to his hip. I must use my other foot and my knee as a block so that Marcel cannot drive his weight into me as I circle my leg free. Marcel continues the drill by underhooking my left leg and once again; I repeat the steps to free my trapped leg. We will continue like this until the drill time has elapsed.

HIP ESCAPE FOOT CIRCLES

Once again, we start the drill with Marcel inside my open guard with both my feet on his hips. This time, Marcel swims his left hand underneath my right leg and pushes my right leg to the floor as if he is doing the over-and-under pass. With Marcel penetrated so deep with such hip control, I will not be able to do the previous escape. Instead, I grab his left wrist with my right hand and hip-escape to my right. This weakens Marcel's hold over my leg as his arm stretches out. Now I have the space and angle to loop my foot counterclockwise to escape his control. Once both legs are inside, I pull my hips back to him and Marcel will keep the drill alive by passing to the other side.

DAY ONE:

SPIDER SWING

FREQUENCY: 2-3 sets of 20

The spider swing is our final drill aimed at keeping the spider guard. This drill focuses on using a rolling motion similar to the shoulder roll to get back to the guard. While practicing, you should allow your partner to throw your legs to the side, but you have to get back to spider guard as quickly as possible. Your opponent has a window of opportunity to attack your arm, so try to keep it close to your body and be aware of your openings as you transition.

DAY TWO:

FREQUENCY: 3 sets of 8-20

As with all of my positions in jiu-jitsu, I am always linking speed, timing, rhythm, balance, and strength to my technique. When I think of strength in the spider guard, I do not think of raw superhuman power; instead, I am thinking of the strength to be able to sweep a person one minute into my first match or seven minutes into my last one. Make sure that you condition your body so that it is always ready for the battle call. All of the sweeping skills and technique in the world will not matter if you do not have the strength to execute. With this drill, you will get a great leg-lift routine, so expect a hamstring burn. However, you will also get a great lesson on balance and leverage for the tomoe-nage, or superman sweep. Keep your opponent balanced over your hips and feel how easy it is to lift him—at least for the first few repetitions!

Keeping the Spider Guard Cont.

I am holding Marcel in spider guard. To get rid of my control, Marcel loops his hands around to the back of my legs, grabbing my pants at the calf level and pushing my feet off his biceps. Without control of his arms, I am unable to prevent Marcel from easily throwing my legs to the side as if he is passing the guard. I do not resist the throw, and I shoulder roll to the side. While I roll, I keep my left arm as close to my side as possible to avoid a potential armbar. With the threat of submission in mind, I quickly shoulder roll back to the original guard position and resume the drill.

Spider Strength

SUPERMAN LIFTS

I start with Marcel posturing forward in my spider guard. I am gripping both his sleeves, and I have moved both my feet to his hips. With Marcel leaning forward, it is easy to pull him slightly forward to load him onto my legs. From here, I simply extend my legs upward to lift Marcel, holding the position for a few seconds without locking my knees. Then, I slowly bring Marcel back to me. I will repeat this leg lift until my set has been exhausted. While practicing, I can lift Marcel either explosively or gradually. Just be careful that you do not accidentally throw your partner (this disrupts your rhythm) and that you always try to recover (negative phase) over a slow 2–3 count.

DAY THREE:

SPIDER HOOKS

FREQUENCY: 1x 5-10 minutes

Your ability to move and adapt your spider hooks to different situations is an integral part of the spider guard. Try to avoid developing a guard that is too stiff to change the position when the time calls. You should use this drill to learn more about what it means to be successful in the spider guard, as well as what the spider guard is. Personally, I see the spider guard as any situation where you control your opponent's sleeves (one or both) and then use your hooks to frustrate and play with him like a marionette. To be the most offensive, you should constantly poke away at his defense by moving your hips and hooks as you shift and prod your way to where you want to be.

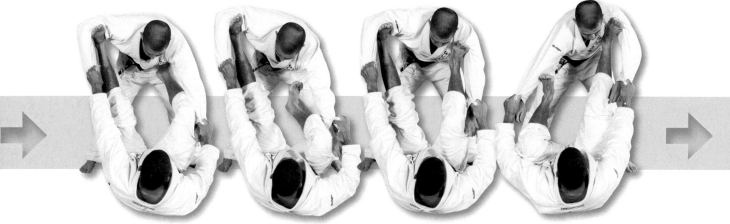

FREQUENCY: 3 sets of 20

The moving spider drill is a great way to feel how to control your opponent in the spider guard as he tries to move from side to side to gain an advantage to pass. At the heart of this drill is your ability to extend and retract your legs to keep your partner off balance and uncomfortable. When done correctly, your partner should feel similar to the way he did when you drilled the same-side arm drag and tug and push drills on him. Sure he is moving to the side, but it feels as if he could be swept at any second! Practice this movement often if you want to master the basic spider guard sweeps.

Spider Guard Movement

I start in the spider guard with Marcel standing. I have control over both his sleeves and have my right foot on his hip and my left foot on his biceps. First, I extend my left foot and then bring my right foot onto his left biceps. I must always move one leg at a time to keep the connection between us. Next, I extend my right foot and drop my left foot down to hook behind Marcel's knee. With my right foot still extended, I bring my left foot to Marcel's hip. Once secure, my right foot also follows to his hip. While practicing, I can use any combination of foot placement as long as I move one at a time and use all of the different placements.

MOVING SPIDER

I begin in the spider guard with both feet on Marcel's hips. Immediately I transition (one at a time) both feet to Marcel's armpits, and I am ready to go. As Marcel starts moving to his left, I chamber my right leg to my body while I straighten my left leg to disrupt his balance. Marcel should not feel comfortable here and he will back up and reset the position. Marcel will continue the drill by trying to move to other side, and once more, I will disrupt his balance with my extending and contracting legs.

DAY FOUR:
SPIDER LASSOS

FREQUENCY: 2-3 sets of 20

Your ability to lasso your opponent's arm is fundamental to spider guard attack and defense. With this hooking action, you can set up triangle chokes, omoplatas, sweeps and take the back. If your opponent is a great passer, this can frustrate him and impede his passing attempt (he has to address his trapped arm), buying you the time you need to get back on track and switch to offense. Try to make the lasso second nature, and get ready to implement your new tool during tomorrow's spider guard attack training.

DAY FIVE:

FREQUENCY: 3 sets of 20

For your first day of spider guard attacks, you are going to get a great lesson in the principle of action and reaction. This drill is simple and effective when used during sparring. The idea is for your opponent to be compliant and resist where he should. As you push your opponent with your legs, he is going to push back to avoid a perceived sweep. When he does this, you let your legs slip through and you can pull him right into the triangle. His resistance will actually work as a force multiplier with your pull, maximizing your speed and efficiency in getting to the submission position. Practice with a strong pull!

Spider Hooks w/Movement

I start the drill with Marcel in my spider guard. My left hook is pressing upward while my right leg hangs loose. I do not want my right leg to remain idle, so I "lasso" it over Marcel's elbow. The position is consolidated as I hook my right foot behind his triceps. I will need this hook if I want to open up Marcel's elbows with my legs. Having achieved the lasso, I unwind my hook and transition back to the spider guard with both feet on his biceps. As I unwind my leg, I can always pull my opponent into me as his arm becomes free. Use this later to set up triangle attacks.

Spider Attacker

WEEK TWO:
Spider Guard

SPIDER TRIANGLE

For the spider triangle drill, Marcel starts inside my spider guard with both my feet on his hips. I push into Marcel with my hooks, and when I feel him resisting into me, I slip my right leg over his shoulder and my left leg under. At the exact same moment, I pull him into my triangle position, using the forward momentum off his resistance to help me. Often enough, your force is so strong that you can pull all the way to the tight triangle! Instead of submitting Marcel, I release the hold and we continue to the other side. We will continue like this for the rest of the set.

DAY FIVE:
SPIDER LASSO TO TRIANGLE

FREQUENCY: 3 sets of 20

For your last submission on day five of spider guard attacks, focus on using the spider lasso to set up the triangle. Don't just go through the motions with this drill; as you unwind your lasso grip, pull that arm down as you climb your hips into position. Focusing on your hip climb, be sure to use your partner's hip as a step so that you can easily get the reach you need with your hips. This movement will not be successful if you do not pull and lift at the same time. Think of it as a meeting point where your pull is so exaggerated and your lift is so explosive that your hips and his head have no other option but to meet at the triangle choke.

DAYS I & II:

FREQUENCY: 2-3x 3-5 minutes

The focus of this week is on using transitioning into and out of specific guards. Hopefully, these drills allow you to see different guards as part of a much bigger picture and this creates an open-minded willingness to move freely instead of rigidly adhering to one type of control. In this situation, you will use your De la Riva hooks without grips to circle around your opponent. Be sure to push him and pull him with your feet as you use your hips to slide around his back and to the front. De la Riva guard mastery depends on controlling your opponent's posture and legs while opening pathways to the back, not just inserting an outside hook!

Spider Attacker Continued

Once again, we begin in the spider guard with Marcel standing. I straighten my left foot and then circle my right foot counterclockwise to get the lasso, again hooking my right toes behind his lower triceps. Keeping my grips, I release my right leg by circling it clockwise. As I do so, I relieve the pressure on Marcel's left arm and use this as an opportunity to pull his left arm to my body. Meanwhile, I have dropped my right leg onto his hip. Using his hip as a step, I climb my hip upward while I slip my left leg over his shoulder to set up the triangle. I release my foot from his hip and lock the tight triangle, using my body weight to pull Marcel down. I will continue the drill by releasing the choke and attacking to the other side.

De La Riva Transitions
DE LA RIVA TO BACK

I begin in an open guard with Marcel standing in front of me. To transition to the De la Riva guard, I circle my left foot counterclockwise, hooking my left foot behind his right knee. My right foot pushes on his left thigh. To make Marcel show me more of his side, I push his left leg away while hooking his right leg toward me. With his back exposed, I circle my right leg counterclockwise, hooking it behind his right knee as if I were taking his back. I continue the drill by circling my left foot to the front while inserting my right De la Riva hook. For the next repetition, I will transition to Marcel's left side instead (using the De la Riva hook I already have in place).

DAYS III-V:
X-GUARD MOVEMENT

FREQUENCY: 2-3x 3-5 minutes

For the second half of week three, focus on getting into the x-guard, transitioning to the back, and then returning to the front. You should shuffle your hips all the way underneath your opponent's hips to get to x-guard, and you need to use your outside hand to tuck your head underneath the head-side leg to sneak out the back. One last pointer, just as you always keep at least one leg in contact with your opponent while you transition to different spider guard controls, you should also do the same with your hooks. If you try to move two hooks at once, you are begging to have your guard passed.

DAYS I&III:

FREQUENCY: 3 rounds of 5-10 minutes

One-handed sparring is the first training method that involves handicapping both you and your partner for specific gains. In this case, you both severely limit your control by eliminating one arm and one grip. From here, you will have a regular sparring match, using the same movements you have learned during months of drilling. The result should be a better use of your legs and hips to move and control your opponent. Depending on the focus of your training, feel free to change this drill so that either your partner or you have one or both arms either available or eliminated.

The X-Guard Transitions

I begin with Marcel standing in my hooks guard. To get to the x-guard, I first move my right hook in front of Marcel's right quadriceps. I must use my left leg to control Marcel while I make this transition. Then, I reach my right hand under Marcel's left leg and shimmy my hips underneath him. To continue, I swim my right hand underneath Marcel's left knee and lift his knee away from my head. This allows me to pop my head to Marcel's back side. From here, I remove my left hook and place it behind Marcel's left thigh as if I were taking his back. To continue, I will retrace my steps to get back to Marcel's front side and then I will repeat the drill to the other side.

Fighting One-Handed
ONE-HANDED SPARRING

For one-handed sparring, both Marcel and I hide our left hands under our belts. From here, we will start sparring from the standing position. From this position, we can do any technique we want or just limit the focus to guard passing or escapes against the top position. If you take your hand out at any time during this drill, you have to do some push-ups as a penalty, so keep your hand hidden. The goal is not necessarily to "win" in this situation, but to move and transition between positions. This is often harder than regular sparring, so be prepared for a great core workout.

TWO-HANDED VARIATION

DAYS II, IV, V:

BALL SPARRING

FREQUENCY: 3 rounds of 5-10 minutes

Ball sparring is now one of my favorite training methods. I originally learned this from Leo Vieira while training with him in São Paulo, and I always loved it. You still get to use your hands to push and your arms to hook your opponent, but you can no longer rely on holding the gi to slow down the match. I like to make all submissions and transitions "legal" in this training. Although I have introduced this handicapped sparring late (in the hopes that you would focus more on drilling than fighting), I really hope you add this to your future training in all positions, not just the guard. Expect to see nearly immediate gains in your body movement. Take the gi off for an additional speed boost while training.

MONTH TEN:
In Review

Although the guards in Month Ten are slightly more advanced than those in Month Nine, they still depend on the same basic movements to be successful. Continue to work on your hip mobility as you incorporate the spider, De la Riva, and x-guards into your repertoire.

When it comes to the guard, certain attributes like flexibility will pay off in spades. Although you do not need to have a yoga master's flexibility, you will want to have at least an average to above average range of motion when playing with these guards. This will allow you to have a greater limit on your sweeps as well as providing you with a limber body that is more resistant to passing pressure. I recommend forward and butterfly stretches as a great starting place. You can also go back to Month Two and warm up with the stretches and strength drills to get your body loose and limber.

This month, remember to focus on your legs and hips more than your arms. Your arms' efficacies depend on strength, while your legs and hips need to be agile and in constant motion to be effective. In the long run, if you master hip and leg movement over arm strength, your guard will be much harder to crack.

Sparring w/Balls

The purpose of this drill is to move, so I fight the tendency to cheat by grabbing Marcel with my pinky fingers. At this point in the training, I am trying to pass his guard and make space while Marcel tries to transition to keep me in his guard. To make the drill even more playful, we can work our hand-eye coordination by trying to knock the balls out of each other's hands (giving the losing player a 10–20 push-up penalty)!

WEEKEND WORK:

Once again, you should open your weekend work by executing the Submission Training Flow Attack from closed guard. Again, aim for ten minutes per session of this drill. Then, move on to spider guard, x-guard, and De la Riva training. In this situation, your partner will hold tennis balls, while you play with any of these guards for 3 rounds of 15 minutes. Your goal is to transition between the guards while attacking with sweeps and submissions while your opponent tries to pass the guard. If either happens, start over from a different open guard position. While training, put it into your mind to continually change guards, hips, and positioning. If you have been in the same guard for over a minute and nothing has happened, it's time to change!

MONTH ELEVEN:

Think of this month as a bridge between all the drills you've been practicing so far this year. Now you have the tools to train every position in jiu-jitsu. This month, you will put them together and drill with a partner, who will also get a lot out of the drills. The title of this month is Chain Reaction and for good reason—all the drills get both partners better at the same time while chaining different types of techniques together into one fluid drill.

This month, there are two types of combination drills. Looping consists of movement cycles where both partners get to move through all the techniques and the rotation between the partners is built into the drilling. The other type is trading. These usually involve trading offensive for defensive techniques, where each partner only plays his own role and will not cycle through his partner's moves.

You should always practice with both types of combination chains. The looping chain often works better at flowing and does a good job of mimicking sparring. In addition, both players get to work on becoming more well rounded. Trading drills are often very beneficial for working one specific movement chain and practicing this until mastery. This is what I would see Terere do with his guard passing to the back combo drill before every major tournament. With trading drills, you also get to feel the counters to attacks as you play your role in the drill. Then, when you switch, you get to feel what it is like to attack and be countered. Both are great for learning what your opponent could do in any situation.

I provide combination drills here, but you can be creative and make your own as well. Play around with techniques from the previous months and develop some drills that focus on what you want to work on. While creating your combination drills, try to see your movement through to the submission. Here's an example: Say you want to work on guard passing and transitioning out of the side control. Devise a drill where you pass, immediately take the mount/back/knee-on-belly and just as quickly go right into the submission. This way you will teach your body never to stop for positions and to always aim for the finish.

Week one's drills originate with positional and submission defense. Don't let the theme of this week, Defensive Start, mislead you. They are only called defensive drills because that is the origin point. All of these drills have some offense, therefore someone is getting that routine. However, if you are designing the workout for yourself to get out of submissions or bad positions, then it is a defensive com-

DAYS I-IV:

FREQUENCY: 2-3x 3-6 minutes

As with all of the positional defense drills, I categorize the combination drill by its point of origin. With this "trading" style drill, you will work your defense as you recover guard from the north-south position while your opponent gets to be more offensive with an under-the-leg pass. The repetition frequency refers to being on the bottom, but you should work the same for your partner, giving you an excellent guard pass training as you come to the top. As with all combination drills, you really need to focus on continued movement instead of a frantic pace. You should be used to all of the moves in this chain by now, so let your technique shine!

Chain Reaction - Combination Drills

bination drill (regardless of your opponent getting offensive training).

Most defensive drills work on a cycle of partner A defends, partner B creates offense (passing, attacking, or transitioning), and partner A defends. This defense-offense-defense cycle continues and you can see how it gets one person's defense really strong while the other gets to focus on his dominance.

In week two, the drills originate with guard passes. The passing origin drills range from failed passes (usually loop drills) to trading drills that really help focus on passing and the jiu-jitsu endgame. These not only help you get your body used to feeling the passes, but they also help your partner to practice guard recovery.

My favorite drills are ones where I pass the guard and take the back. I like to allow my partner to pick the guard and I create the drill. Just as long as I end up on the back, the drill is a successful one. Once you finish this week, you will have the skills to begin creating your own drills as well. Get creative and play to your strengths. If you love finishing from the mount, create chain drills that begin with a takedown, then pass the guard or sweep to mount, and finish. This is where jiu-jitsu allows you to be a puppet master. You can take control of your training and get better at all positions!

Weeks three and four focus on chain drills that originate from the guard. You'll notice this group of drills is so large that it takes two weeks to get through. All of these drills are looping drills and both players will get to work with this pattern: offensive-offensive-defensive.

There are so many types of guards that your drilling possibilities are really endless. Focus on developing a well-rounded game built from guard attacks.

By the end of this month, you have every tool you need to become a champion. I have given you all my tricks of the trade. Once you finish this month, you will move on to the final exam where you can test your progress and find out just how much drilling improves your jiu-jitsu! Whatever you do, never stop drilling. It is the most important part of my training routine, and I hope you have discovered it works for you, too!

Positional Defense
BRIDGE TO UNDERHOOK PASS

We begin with Marcel in the north-south position; my arms are hidden underneath his armpits for protection. To get Marcel away from me, I bridge upward while extending my arms over my head to open a big space between our chests. Immediately, I curl into a ball and I drive my right knee into the space between us. Then I roll counterclockwise to escape, pulling my bottom leg through as I do so. As I escape, Marcel catches my left leg and pins his head to the outside. He then passes by sprawling his legs so my bottom leg cannot catch him, and then he circles toward my left while pressing into my leg. Marcel passes all the way to the north-south for control, and once more, I begin my upa and north-south escape. We will continue to flow through the drill for the duration of the drill.

WEEK ONE: Defensive Start

DAYS I–IV:
SIT-UP HIP ESCAPE W/CARTWHEEL

FREQUENCY: 3x 3-5 minutes or 2x the length of the mat

The second positional defense combination drill is also a trading exercise. Once again, your partner will get to work his offensive game as he controls and breaks your guard posture and repeatedly passes your guard, while you get to work two different styles of escaping—the head push and the sitting hip escape. Be sure that on the bottom, you do not make the mistake of going flat to your back when your opponent jumps toward your exposed back side. This will give him the pass! Instead, keep the game moving from the position you arrive in.

DAY FIVE:

FREQUENCY: 2-3 sets of 20

For your day on submission defense, I only want to encourage you to think outside of the box to create your own attack and defense chains. Make sure that you have one person attacking while the opponent does a bona fide defense that leads into an attack on the other side. A great example of this is the omoplata defense drill. Both you and your partner get a great moving drill that flows from side to side. For the student on top, it is important that you revert to your head post training and that you use your posted hands on the mat along with your hips to push your body across your partner's to escape.

Positional Defense Continued

The drill starts with Marcel pinning me in my flattened butterfly guard. He moves his head to my right side and jumps his legs to my left to pass his guard (always realigning his body). I defend before he can consolidate the position by bridging and pushing his head to my left side so that his head is on the same side as his legs. Before I can hip escape him back into the guard, Marcel counters by jumping his legs to the other side. With my back exposed, I have to act immediately. I grab his right shoulder with my right hand, sit up to my left elbow, and then escape my hips away from Marcel to recover the butterfly guard. From here, Marcel will drive me back to the flattened position and we will continue the drill.

Submission Defense

WEEK ONE: Defensive Start

OMOPLATA DEFENSE

I begin the drill inside Marcel's guard. Using his traditional collar-and-sleeve grip, Marcel forcefully pulls my left arm to his hip while his left thigh crashes into my armpit for the omoplata shoulder attack. Marcel keeps his legs heavy on my shoulder, and I really cannot get out. I must go to plan B, so I post my left hand on the mat and I execute a head post to get my legs to his right side. This changes the angle of my attacked arm as my body realigns and it saves me from the submission. From here, Marcel must hip-escape to recover guard. Once in guard, he will immediately attack my other arm with the same submission, and the drill will start anew. As I practice, I must develop the tendency to react fast before Marcel can sit up and grab my waist. This is one of the things drilling helps—timing!

DAY ONE:

TURTLE MASTER

FREQUENCY: 3x 5 minutes

The turtle master is your first looping combination drill of the month. While practicing, both players will have the opportunity to work their in-between game, because neither player ever gets to consolidate any position. In this situation, you will take the back while being guard-passed, pass the guard without establishing side control, and recover the guard (momentarily off of the turtle position). This is both an excellent offensive and defensive drill as you quickly transition into one and out of the other.

DAY TWO:

The drill begins with me standing in Marcel's open guard. Both of his feet are on my hips for control. As I reach down to grab Marcel's right lapel and left hip, I can feel him trying to load me up for a tomoe nage or "Superman" sweep. I anticipate his action and I will pass off of it. As Marcel kicks his legs up for the sweep, I kick my legs into a cartwheel. My hands on Marcel's body will provide base while pinning Marcel to the mat—lessening the chance of reversal. I "round off" my cartwheel to land square to Marcel's head, and he continues the drill by "chasing" me with his north-south recovery technique. If I wanted, I could pass off of his recovery attempt, but instead I will continue with the current drill.

Failed Pass to Recovery

This dynamic drill begins with Marcel controlling my hips within my butterfly guard. To get the drill going, Marcel jumps over my guard to my left side. Before he can establish the side control, I underhook his left arm with my right and I kick my right knee to my body as if I were curling into a ball. As Marcel continues to pass, I then kick my leg downward to bring my body to Marcel's navel level. From here, I sneak out the backdoor to my knees and I pull myself to his back. Marcel immediately defends the back before the situation gets any worse by placing his left instep on my hip and then sitting down to his right hip. As he does so, he pulls my left elbow open to make room for his bottom leg to slide through to the guard position. Marcel establishes the butterfly guard and I will continue the drill by passing his guard to either side.

Failed Pass Workout
CARTWHEEL & RECOVERY

WEEK TWO:
Passing Starting Point

FREQUENCY: 3 sets of 20

Although this drill provides the bottom player with an excellent guard recovery and leg workout through the sweeping motion, it really does wonders for the top player's strategy. This is a chasing drill. As the person on top, you set the pace that you are going to pass the guard and you pass off of his attempted counter. Then, he has to counter to recover. This is predictable, and this is excellent for working your dominant game. While practicing this trading style drill, focus on your opponent's recovery and feel what passes you could do before he even rolls. If you are more advanced, you can pass off of the recovery—just make sure that your partner can transition back to the beginning to keep the drill moving.

DAY THREE:
DOUBLE UNDERHOOK PICKUP

FREQUENCY: 3x 5 minutes

The looping drill double underhook pickup is both an amazing workout and a functional way to link your defense to your offense. Expect to do some explosive training as you flip your opponent over and shoot in for the double-leg takedown. While practicing, mix hard and soft aspects. You will be soft and supple as you allow yourself to be rolled, but you will be hard and fast as you shoot in for the takedown. Likewise, you will be overwhelming when you flip your opponent with your hip power and you will be light as a feather as he takes you down. Feel this interplay so that you know when it is time to be the rock and the water.

DAYS IV&V:

FREQUENCY: 3x 5-10 minutes

If you ever wanted to know the secret as to why my former instructor, Fernando "Terere" Augusto, was always able to pass his opponent's guards so fast and take the back to finish so quickly, then this is the drill with the answer. Whenever Terere trained for a tournament he would do this exercise fifty-plus times while the rest of the class sparred. He said that he wanted the movement to be automatic. The results were outstanding, when his opponent pulled guard, Terere would immediately pass, take the back, and finish. It was fast, but it was the result of drilling, not natural talent. Even today, we use this drill at Team Atos, and we practice it often before every tournament. When you practice, feel free to combine different guards, but make sure that you always follow this formula—pass the guard, opponent turns away, you take the back, and you finish!

Pick Up & Put Down

Marcel starts the drill by underhooking both of my legs from a standing position. Both of his hands grip the back of my trousers. As Marcel stands from a power squat he lifts my hips and rolls me over my right shoulder. Marcel's power helps me counter as I go with his momentum, rolling all the way through to my knees. Without delay, I shoot in fast for a double-leg takedown, driving Marcel to his back. From here, I immediately shoot my arms inside for a double underhook pass, and I will continue the drill when I flip Marcel to his knees.

Pass to Transition

PASS TO BACK

I begin inside Marcel's open guard; he has both of his feet on my hips and he is grabbing my collar. I immediately pass by pinning Marcel's hips and left knee to execute an around-the-legs pass to Marcel's right side. As I move to Marcel's side, he must turn away to continue the drill. When he does this, I slide my left (bottom) hook under his left leg, control his body with an under-and-over grip, and pop my right hook in front inside of his right thigh. From here, Marcel continues to roll, and I ride him to the belly-up position. From here, I switch my grips to a choke and I quickly finish. Without stopping, we will reset our starting position, choose a guard, and I will commit to the same style of pass with the same ultimate finish—the choke from behind.

DAYS IV & V:
DOUBLE UNDERHOOK FLIP TRANSITION

FREQUENCY: 3x 5 minutes

This move combines the same flip-over movement as yesterday's drill, but this time the partner on top is going to stay offensive, while the bottom player gets to work his defense. This is a great drill for both players to learn to start executing their movements early. Looking at this from a points perspective, neither person has gained any points in their offense or defense (though there is an advantage for forcing Marcel to scramble out of the turtle), but both clearly get to exhibit a lot of movement and great jiu-jitsu. In this situation, you will be passing and transitioning to your partner's back off of the roll attempt. To be successful with your drill you should already be thinking of his back before he even lands on his knees. Likewise, you should also be planning your turtle escape well before your opponent lands on your hips as he transitions to your back while playing on the bottom. Make your plan and start executing the early transition instead of being tardy!

I begin the drill inside Marcel's open guard with both underhooks. While grabbing Marcel's pants for control, I first stand my left and then right leg to get upright. Lifting with my hips, I pull Marcel's lower body off the mat and I force him to flip backward. As he lands on his knees, I sprawl onto his shoulders and then transition around his right side to get to his back. As Marcel senses me nearing his hips he rolls on his right (inside) shoulder so that he can bring his left (outside) leg around to recover the guard. I see this coming, and I keep my hands low so that he lands in the double underhook position. Once again, I control his pants, lift him off the mat, and continue the drill to the other side. As I get better and better with this drill, I should always preemptively set up the next step before my opponent arrives. This is integral to faster and smoother transitions.

DAYS I-V:
OMOPLATA SWEEP AND ESCAPE

FREQUENCY: 2-3 sets of 12-20

This last drill is probably the most dynamic of all the sweep and escape combination drills. It includes an omoplata, an omoplata sweep off of a defense, a transition from side control to the mount, and an elbow escape back to the guard. With the omoplata being one of my favorite attacks in jiu-jitsu (I love it because I am able to get my body out from under my opponent's body weight), I was naturally drawn to this drill. To keep the drill flowing, make sure that you roll out of the omoplata as your partner tries to attack. This will put you in the proper range for him to sit up to the mount. As your partner sits to the mount, trap the lagging leg, not the leg that comes over the top. This leg is easier to catch and will make for a much faster transition back to the guard.

FREQUENCY: 2-3 sets of 12-20

Your penultimate week of drilling this year will focus on drills that always combine guard sweeps with escapes and guard recoveries. You will be practicing several different sweeps everyday this week, and you should start to feel great improvements in your escaping skills and basic sweeping skills. For your first drill, you will work on the scissor sweep and mount defense. When sweeping, you need to pull your partner onto your top leg to "load up the sweep," and you should leave your hand on the collar to set up your partner's upa escape.

Mastering Sweeps & Escapes

I begin inside Marcel's closed guard. Marcel gets a collar and sleeve grip, pins my left hand to his hips, and throws his right leg into my left triceps for the omoplata attack. As he pushes his legs to the mat to control my posture, I decide to roll out of the attack to avoid the submission. While I roll, Marcel sits up to my side control to finish the sweep. Immediately, he steps his left leg over my body to mount. As he does this, I trap his right (lagging leg) in my half guard. With one leg trapped, I face Marcel's left leg. I place my hands on his left shoulder and hip-escape to recover my trapped right leg. I finish in the closed guard and now I am ready to continue to the offensive phase of the drill.

SCISSOR SWEEP & MOUNT DEFENSE

I begin with Marcel inside my closed guard; I have a cross-collar grip with my left hand as my right hand controls the end of his left sleeve. Quickly, I hip-escape to my left and slide my left shin across Marcel's abdomen. Next, I pull Marcel onto my shin and when I feel his weight come over me, I scissor my legs. I straighten my right leg and move it to Marcel's left knee, sweeping his leg out from under him as my left leg drives him to his back. I take the mount position with the same grips. Marcel then counters by grabbing my elbow and sleeve, while trapping my right leg with his left foot. He then bridges over his left shoulder to reverse me back to the starting position. We will continue this drill until the set is finished.

DAYS I–V:
SPIDER SWEEP & GUARD RECOVERY

I begin inside Marcel's spider guard with his feet on my hips. Marcel hip-escapes slightly to his right and places his left foot on my biceps to set up his sweep. Then, he uses his left foot to pull me forward, making my left leg lighter as my rear moves away from my heels. Using a scissor motion, Marcel kicks me off my feet and I land on my back. I immediately go to work, pushing his knee away as I hip escape to my left. I free my right leg and then I hip-escape to my right to escape my left leg. Once free. I can recover the spider guard and continue with a sweep of my own.

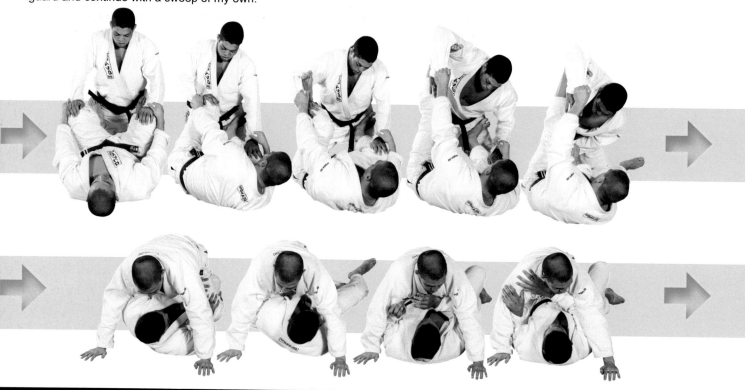

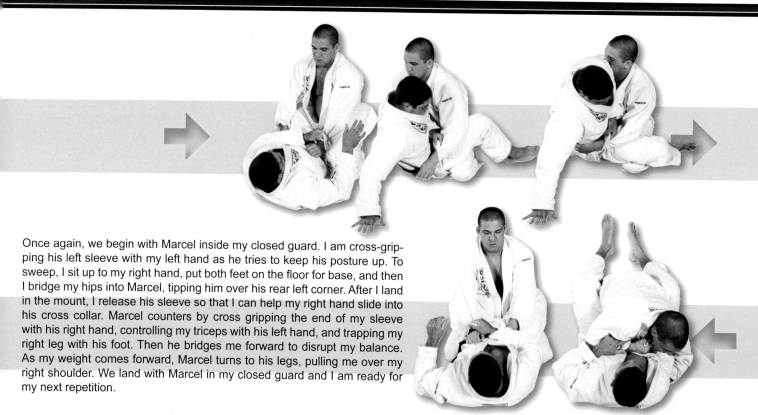

Once again, we begin with Marcel inside my closed guard. I am cross-gripping his left sleeve with my left hand as he tries to keep his posture up. To sweep, I sit up to my right hand, put both feet on the floor for base, and then I bridge my hips into Marcel, tipping him over his rear left corner. After I land in the mount, I release his sleeve so that I can help my right hand slide into his cross collar. Marcel counters by cross gripping the end of my sleeve with his right hand, controlling my triceps with his left hand, and trapping my right leg with his foot. Then he bridges me forward to disrupt my balance. As my weight comes forward, Marcel turns to his legs, pulling me over my right shoulder. We land with Marcel in my closed guard and I am ready for my next repetition.

Mastering Sweeps & Escapes

FREQUENCY: 2-3 sets of 12-20

This next drill follows the same scissoring concept as the previous sweep, but this time you will apply the sweep from the spider guard. In addition, this is a looping drill, so both partners will get to execute a nice range of jiu-jitsu with the sweep, mount, mount escape, and transition to spider guard. As with the last drill, work on bringing your opponent toward you to make his legs lighter and therefore more susceptible to being swept. Beyond this, never stop in any position—the key is to transition! This is nowhere more apparent than when your partner takes the mount after the sweep. There is a moment where his weight has not been established yet, and that is your best time to escape. The longer you wait the harder the escape—even when drilling!

HIP BUMP SWEEP W/MOUNT DEFENSE

FREQUENCY: 2-3 sets of 12-20

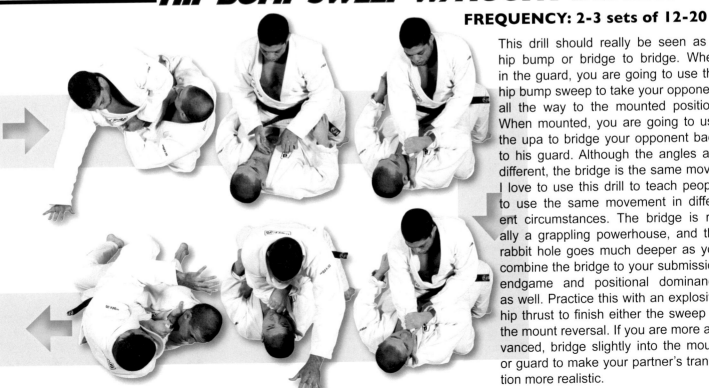

This drill should really be seen as a hip bump or bridge to bridge. When in the guard, you are going to use the hip bump sweep to take your opponent all the way to the mounted position. When mounted, you are going to use the upa to bridge your opponent back to his guard. Although the angles are different, the bridge is the same move. I love to use this drill to teach people to use the same movement in different circumstances. The bridge is really a grappling powerhouse, and the rabbit hole goes much deeper as you combine the bridge to your submission endgame and positional dominance as well. Practice this with an explosive hip thrust to finish either the sweep or the mount reversal. If you are more advanced, bridge slightly into the mount or guard to make your partner's transition more realistic.

DAYS I-III:
BACK & FORTH SUPERMAN SWEEP

FREQUENCY: 2-3 sets of 20

Your last week on guard combination training focuses on trading sweeps with these looping drills. Your first drill will have you revisit the now familiar tomoe nage, or Superman sweep. Both partners will get to break their opponent's posture, execute an overhead sweep, back-roll to mount, and recover guard. Key to this movement is how you gain momentum. Always start from a sitting position so that you can gain more pulling force as you fall to your back and scoot your hips toward your partner. This will bring him on top of you while loading your legs up for the sweep. Think of creating momentum through body movement in all of your drills and techniques. It will make you feel much stronger than you are in actuality.

FREQUENCY: 2-3 sets of 12-20

After all of that practice with the shoulder roll from the closed guard, it is about time that you get to practice sweeping with this technique! Think of this movement as a shoulder roll to a single-leg takedown. Just be careful that you keep your body below his knee line as you come to your knees. If you get your flank much higher than his knee, he can use his trapped leg to trap your arm, setting up a possible crucifix. Drill this movement to learn to be tight with the low single-leg takedown. As an added benefit, you will get a good leg and base workout as you stand in the closed guard.

Sweep to Sweep

I start the drill with Marcel on his knees inside my butterfly guard. I am gripping the outside of both of his sleeves at the triceps level. To create momentum, I scoot my rear to my heels and I fall back to the mat. As I do this, I pull Marcel's body forward so that his head crosses my own. With Marcel out of position, I can easily lift my hooks upward to skyrocket him into an over-the-head Superman sweep. Marcel lands on his back, and I use a back shoulder roll to follow him to the mount. From here, Marcel grabs my pants at the hips and bridges. At the height of his bridge, he drops his hips to the mat, stiff-arming me to keep my hips elevated. Immediately, he tucks both knees into the space he created between our hips. Marcel then pushes me away with his hooks and ends in a seated butterfly guard. Now, he can continue the drill with a sweep of his own.

STANDING SWEEPS

We start the drill with Marcel standing in my closed guard. I quickly hook my right arm behind Marcel's left ankle and I place my left hand on the mat as if I were attempting the basic bridging sweep. Marcel counters by stepping his right leg back in base. As he does this, I circle my left foot clockwise toward my right leg. As I do this, I push off the mat so I escape my legs with a right-sided shoulder roll. As I get to my knees, I keep my body below Marcel's knee, and I pick his left foot off the mat while I drive into his shin to topple him to his back. Having swept Marcel, I turn the corner to approach his closed guard. Marcel closes the guard and I stand up in base. From here, Marcel will hook my leg, sweep, and continue the drill.

FREQUENCY: 3 sets of 20

The rolling sweeps drill is an excellent way to get used to loading your opponent onto your shins and then back-rolling to reverse positions. This is probably my favorite style of sweep, and I have seen it used with great success in competition by smaller fighters like Ricardo Vieira and Rafael Mendes to big men like Roger Gracie. Originally, I learned this move while training with Terere and Ricardo Vieira at the old Master Team, but later I started working it into the beautiful drill below. While practicing, make sure that you pull your partner's weight onto your shins. From there, you can easily handle their weight and reverse them by kicking your feet and back rolling. This drill is poetry in motion.

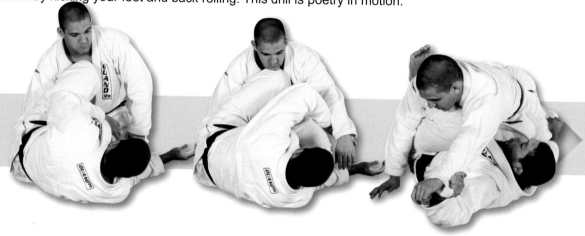

Sweep to Sweep Continued

I start with Marcel inside my half-spider guard. My right leg is between his legs and my left foot is on his right hip with my knee angled toward his face. My shin blocks Marcel's forward progress. To get the sweep in place, I grab my left hand under Marcel's left sleeve with my thumb pointed toward his head. My right hand grabs his pant leg. Immediately, I pull Marcel forward so that his weight loads onto my bent legs. To sweep, I push Marcel's arm away from me and I kick my feet toward my left shoulder to emphatically flip him to his back. I ride his momentum to the top and I land in the same starting position. From here, Marcel takes the same grips, pulls me onto his legs, and sweeps me back to the start of the drill. We will continue trading sweeps like this until our set is completed.

DAYS IV & V:
SNEAK TO BACK
WEEK FOUR: From the Guard

FREQUENCY: 2-3x 5 minutes

As with every position, it is important that you look at the closed guard as angles of attack. In this situation, you will transition to the back the same way that you did during last month's x-guard transition training. Then, you should take the back and allow your partner to escape to the guard. I think of this movement as a trademark of many of my students at Team Atos, and it has been incredibly successful, especially in our smaller guys. The back is a huge target, and hopefully this drill gives you the confidence to attack it, even when it seems so far away! Practice this at a medium pace—it is more important to control every step of the way than to move explosively.

Sweep to Transition

We start the drill with Marcel standing inside my closed guard. I hook Marcel's left leg as if I were attempting a bridging sweep. Instead of sweeping, I scoot my hips slightly to the left and I bring my left hand inside Marcel's legs. In one motion, I open my legs and I use my left hand to pull my head between Marcel's legs. Between Marcel's feet, I push Marcel forward with my hands while I tuck my knees behind his thighs. I grab Marcel's belt and kick my feet away from me to send Marcel falling into my lap. I place my right hook in front of Marcel's thigh, and he counters by escaping to his left. I do not resist Marcel's escape. Instead, I transition to the top. As I do so, Marcel first recovers half and then full guard. Now inside Marcel's guard, I am ready to continue the drill as I move to a standing posture.

MONTH ELEVEN:
In Review

The most important lesson to take from Month Eleven is to be a versatile jiu-jitsu player. Do not build your game around being a one trick pony. Although single techniques can and certainly do work, your success rate will drop as your partners become more and more advanced or are savvy to your style of jiu-jitsu.

Build a game that can dominate through angle changes and constant attacks. Return to previous chapters to find the right drills to piece together and practice these movements. Drilling angle changes and attacks (sweeps or submissions) will greatly influence your chances of success in tournament. When you can put them all together, your game will be unstoppable!

However, think of combinations in all aspects of jiu-jitsu, not just offense. Just as the triangle feeds the omoplata, the bridge also feeds the elbow escape. Jiu-jitsu is one big chain of movements. Whether you are attacking or defending, you'll need to piece together the techniques you've learned over the last eleven months to create a flawless game plan.

Combination drills not only add fluidity and an element of attack to your jiu-jitsu, but they also provide what I call "jiu-jitsu cardio" or the ability to continuously attack or escape without tiring easily. This is a great workout. Use combination drills both to practice your techniques and to get your endurance ready for competition!

WEEKEND WORK:

To change things up for this penultimate month of training, you should create your own combination drills from at least three different starting points. Try to incorporate at least three different but similar techniques and two to three positions. You can use any combination and feel free to use both attacks and escapes.

Every good guard starts with control. Here I am using one of my favorite guards, the half-spider guard in a match against the always tough Roberto "Cyborg" Abreu. *(Photo: John Lamonica)*

MONTH TWELVE:
Final Exam - Putting It All Together

This final month of training will look at two elements. First is strengthening those areas in your game where you are weakest. The first three weeks you will spend working on your worst positions of the past five months, while your last week will be spent working on your so-so areas. As with the midterm, you should work at as intense a pace as possible. The end is in sight, but I want you to race through the finish instead of stopping at the goal line.

The second element of this final review month is to go through the previous twelve months of training and critically evaluate three elements: your diet, your balance and conditioning, and your technical application. With your diet, you need to be fueling the machine with good foods and getting plenty of rest. Make sure you have the proper health to achieve your goals. As your jiu-jitsu improves, be sure to continue the less enjoyable physical training. Stretch daily and do those hill runs so you have the conditioning to continue through the rough spells. Finally, be your own biggest critic. No one will ever give you enough of the criticism that you may need or want to hear, so do this for yourself. Do not rest on your laurels. You do not have the best guard, escapes, passing, or jiu-jitsu in the world (neither do I), so seek continual improvement and always strive to match your knowledge with your ability to apply these techniques in sparring or competition.

Frequently Asked Questions:

Q: I tend to fall over/lose my balance as I move from side to side during the torreando guard pass.
A: The balance of the torreando depends entirely on the relationship between your posting hands and your leg movement. Oftentimes, you will start the torreando pass with your hands on your opponent's shins and then step to the side. The problem is that you continue to hold the legs as your body shifts upward to take the side control. Instead, get used to inserting a knee on the belly instead of going directly to side control. This way, you will alleviate the sensation that you are falling as you transfer to the side. If you prefer passing to the side, try to use the hip and knee pin variations.
   Action: Begin with the bear crawl to push-up (pg 34), then transition to monkey walking (pg 144). Next, practice torreando to knee-on-belly (pg 146) and then torreando to armbar (pg 147).

Q: I am very good at under-the-legs style of passing. Do I really need to master around- and over-the-legs?
A: You will definitely need more in your bag than just one area of passing. If you face a flexible guard player, you will need an outside (around-the-legs) and direct (over-the-legs) style of pass to keep his guard confused. Don't make the mistake of thinking that you need a million passes from each area. You only need one or two passes from each field, but be sure they are passes that can be combined with others. For example, if you pass with an underhook and are blocked, develop the transitional sensitivity to immediately pass over or around the legs to the other side. You will need to work combinations in passing just as much as you do in submissions.
   Action: Choose complementary guard passes and drill them in succession—over-and-under pass drill (pg 162), headstand pass (pg 167), etc. Get creative and build your own game!

Q: I am a good guard passer, but my opponent always instantly recovers guard before I can establish the position.
A: This is a common problem and one to which I am susceptible as well. If you cannot comfortably anchor your position, prepare yourself for the escaping action. Your opponent can only escape toward or away from you, and his options are recovering guard or going to his knees to turtle or attack your legs. Therefore, develop your drills to combat these predictable scenarios. Work your favorite guard passes during positional sparring and drilling and have your partner immediately transition to guard or to his knees. As he does so, immediately circle to his other side or back using one of the side control transition drills. This is how you develop the sensitivity to pass through your opponent's escape.
   Action: Begin with your favorite guard pass, then drill the quarter nelson transition (pg 175), and then back to your favorite pass. Move into the arm control transition (pg 176) and then the Terere pass (pg 152), knee smash pass (pg 180), and back to the Terere pass and finish with the mount flow (pg 187).

Frequently Asked Questions Continued:

Q: I have horrible balance while in the mount or knee-on–belly, and I usually lose the positions when my opponent bridges.

A: Obviously, you have found a weakness in your game and you will need to spend much of this month focusing on balance. However, I also want you to think of other variables, such as your experience, size, and weight in relation to that of your partner(s). Secondly, you should evaluate your strategy. There are no positions that are foolproof in jiu-jitsu. Make sure that the problem is not your strategy. If you are trying to keep the knee-on-belly or mount against a 300-pound bucking bronco, perhaps you should switch to a more tenable position like the side control or back. This is why I prefer to control positions through transition training.

Action: Begin with ball push-ups (pg 20), then knee-on-ball (pg 188), then side-to-side or knee-on-belly step-around, then mount control and mount flow (pg 186).

Q: I think I have a good guard, but I struggle with submissions from the position.

A: Without a doubt, submissions should be your number one goal while in the guard. Personally, whenever I compete or train against a guard player with great sweeps but poor submissions, I can easily impose my passing game. The reason is simple, I am not afraid of his guard. Becoming a submission master will make me fear your every grip and hand placement. A so-so guard becomes great when it is threatening and a beautiful guard is worthless if it cannot instill this fear. Work on the simple 1-2-3 combination chains of attacking either submission-to-submission-to-submission or submission-to-sweep-to-submission until you feel more comfortable with the attack. You may lose the guard more in this process, but the long-term payoff is a devastating position.

While drilling, look for positions where you will not have to change to a radically different grip. One example is sitting up for the guillotine, attacking the hip bump sweep, and then finishing with the kimura. All three are right at your fingertips from the starting position and can be overwhelming if done in succession. Drill your chain attacks and take this game plan to positional sparring.

Action: Start with hip-ups (pg 208), then triangles (pg 209), then master attacker (pg 225), followed by closed guard standing sit-ups (pg 26). Next, drill the bridge (pg 64), hip bump (pg 219), kimura (pg 220), and finally, knee-inside-omoplata (pg 218).

Q: Whenever I play butterfly guard, my opponents always back out and pass easily. Sometimes I feel like this is not a modern position.

A: Your problem is twofold. First, you need to address your partner's range, which is the most important factor in defending the guard. This can be done from any open guard type and should always dictate your attack and defense. Second, and specific to the butterfly guard, you must attack. Don't make the mistake of thinking the butterfly guard is obsolete, judging from the success that Terere, Marcelo Garcia, and I have all had with it, it is anything but antiquated. Instead, look at it as an effective attacking position. Develop an attacking style and always have another guard to which you can easily transition. I recommend the half guard or sitting guard as two positions that you can easily transition to as your opponent closes in or retreats.

Action: Try this series: Follow the leader (pg 210), then hip escape foot circles (pg 253), followed by rocking chair (pg 235). Then, butterfly sit-up (pg 226) and butterfly kick-out (pg 228), followed by x-guard movement (pg 262), sit-up drill (pg 230), tug and push (pg 233), sit-up hip escape (pg 60), and finally, pass block to triangle (pg 241).

Lyoto Machida 4 DVD Box Set

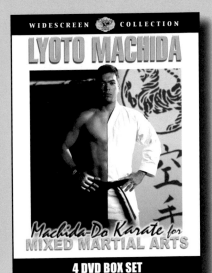

DVD 1
Movement and Fundamental Strikes

DVD 2
Striking Attacks and Takedowns

DVD 3
Intercepting Attacks, Takedown Defense, and The Clinch

DVD 4
The Ground Game

INSTRUCTIONAL DVDs BY ANTONIO RODRIGO NOGUEIRA

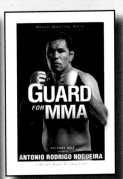
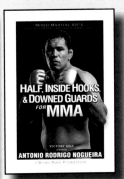

INSTRUCTIONAL DVDs BY ANDERSON SILVA

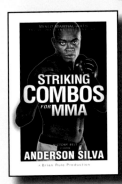
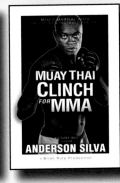
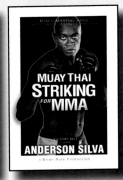
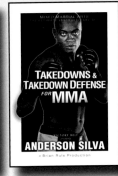
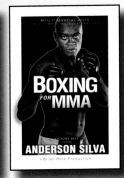

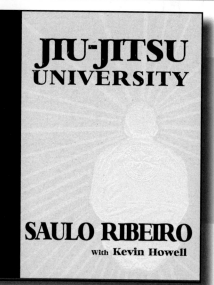

JIU-JITSU
UNIVERSITY

SAULO RIBEIRO

with Kevin Howell

JIU-JITSU UNIVERSITY
SAULO RIBEIRO

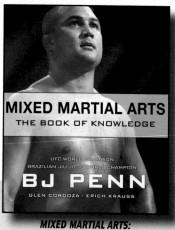

MIXED MARTIAL ARTS:
THE BOOK OF KNOWLEDGE
BJ PENN

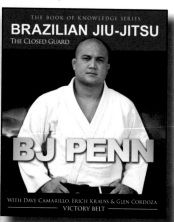

BRAZILIAN JIU-JITSU:
THE CLOSED GUARD
BJ PENN

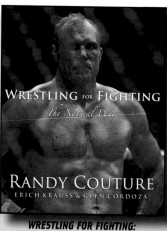

WRESTLING FOR FIGHTING:
THE NATURAL WAY
RANDY COUTURE

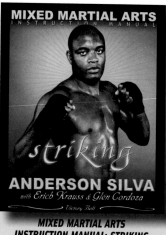

MIXED MARTIAL ARTS
INSTRUCTION MANUAL: STRIKING
ANDERSON SILVA

MASTERING MIXED MARTIAL ARTS:
THE GUARD
ANTONIO NOGUEIRA

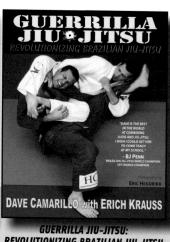

GUERRILLA JIU-JITSU:
REVOLUTIONIZING BRAZILIAN JIU-JITSU
DAVE CAMARILLO

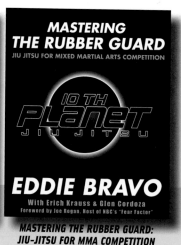

MASTERING THE RUBBER GUARD:
JIU-JITSU FOR MMA COMPETITION
EDDIE BRAVO

MASTERING THE TWISTER:
JIU-JITSU FOR MMA COMPETITION
EDDIE BRAVO

**XTREME TRAINING
THE FIGHTER'S ULTIMATE FITNESS MANUAL
RANDY COUTURE**

**ADVANCED BRAZILIAN JIU-JITSU
MARCELO GARCIA**

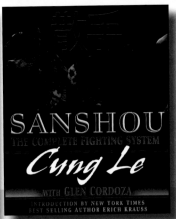

**SAN SHOU
THE COMPLETE FIGHTING SYSTEM
CUNG LE**

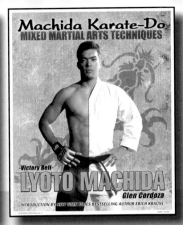

**MACHIDA KARATE-DO
MIXED MARTIAL ARTS TECHNIQUES
LYOTO MACHIDA**

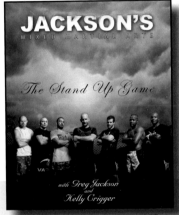

**JACKSON'S MIXED MARTIAL ARTS
THE STAND-UP GAME
GREG JACKSON**

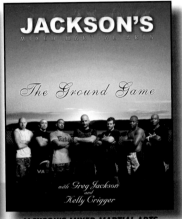

**JACKSON'S MIXED MARTIAL ARTS
THE GROUND GAME
GREG JACKSON**

**FEDOR: THE FIGHTING SYSTEM OF THE
UNDISPUTED KING OF MMA
FEDOR EMELIANENKO**

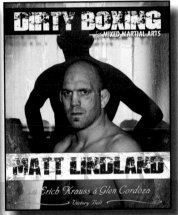

**DIRTY BOXING
FOR MIXED MARTIAL ARTS
MATT LINDLAND**

**THE X-GUARD
GI & NO GI JIU-JITSU
MARCELO GARCIA**

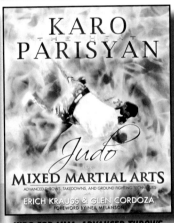

**JUDO FOR MMA: ADVANCED THROWS,
TAKEDOWNS, AND GROUND FIGHTING
KARO PARISYAN**

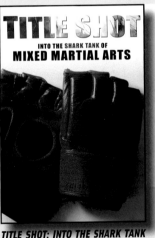

**TITLE SHOT: INTO THE SHARK TANK
OF MIXED MARTIAL ARTS
KELLY CRIGGER**

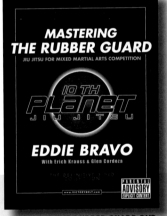

**MASTERING THE RUBBER GUARD DVD:
JIU-JITSU FOR MMA COMPETITION
EDDIE BRAVO**

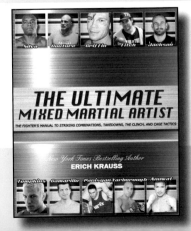

**THE ULTIMATE MIXED MARTIAL ARTIST
THE FIGHTER'S MANUAL TO STRIKING
COMBINATIONS, TAKEDOWNS,
THE CLINCH, AND CAGE TACTICS
ANDERSON SILVA
RANDY COUTURE
FORREST GRIFFIN
JON FITCH
GREG JACKSON
SHAWN THOMPKINS
DAVE CAMARILLO
KARO PARISYAN**

CONTRIBUTORS

Marcel, Andre, Haley, Kevin, and Brian after a long day of shooting *Drill to Win*.

Andre Galvao is one of the most well-respected jiu-jitsu athletes of our time. He is a State, National, Pan-American, and World Champion, having won the Worlds at every belt level including twice at the black belt. Currently, Andre is the co-founder of Atos Jiu-Jitsu and is fighting MMA for the Strikeforce organization.

Kevin Howell is the co-author of the best selling *Jiu-Jitsu University*. He holds a brown belt in jiu-jitsu under Leo Vieira and teaches at Fight Zone USA in Signal Hill, California. When away from jiu-jitsu, Kevin enjoys teaching Political Science, family time, and surfing.

Marcel Louzado is a world champion from Sao Paolo, Brazil. He holds a black belt in Brazilian Jiu-Jitsu and a black belt in Judo. He is a friend and former training partner to Andre Galvao and is currently teaching out of Southern California.

Brian Rule is a well-respected photographer, graphic designer, and videographer. Currently residing in Richmond, Virginia, Brian spends his free time making experimental films and hanging with his four-legged friend, Stinky.

Haley Howell made her professional graphic design debut with Saulo Ribeiro's *Jiu-Jitsu University*. She currently resides in Southern California.